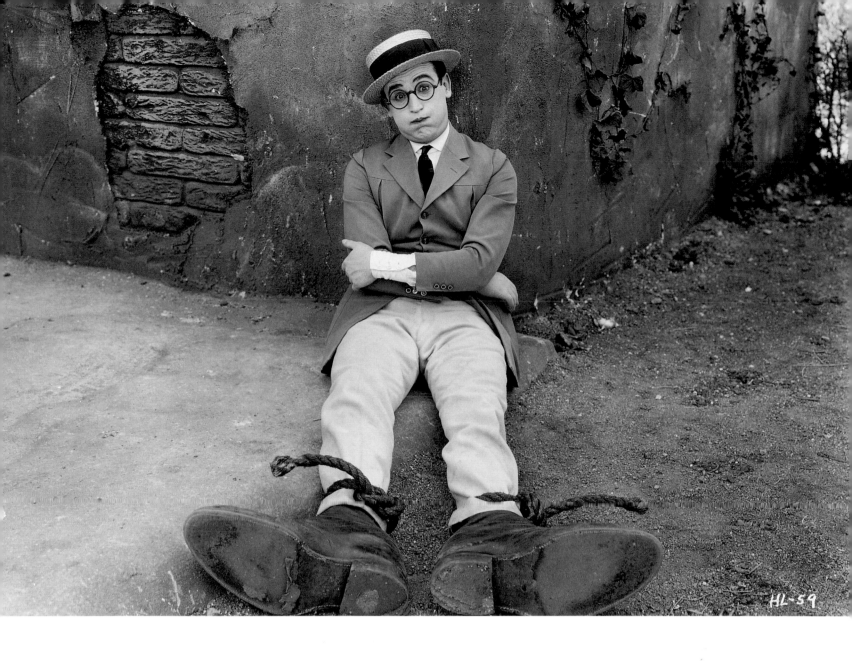

Harold **Lloyd**

Harold Lloyd Master Comedian

Jeffrey Vance and **Suzanne Lloyd**

Introduction by **Kevin Brownlow**

Manoah Bowman, Photographic Editor

Harry N. Abrams, Inc., Publishers

*This book is dedicated to my beloved
grandparents Harold and Mildred,
to Gloria (my mother) and Harold, Jr.,
to Jack Lemmon, and to my children,
Christopher and Jacqueline.*

With love,
Suzanne Lloyd

Contents

The Harold Lloyd Stills: A Note on the Photography

When one thinks of Harold Lloyd, several things may come to mind: his work as a silent-film comedian; his famous estate, Greenacres; his fascinating collection of 250 personally inscribed photographs of celebrities, known as "The Rogues Gallery"; or Lloyd's own prizewinning 3-D stereopticon photography.

Lloyd's enthusiasm for photography was not an interest that began after his retirement from films; it was an outgrowth of his interest in cinematography. His silent feature-length comedies (photographed by the superb cinematographer Walter Lundin) were some of the best-photographed films of the period. As Lloyd strove for perfection in all aspects of his work, it is no wonder that there are so many exceptional stills from his films. Gene Kornman, Lloyd's still photographer throughout most of the 1920s, was responsible for many of these wonderful images. It is important to note that most still photographers from the silent-film era were rarely credited for their work. This makes Kornman an anomaly of sorts. While not always credited on the publicity stills that were sent out to magazines and newspapers for publication, he was usually credited on Lloyd's personal set of prints. Another largely forgotten photographer of the time, J. C. Milligan, responsible for the wonderful stills taken for many of Lloyd's one-reel and two-reel comedies made during 1919 and 1920, was also credited on Lloyd's prints. These razor-sharp, beautifully lit, and highly animated photographs brilliantly capture the spirit of Lloyd's films.

Lloyd's collection aided co-author Jeffrey Vance and me immensely in creating a unique and definitive photographic overview of Harold Lloyd's life and films, and allowed us to give all photographers, when known, proper credit . Having worked with the personal collections of Charles Chaplin, Buster Keaton, and Harold Lloyd, I must admit that there are more consistently marvelous photographs to choose from among Lloyd's material than that of any other silent comedian. This made my job as photographic editor extremely challenging. Whereas with Chaplin one gets the classic iconic images, and with Keaton the famous gag shots, with Lloyd one gets perfectly composed and fluid scene stills that somehow represent not only the action of the films but the personality and motivations of the characters. This quality is especially noteworthy in Lloyd's photographs from the 1920s, an era when photographs were typically stiff, staged, and static. This was mainly owing to the 8 x 10 camera format typically used that required the actors to remain frozen in a pose for several seconds. The fact that most of the photographs from Lloyd's films do not suffer this malady is a testament not only to Lloyd's charisma but also to the talents of Gene Kornman and J. C. Milligan.

It is not surprising that Lloyd became averse to posing for publicity portraits and gag photos after his terrible accident at Witzel Studios in 1919, when a prop bomb turned out to be real and nearly destroyed his

Publicity portrait of Harold Lloyd from *Speedy* (1928).

right hand and the side of his face. There is irony in the fact that Lloyd, famous for the extremely risky stunts he performed in his "thrill" comedies, had his only serious accident posing for a still photograph! Despite the accident, many famous photographers did manage to photograph him — James Abbe, Strauss-Peyton, Edward Steichen, Eugene Robert Richee, John Engstead, and Philippe Halsman, just to name a few.

Lloyd's massive collection of original still photographs documents his entire career on the screen, as well as many other aspects of both his public and personal life. The Harold Lloyd Trust collection includes two filing cabinets filled with loose original stills, several family photograph albums, and a collection of more than five hundred 4 x 5 glass negatives that have been carefully catalogued and archived by Jeffrey Vance. There are also keybook albums of stills for nearly all of Lloyd's feature-length films and his two- and three-reel comedies, as well as more than eight hundred original prints from the earliest Lonesome Luke and Glass Character one-reel comedies (1915–19), and nearly three thousand original 8 x 10 nitrate still negatives that Suzanne Lloyd donated to the Academy of Motion Picture Arts and Sciences in 2001.

Robert Cushman, photograph curator of the Academy's Margaret Herrick Library, served as the photographic coordinator, and the book greatly benefited from Robert's exemplary conservation work. He assumed the arduous task of removing, cleaning, and reglossing the photographs that were glued to the acidic black scrapbook paper in the keybook albums. In 1999, the Academy started production of master archival fiber preservation prints from the original 8 x 10 nitrate still negatives, and I was given the responsibility of creating the prints in the darkroom. We got to them not a moment too soon; several of the negatives — particularly from *Girl Shy* (1924) and *Speedy* (1928) — had by then started to become sticky. Since then, many of this small group have deteriorated beyond printability, despite the temperature- and humidity-controlled storage in which the Academy has placed them.

As a final point of interest, approximately 90 percent of the photographs appearing in this book are first-generation images — modern archival prints created either from the original camera negatives or (to a much lesser extent) from original vintage prints. This book could be double its size and still not showcase all of the great photography from the Harold Lloyd films — certainly a highly unusual circumstance. It is to Lloyd's credit that he meticulously saved much of the original photographic material. The existence of this rich resource results in a legacy that promotes and secures Harold Lloyd's legendary status as we move into the new century.

Manoah Bowman

Foreword by Jack Lemmon

Charlie Chaplin, Buster Keaton, and Harold Lloyd were three of my movie favorites when I was very young. I think that is where Harold Lloyd rates in his influence and importance to film history and, in my estimation, one could not be in greater company.

I had the good fortune to become friends with Harold Lloyd. Harold was the first film star I ever met. I was introduced to him almost immediately after coming to Los Angeles in the early 1950s. My former wife, Cynthia, and I were close friends with Harold's daughter Gloria (Cynthia and Gloria used to share an apartment in New York City before we were married), and I met Harold through my friendship with her. I vividly remember first meeting Harold at his house, Greenacres. I use the word *house* loosely, as Greenacres was a huge mansion on sixteen acres in Benedict Canyon, Beverly Hills. I had never seen anything like it. There was an enormous Christmas tree in the sunroom, a huge organ in the living room, elaborate gardens, and an Olympic-size swimming pool. As a kid, I had always imagined Hollywood to be like that amazing estate.

I was in awe of Harold Lloyd, but he immediately put me at ease. He was very open, with absolutely no ego or conceit. He could not have been less concerned about himself or trying to impress people. He was inquisitive about me and what I was doing. I remember him saying, "How are you, young man?" "What are you doing?" "Isn't that wonderful, you're just starting out." He was very warm, very ingenuous, very gregarious, and lovely. I took an instant liking to him personally. He was simply one of the kindest, sweetest, most dignified men I have ever known, in this business or elsewhere.

Harold was not the kind of man who would give unsolicited advice. However, if one asked him, he was more than willing. Although I had had experience before cameras in live television, I had no motion picture experience at the time. I remember discussing film acting with him while I was in rehearsals for my first film, George Cukor's *It Should Happen to You* (1954). His advice was "less is better." It was excellent advice for a fledgling film actor. I played opposite the incomparable Judy Holliday, and the film contains a scene where I have an enormous argument with her, make an exit, slam the door, and then open the door immediately and say, "So, are we still on for Friday lunch?" She responds, "Certainly," and I say, "Thank you very much!" and slam the door again. It is a wonderful scene that really lets out all the stops. While filming the scene, in the back of my mind I was thinking, "Less is better." However, I think I was trying to do two things at once: play the scene fully and pay attention to this sage advice. Fortunately for me, the film and my performance received good reviews, but I was anxious to get Harold's reaction. When I saw him next, I asked him if he happened to see the film. He said, "Yes, I did. I loved it. I especially liked you and your work." I was delighted, as Harold was

not the kind of person to say something like that just to be polite. I said to him, "About the one big scene, where I blow up, make the false exit, come back in, and leave. . ." "Yes," he said. "I tried not to go overboard and do too much. What did you think?" He smiled and said, "Close, wasn't it?" And he just looked at me. And from that day to this I have tried desperately not to give in to overplaying, no matter how right it may feel at the moment. Less is indeed always better.

In January 1963 I was asked to help moderate a gala evening for Harold Lloyd and Mary Pickford at the silver anniversary for Delta Kappa Alpha, the national honorary cinema fraternity, held at USC. It was a wonderful night for Harold, with Steve Allen and I asking him questions about his career after film clips were shown. The evening was one of the biggest thrills of my life, for it was at this celebration that Harold announced that he wanted me to play him in a film version of his life that Jerry Wald wanted to produce. To be Harold's choice was a great honor, and with his help perhaps I could have done him justice. However, the film was never made, and in a way I am rather relieved. The onus of trying to recapture someone like Harold Lloyd, who was famous because he was unique, would have been too great for me to have enjoyed the experience.

Harold Lloyd was one of the most charismatic innovators of film comedy, an excellent actor, and a consummate filmmaker. His films should be seen, not just for their historical value, but for their sheer pleasure. Unfortunately, Harold chose not to reissue his best films during his lifetime, and as a result has lost his place in film history. It is for that reason alone that he is not as well known today as Chaplin or Keaton. However, for me, Harold Lloyd is not forgotten and I am confident that this book will make it possible for him to become a cult favorite all over again.

Jack Lemmon and Harold making a spectacle of themselves at Greenacres, c. 1962.

Introduction by Kevin Brownlow

Compared to Charlie Chaplin and Buster Keaton, Harold Lloyd has been treated shabbily by history. There have been some excellent books about him, but for the general public he has meant very little for far too long. It was partly his own fault. He held on to his films, anxious that they be handled with respect—but he held on to them too long. Instead of creating a sense of mystery and expectation, he caused the public to lose interest. And the critics did not help. Lloyd tended to be dismissed as a "mechanical" comedian, too commercial, too concerned with laughs for their own sake. Gilbert Seldes, chronicler of the popular arts, declared that Lloyd had no tenderness.[1] In this era, when people deride Chaplin for being too sentimental, one might think this would prove an advantage. But it was not true in any case. For a variety of reasons, Lloyd has been relegated to a place far below Keaton, somewhere among those talented and neglected comedians like Charley Chase and Harry Langdon, whose films are seldom seen these days.

In the 1980s, when David Gill and I had completed television documentaries on Chaplin and Keaton for Thames Television, we felt we owed it to Lloyd to make a film about his career. We came up with the title *Harold Lloyd: The Third Genius* (1989).

As we quizzed people, we realized that most had seen the still of Harold on the clock, a brief clip on television, and that was the extent of their knowledge. A handful had seen *Safety Last!* (1923) and perhaps a short. Otherwise, it appeared that Lloyd's career had been erased from the public consciousness. His had become a name people automatically added to Chaplin's and Keaton's without really knowing why.

Working on a program about a figure like Lloyd to the exclusion of virtually anything else for months on end could too easily have bred a tedium, but it proved fascinating. We were discovering things about the man right up until the deadline—and beyond. Perhaps the most important fact we learned was that, besides being a great actor, Lloyd was a film-maker of brilliance, who never took screen credit for his contributions. Like Irving Thalberg, he did not need to.

In the 1920s, no one cared who directed what unless it happened to be D. W. Griffith, Rex Ingram, Erich von Stroheim, or Cecil B. DeMille. Audiences went to see *him*. Literally. That was what he was called around the world—*Lui* in France, *Er* in Germany—until his big feature films arrived and posters advertised "Harold Lloyd." They

Harold with arguably his two greatest cinematic influences: Charles Chaplin and Douglas Fairbanks, July 1932.

still called him *Lui* and went to see him in such numbers that he rivaled Chaplin at the box office. Lloyd made eleven silent feature-length comedies in the 1920s compared to Chaplin's four.[2] The Chaplin films made more money, so his box-office achievement is clearly the greater. But Chaplin had slowed down, so that his films were Great Events. Lloyd catered to the regular moviegoer, turning out at least two films a year. And his films were eagerly awaited.

It is impressive to see how Lloyd tried to vary his character from film to film. He increased the number of gagmen, and one can imagine the intensity of some of the meetings as they tried to find new story angles, new gags. He was a man who always looked on the bright side, hated sadness, and was invariably positive. But production stills betray his expression of anxiety, as do certain interviews, which catch his basic insecurity.

Lloyd believed in positive thinking—mind over matter—and *Grandma's Boy* (1922) exemplified his convictions. The film that followed, *Dr. Jack* (1922), took this belief to its logical conclusion: a doctor treats his patients with a breath of fresh air and a blast of excitement instead of medicine. It was amusing and diverting and did well, but "mind over matter" was not what people had enjoyed about *Grandma's Boy*. It was the sleight-of-hand jokes and the character of the boy—one with which we could identify, since we are all cowards at heart. Harold's triumph over the bully was exhilarating, and the gags made the viciousness of the fight all the more thrilling. And it was thrills as well as laughs that Lloyd's public expected from him. He gave them so many in *Safety Last!* he could have retired and left the film as his memorial, to run as long as there were theaters. It was a smash hit, and heightened the expectations of his audience. Harold was indelibly imprinted on our memory as the man on the clock, and what they wanted to see was the same thing again—only different.

How well he succeeded—and succeed he did—one can discover in this book. He set his sights high; for every feature he made, his preparation was intense, and he provided the highest possible value for the money of any moviegoer.

So if his work is so brilliant, why has it been so underrated? Largely because the vagaries of access introduced latter-day audiences to Lloyd via the wrong films, and denied them the right ones. From 1915 to 1919, he made scores of comedies that, like the Chaplin films made for Keystone in 1914, were of no more than ephemeral value. They were indeed "mechanical," and, while they had legions of fans, have not stood the test of time. Lloyd was a slow developer and, unlike Chaplin whose work began to show signs of brilliance as early as 1915, he did not flower until 1919. Yet it is precisely the early films that have been available for home movie use for years, suggesting that Lloyd was just, well, ordinary. And at that early stage he was. It was only with the later shorts and features that the brilliance was revealed.

Two years after Lloyd died in 1971, Time-Life signed a distribution deal for his films and handled them with a tragic lack of understanding. The shorts were packaged with a commentary in the style of Pete Smith ("Poor Harold! It's doom for the groom unless he gets to his room!"), which effectively sank them without a trace. The features were spared the commentary, but insensitive, honky-tonk scores and the elimination of entire sequences often crippled their effect.

Television is not the ideal medium for silent comedy, which depends on the shared laughter of large audiences. But it was the only way that people could expect to make contact with the great comedians of the past. When David Gill and I were preparing our documentary, we encountered a handful of young admirers of Lloyd, but we found no group of aficionados who studied his work with the devotion of those committed to Chaplin or Keaton.

Harold Lloyd was a far more influential comedian than he has been given credit for. We were surprised, for instance, at the number of Lloyd gags that turn up in Buster Keaton films. Of course, there was an interchange of gagmen between the two, and later on, Lloyd borrowed gags from Keaton. Then again, all the major comedians incorporated "high and dizzy" routines into their work once Lloyd had proved how popular they were—think of the cabin on the edge of the cliff in Chaplin's *The Gold Rush* (1925) and the waterfall scene from Keaton's *Our Hospitality* (1923).

Once he adopted his trademark glasses, Lloyd's comedies became a much more precise mirror of the 1920s than Chaplin's or Keaton's. Falling afoul of the highly regimented society into which he longed to be accepted, Harold's character tried desperately to atone. If he was late for work, he would spirit himself aboard an ambulance to beat the traffic. Assumed by his girl to be a successful department store manager, he would go to excruciating lengths to maintain her illusion, despite the risk to his real job as a sales clerk.

Embarrassment was the emotion he made us suffer with him. It is a considerable achievement to be able to convey any kind of emotion on a strip of celluloid, and Lloyd did it exceptionally well—perhaps too well; some people still reject him for making them feel uncomfortable.

Lloyd's nickname was "Speedy"—the title of his last silent—and all his films have terrific pace. He filmed several maniacal races through crowded streets that were forerunners of the ones in *The French Connection* (1971) and *Speed* (1993). The chase in *Girl Shy* (1924), intercut with a wedding that Harold must stop, is a breathtaking piece of cinema—one that influenced the makers of *Ben-Hur* (1925) when they shot their chariot race the following year. It is time that his features are put in the category they deserve: masterpiece.

When I was young and saw Lloyd's best-known film, *Safety Last!*, uncut and in an excellent print, together with *Dr. Jack*, in a Wardour Street film library, I was encouraged to write a fan letter to the great comedian. One day I planned to write a book about the silent era, and with this in mind I asked him questions about his career. Lloyd did not reply. He was a successful businessman, after all, hardly likely to have the time to answer letters from fledgling film historians. A pity, but there it was.

By then I had left home, joined the film industry, and was living in a bed-sit in Hampstead, North London. It was Saturday, June 2, 1962—my twenty-fourth birthday. I was sleeping late, having a most delightful dream: D. W. Griffith was conducting me through the corridor of a spacious clapboard building somewhere in the United States (I had not yet been there). It was a home for retired movie people. He gestured at one door and mentioned the name of a famous film editor; at another, a great cameraman. Before we had time to meet any-one, a telephone began to ring at the far end of the corridor. We set out toward it, and I woke up, realizing the phone was ringing in *my* corridor. I staggered out of bed, down the hall, and picked it up.

"This is Harold Lloyd."

I was young enough to have friends who played practical jokes, and I had often been taken in. But there was an authenticity about the voice that, coming out of my dream, caused me to hesitate. It was indeed Harold Lloyd. He was in London for a few days; was I free for lunch? Come over to the Dorchester . . . how about 11 o'clock?

What better birthday present could any film historian have? Nonetheless, I was apprehensive. Many comedians are dour and humorless offstage. I remembered meeting Groucho Marx, after a scintillating appearance at the National Film Theatre, in which he had us all in fits, and being astonished at his coldness. He had done his act, and now he was off—that was it.

Lloyd, by contrast, was charming. He was in his late sixties, still good-looking, with a dazzling smile, and a naiveté reflected not so much in what he said as in how he said it. He spoke with the inflection of an eager midwestern youth, with a smattering of "Gees" and much laughter. The glasses were now permanent. When we shook hands he used his left, and I saw that his right hand was missing both thumb and forefinger. Not until later did I learn about the bomb that had shattered his hand and nearly wrecked his career during a still photo session.

Lloyd put me at ease, answered all my questions, and behaved exactly as I wanted the characters in my dream to behave. He conjured up the challenge and excitement of making pictures in the silent days with effortless ease; his heart lay in that era, and he soon recognized that mine did, too.

Lloyd had that effusive, hail-fellow-well-met manner that in younger people makes me instantly suspicious. With many, it is simply a sign that they have read Dale Carnegie's *How to Make Friends and Influence*

Filming *Spring Fever* (1919). Director Hal Roach consults with cameraman Fred Guiol. Harold and Snub Pollard are pulling diminutive Sammy Brooks in front of the camera while Bebe Daniels converses with Paul Brunet (vice president and general manager of Pathé) off camera.

People, and it reveals them as door-to-door salespersons, real-estate agents, or film producers. With Lloyd, the sincerity and bonhomie were genuine. It was as though he was the model on whom Dale Carnegie based his book.

I was surprised to discover that Lloyd had no more time for unmotivated slapstick than I had. "I get very upset when people refer to my pictures as slapstick. Sure, there's slapstick *in* them — but you can't call them that as a whole. My Glass Character never did anything that wasn't possible — except in *Get Out and Get Under* (1920) where I went further into my Model T Ford's hood, until finally my feet disappeared. And we thought the old T Ford could run on anything, so there's one scene of my stopping the car and opening the hood and finding no engine."

Lloyd was careful to discriminate between the later films and the early slapstick one-reelers. He was somewhat apologetic about his early attempts with characters inspired by Chaplin: Willie Work (stovepipe hat, Prince Albert coat, and cat moustache), the character in *Just Nuts* (1915) (a variation even closer to Chaplin), and Lonesome Luke, who sported an outfit as tight as Chaplin's was baggy. He tended to regard his career proper as starting with the arrival of what he called the Glass Character — the ordinary-looking young man who wore a straw hat and horn-rims and came into being in a one-reel picture called *Over the Fence* (1917).

Of the later Lloyd, I had seen only a couple of two-reelers and features. I had no idea of the range of which this Glass Character was capable until Lloyd invited me to a midnight premiere of a film he had compiled called *Harold Lloyd's World of Comedy* (1962). It was an exhilarating event; the Columbia Theatre on Shaftsbury Avenue was packed with comedians—Peter Ustinov, Frankie Howerd, Bob Monkhouse, and Peter Sellers among them. The barrage of laughter proved that Lloyd's films still worked, even for hardened professionals.

In the early 1960s most people, even those in the business, expected silent films to be crudely photographed, and it came as a surprise to the audience that the pictorial quality was so good. The extracts were well chosen, well integrated, and although as a purist I objected to the use of sound effects, the film was accompanied by a lively orchestral score by Walter Scharf, rather than the interminable piano usually thought sufficient for silent films.

Harold Lloyd's World of Comedy proved Lloyd's talent beyond doubt, but it did no more than hint at his genius. Lloyd said it had more laughs in it than any of his other films, and I inferred from this that he had chosen the best scenes, and that the rest of his features would be full of padding. Later I found this was not so; in fact, splendid as *Harold Lloyd's World of Comedy* was for its time, its format prevented it from being as absorbing or as funny as the best of his silent features.

The following year, Lloyd reissued *The Freshman* (1925), his most popular film, in another compilation, *Harold Lloyd's Funny Side of Life* (1963). *The Freshman* was virtually complete, with most of its original titles. The music was again by Scharf, and there was a song, with lyrics by Ned Washington, entitled "There Was a Boy, There Was a Girl." I loved the film but hated the song. Lloyd was not averse to criticism, and when we met after the show I was impressed by the seriousness with which he listened to my objection. I can imagine how this combination of concentration and respect for an opposing point of view endeared him to his directors, gagmen, and even his carpenters, and how he encouraged them to come up with better ideas. I am sure this was not a pose; Lloyd was no more confident of his own judgment than any other artist, and he responded well to enthusiastic discussion, even when it went against his own convictions.

I became friends with Lloyd, visited him at Greenacres, his amazing estate in Beverly Hills, and saw more of his films. I was overwhelmed—as I still am—not only by the comic talents but the sheer film craft. If ever I want to convert someone to silent films, I simply run a Harold Lloyd feature. I got to know Lloyd's granddaughter, Suzanne Lloyd, in the 1960s, and she worked closely with David and me on *Harold Lloyd: The Third Genius*. She supported us when we presented several of the Lloyd silent features with live orchestra and produced a series of them for Thames Television. She has also supported restorations by the UCLA Film and Television Archive funded through the David and Lucille Packard Foundation and the Packard Humanities Institute in cooperation with The Harold Lloyd Trust. She has always been anxious to get the message about her grandfather across to a wider public, and if Harold Lloyd is better known now it is largely due to her.

There has long been a rivalry among fans of Chaplin, Keaton, and Lloyd—admiring one of them and denigrating the others, rather as if, in the eighteenth century, people had enthused over Mozart while rejecting Haydn and Beethoven. This has always bewildered me. The silent era was incredibly rich in comedy, and we should appreciate our luck that so much is still available. The work of Harold Lloyd includes some of the finest comedies ever made, and they will continue to delight audiences as long as there are methods of projecting moving images upon a screen.

His Early Years

IN THE GOLDEN AGE OF SILENT FILM COMEDY there were many clowns, but only three truly great artists—Charles Chaplin, Buster Keaton, and Harold Lloyd. However, Harold made more films than Chaplin or Keaton, and his films often rivaled Chaplin's and always surpassed Keaton's at the box office. Harold did not learn his craft on the vaudeville stage, as virtually all the other silent clowns had, yet he is regarded as one of the finest comic actors ever to appear on film. Unlike Chaplin and Keaton, whose innate gifts destined them for success, Harold Lloyd relied only on luck and hard work to become one of the greatest cinema artists of his era. Harold was a genius because he worked at it, and a success because he never gave up. His values are uniquely American; Harold Lloyd lived the American dream.

Harold Clayton Lloyd was the second son of J. Darsie and Elizabeth Lloyd, born in a modest frame house located at 24 Pawnee Street in the small Nebraska town of Burchard on April 20, 1893. His elder brother, Gaylord Fraser Lloyd, was born in 1888. Harold's father

was born James Darsie Lloyd in Ebensburg, Pennsylvania, in 1864. His parents had come to the United States from South Wales and settled in Toulon, Illinois, before moving to Pawnee County, Nebraska. Harold's mother was born Elizabeth Fraser in Toulon, Illinois, in 1869. Her forebears were of English and Scottish extraction. It was in Toulon where J. Darsie and Elizabeth met, and in 1880 they were married in Burchard, Nebraska.

J. Darsie Lloyd acquired the nickname "Foxy" because, as a Singer sewing machine salesman, he devised a successful scheme to recover lost machines. Harold's mother worked as a milliner. Music lessons that she took in her youth had inspired her ambition to be a concert singer, but her dream was quashed by her family. Although Harold's mother had wanted him to become a civil engineer, both his parents supported his theatrical ambitions.

Harold learned to be resourceful and industrious at an early age, and often likened his upbringing to the fictional life of Tom Sawyer. Like Mark Twain's character, Harold performed numerous odd jobs, including delivering newspapers, selling popcorn, and entertaining both children and adults with illusions and sleight-of-hand tricks he created (which

A collage of photographs from Harold's portfolio created to demonstrate the range of his makeup talents (Harold is without makeup in the lower right). At this period Harold was looking for character roles and was not interested in being a comedian, nor did he consider himself a suitable leading man. All photos c. 1913.

Right:
Elizabeth, Gaylord, Harold,
and J. Darsie "Foxy" Lloyd,
c. 1894.

Below:
Harold at three years of age,
photographed by his father at
Bennett & Lloyd, the studio
he co-owned, in Humbolt,
Nebraska, 1896.

were performed at a price). Yet the Tom Sawyer gloss over Harold's youth is a bit of a whitewash. Harold's father was a failure. Although he was full of ideas, very few came to anything; he held a variety of jobs and never made anything out of them, often moving his family from town to town in rural Nebraska and later Colorado, looking for work. During Harold's childhood he lived, at various times, in Burchard, Pawnee City, Humboldt, Beatrice, and Omaha, Nebraska; and Fort Collins, Durango, and Denver, Colorado. Harold's mother, who could no longer endure this lifestyle, divorced Foxy in 1910.

Elizabeth instilled her passion for the theater in both Harold and Gaylord at an early age. She read plays to her sons, particularly Shakespeare, and encouraged them to perform. As a child, Harold often play-acted, using various types of hats and masks set up on couches and chairs as characters for which he had no actors. His interest in acting led him to a job as a doorman in an opera house. Harold got his first acting job onstage before his tenth birthday, playing Fléance for a single night in a Shakespearean touring company's production of *Macbeth*. After that rather inauspicious debut, Harold was hooked. He formed his own juvenile acting company, and gave performances in neighborhood barns and on front lawns. He sought out whatever jobs he could find that were located in a theater and immersed himself in the study of the tools of his trade, including acting, staging, and particularly makeup.

At the age of thirteen, Harold met an actor named John Lane Conner, a juvenile lead with the Burwood Stock Company, who took the young Harold under his wing and got him various juvenile parts in plays. His first important role was as Abraham in an Omaha stock company production of *Tess of the D'Ubervilles* that premiered on January 10, 1907. To Harold's delight, the local newspaper (Omaha's *World-Herald*) gave him a good notice:

> *"The part of Tess' little brother was well done by Master Harold Lloyd, who demonstrated that he has a dramatic instinct which will doubtless carry him on to success in the histrionic art."*[1]

Connor was arguably Lloyd's greatest influence as an actor. As the young Lloyd's mentor, he helped improve Harold's acting technique and impressed upon him the desire for perfection that would remain with Lloyd for the rest of his career and even permeate his hobbies.

Harold Lloyd's life was often propelled forward by uncanny collisions of perseverance and luck; the Lloyd family's first (and perhaps only) break came when Foxy was badly injured in a collision with a brewery truck driven by a drunk driver. Foxy was awarded $6,000 in damages, split evenly with his

Bennett & Lloyd   Humboldt Neb.

attorney. Yielding entirely to luck, Harold and his father tossed a coin to determine where they would begin their new life. The head side of the coin would bring them east to New York; the tail side would send them west to San Diego, where Harold's friend John Lane Connor had set up the San Diego School of Expression. Tails won. Foxy used his award to buy a pool hall and lunch counter in San Diego.

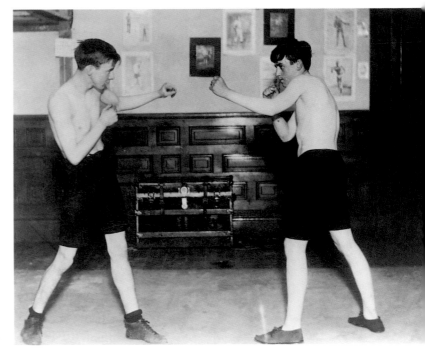

Throughout high school (from which he was never to graduate), Harold regularly acted in various San Diego stock companies and, in 1912, joined Connor's acting troupe and school. At this point in his life, Harold aspired to be a dramatic actor on the stage. He saw his first film, *The Great Train Robbery* (1903), as part of a medicine show in Pawnee City, Nebraska. Although Harold enjoyed it and the French Pathé comedies he saw regularly as a boy in Denver and Omaha, he never considered working in films, as he shared the general disdain for the cinema prevalent among theater people. However, in 1913, Lloyd retreated to films out of economic necessity and made his first appearance in a part less appealing than Fléance, playing a Native American servant in *The Old Monk's Tale* (1913), a one-reel production of the Edison Picture Company. It was in San Diego during this time that Harold experienced the worst economic hardship of his career. When he was down to his last nickel, he bought six sugar donuts and lived off them until he found other work. It was an experience he would never forget and often spoke about in his later years.

That same year, Foxy's San Diego business failed, and Harold and Gaylord moved with their father yet again, this time to Los Angeles. They lived in the Belmont hotel for actors, where the boys found work as bellhops and desk clerks. When work in local theaters dried up, Harold found acting jobs as an extra at the Universal Film Manufacturing Company for three dollars a day, using his knowledge of makeup techniques

Above:
Harold (right, with an unidentified opponent) as a fourteen-year-old amateur boxer at Jacobs' gymnasium, Denver, Colorado, 1907.

Left:
The San Diego School of Expression, 1912. Harold is seated in the center row, second from the right.

to sneak past the studio guard, disguised as a regular extra. He had difficulty getting in at first, not wanting to wait with the other aspiring extras in the waiting area called "the bull pen." Harold later remembered how he managed to get into the studio:

> *I happened to observe that anyone with makeup on got by the old gateman without any difficulty. He saw they were working—they had makeup on—so he permitted them to pass through. So I brought some makeup out, and went around the corner, and slapped on a kind of cursory makeup, and stuck my cap—I used to wear a cap in those days—under my coat, and ambled through the gate, without any trouble. But I made it a point, coming out, to talk with the old gateman. So I had to wear makeup, the first three days, in order to get through the gate. After that he got acquainted with me, and then I could go through, because he felt I belonged.*[2]

Harold would recreate his experience with the gateman in his one-reel comedy *Hey There* (1918) in which Harold attempts to break into a motion picture studio—the Near-Famous Film Company—in search of a glamorous actress (Bebe Daniels).

Harold's cheerful, optimistic demeanor and strong work ethic won him many friends and helped him get bit parts once he made it onto the Universal lot. Soon he was enjoying regular work at the studio. Harold met another extra at Universal who more than any other person would influence his young career, Hal Roach. Roach would become one of the great Hollywood comedy producers—along with Mack Sennett, the creator of the Our Gang comedies—and the one who paired Laurel and Hardy. Lloyd and Roach would learn together how to make movies, and in the process help define motion picture comedy.

Lonesome Luke

Harold in costume for *Just Nuts* (1915), a character even more Chaplinesque than Willie Work.

Harold as Lonesome Luke with his leading lady Bebe Daniels, 1915.

Harold and Hal Roach left Universal during a strike in which extras were protesting a cut in pay. Roach decided to set up his own independent production company, acquired a few thousand dollars, and partnered with Dan Linthicum[3] to form the Rolin Film Company (a combination of the first letters of their surnames) in August 1914. Roach hired his friend, Harold Lloyd, to be Rolin's comedy star, and the two created Willie Work, a character imitative of Charlie Chaplin. In 1914, Chaplin was the emergent king of film comedy and, to be successful, most comedians sought to imitate his indelible Little Tramp character. Lloyd's character's name evoked the question: will he work, or won't he? According to Harold:

> *I experimented with dress and makeup and about the fifth picture settled on a character we christened Willie Work. The name wrongly suggests a tramp; it was, instead, a hash of different low-comedy get-ups, with a much-padded coat, a battered silk hat and a cat's-whisker mustache as its distinguishing marks.*[4]

Unfortunately for Roach and Harold, the one-reel Rolin comedies were not commercially viable; Willie Work was not funny. According to Lloyd, none of the films were ever sold to distribution, and as early as 1928 he believed the films no longer existed, having "been burned long ago to recover the metallic silver."[5] The two friends were almost on the street.

Upper left:
Full-length portrait of Harold as Lonesome Luke, 1915. The character was an imitation of Charles Chaplin's Tramp character. However, Harold adopted tight trousers instead of the baggy trousers worn by Chaplin. The aggressive, Chaplinesque figure proved to be a moderate success. As Lloyd later explained, "It was quite successful but not really good."

Above:
Harold with unidentified players in an early Rolin comedy filmed outside the Bradbury Mansion, located above the Hill Street tunnel at 406 Court Street in Los Angeles, c. 1914. Note the actor costumed as a parson on the far right in wire-rimmed glasses similar to the horn-rimmed glasses Lloyd would later adopt.

Left:
Hal Roach, Harold, and Frank Borzage (at back, left to right) portray the chief eunuchs attending the birth of *Samson* (1914), a six-reel feature film made by Universal. George Periolat (front) is Manoah, Samson's father.

Above:
Harold as Luke de Fluke, a shoe store clerk who cannot resist his female customers in *Giving Them Fits* (1915). Snub Pollard wields the hammer as Bebe Daniels watches from the balcony. The film marked the first appearance of both Pollard and Daniels in a Lloyd film.

Right:
Harold as hired help in a photographer's studio. Larkin (Snub Pollard) and Lucas (Harold) photograph new college graduate Earl Mohan with his diploma in *Ragtime Snap Shots* (1915). Mohan's lensless horn-rimmed glasses would inspire Harold's Glass Character.

However, in a spate of luck, one of the Rolin films, *Just Nuts* (1915), came to the attention of the famed Pathé Exchange in New York . *Just Nuts* is a knockabout comedy, and has Lloyd playing a character even more imitative of Chaplin. Pathé liked the film and offered Roach a contract. Harold parted with Roach, however, over a money dispute: Roy Stewart, the leading dramatic actor in Roach's company, was paid ten dollars a day, twice as much as Lloyd's salary as the principal comic actor, and Harold balked. Without Harold, Roach's comedies featuring Dick Rosson floundered, and Roach soon moved to a directing position with the Essanay Film Manufacturing company, where Chaplin had been starring in a widely popular series of films. Roach's position at Essanay was to use Chaplin's stock company so they would be kept busy earning their salaries between their work in the Chaplin films. Harold was now with Mack Sennett at the Keystone Film Company and appeared in films with Keystone stars Roscoe "Fatty" Arbuckle and Ford Sterling. At Keystone, Sennett never noticed Harold's potential, perhaps because Harold lacked the comic training of Sennett's other actors. In fact, Ford Sterling advised Harold to seek employment as a dramatic actor.

Roach was lured back into independent production after securing a contract with Pathé on the condition that he must sign the three leads of *Just Nuts*—Stewart, Novak, and Lloyd. However, Stewart and Novak were contracted elsewhere, and only Harold was

available. Roach got the permission from Pathé to make comedies with just Lloyd, and in June 1915 Roach signed Harold for fifty dollars a week. Harold, with the assistance of his father and Roach, devised a new character, Lonesome Luke, who was essentially another Chaplin imitation. The character wore the tailored coat of a woman's suit, a black-and-white vertical-striped shirt, a small vest, tight, shortened trousers, a short hat, size 12AA shoes, and a mustache comprised of two dots under his nose. Harold described Lonesome Luke as follows: "The cunning thought behind all this, you will observe, was to reverse the Chaplin outfit. All his clothes were too large, mine all too small. My shoes were funny, but different; my mustache funny, but different."[6]

Pathé had purchased scenarios from the famous sports cartoonist Tad Dorgan to be used for the Lonesome Luke comedies. The first Lonesome Luke comedy was *Spit-Ball Sadie* (1915), a baseball story in which Lloyd at one point appeared in drag and at another hung from a crane hook, anticipating his later "thrill" comedies. The Dorgan stories and other scenarios were soon dispensed with in favor of improvising comedy at a certain locale — a park, a shoe store, a dance hall, etc. Roach directed these early one-reel comedies, which were made in one week for $1,200–$1,500 each. He later remembered:

> *The entire city of Los Angeles was my property room. We would go to Westlake Park or some other location with Harold, a pretty girl, and maybe a policeman and I would start with one idea and we would work with that as a starting point. The actors would make suggestions, but we had nothing written down on paper. The films would end with some kind of a chase. That's how we made the early one-reel comedies. . . . Harold Lloyd worked for me because he could play a comedian. He was not a comedian. He was the best actor I ever saw being a comedian. He was one of the most dedicated actors I've ever met in my life. No one worked harder than he did. He didn't have the music-hall training that Chaplin had, so he had to work harder than the rest.[7]*

Harold as a theatrical booking agent at the Bunko Agency in *Luke Pipes the Pippins* (1916). The fat boy is Dee Lampton, who played in many of the early Lloyd comedies.

Made between 1915 and 1917, the Lonesome Luke films are essentially knockabout chases set in different venues, and foreshadow nothing of the famous Lloyd character and subtle acting that would follow. In the Lonesome Lukes, Harold drew on his athleticism and the training he received at Keystone. The knockabout was such that cast members were frequently injured, and the company had difficulty obtaining insurance for Harold.

The Lonesome Luke comedies eventually expanded to two reels in length and, despite the primitive nature of the films, were commercially successful and very popular in this period when exhibitors were craving Chaplin product—even imitations. The supporting players for the Lonesome Luke comedies included Australian actor Harry "Snub" Pollard, famous for his absurd walrus mustache. Born Harry Hopetown Fraser, he came to the United States with the Pollard Juvenile Opera Company, with whom he had appeared in vaudeville. When the troop dissolved, many of its members took the company name. Pollard had appeared in several of Chaplin's

Above:
Harold dreams he has a double
who gets him into trouble in
Luke's Double (1916). Here
Luke is in prison, visited by his
mischievous twin, courtesy of
some excellent double-exposure
work.

Above right:
Harold is enamored with the
young woman (Bebe Daniels)
who works in an occult shop in
Luke, Crystal Gazer (1916).

Right:
Harold gets into a celluloid
entanglement with projectionist
Snub Pollard while working in a
small cinema in *Luke's Movie
Muddle* (1916). This photograph
anticipates the famous image of
Buster Keaton surrounded by film
from *Sherlock, Jr.* (1924).

Essanay comedies and proved to be a fine comic foil for Lloyd. Harold's leading lady was the vivacious, dark-haired Virginia "Bebe" Daniels, a child actress who had many years of experience in motion pictures at such studios as Vitagraph and Ince before she joined Rolin at age fourteen. However, Bebe was little more than a prop for Harold to play off of in these early Lonesome Luke comedies. Romance was never developed, only travesties of romance. Both Pollard and Daniels first appeared with Harold in *Giving Them Fits* (1915). Another vital member of the Rolin team was Harley M. "Beany" Walker, a former sports editor for William Randolph Hearst's *Los Angeles Examiner*, who wrote the clever intertitles for the Rolin comedies.

One night Harold and Bebe went to the cinema to see one of their comedies, and as Luke appeared on the screen, a boy sitting next to Harold said, "Oh, here's that fellow who tries to do like Chaplin." That was the last straw for Harold, who decided then and there that "I wasn't going on forever being a third-rate imitator of anybody, even a genius like Chaplin."[8]

Lloyd determined at that moment to abandon the Lonesome Luke character. However, Pathé had invested a considerable amount of money exploiting Lonesome Luke and was making money from the films. The company was reluctant to lose a successful known quantity for something new and uncertain. Competitive and ambitious, Harold believed he could rise to the level of Chaplin, but such an ascent could not be accomplished as Lonesome Luke. He persuaded Roach and Pathé to see things his way. Harold recalled:

> *I had the feeling, and rightly so, that I would never get any farther with Lonesome Luke than I had, because underneath it all, he was a comedy character and couldn't possibly rise to the heights that Chaplin had. And while you didn't try directly to imitate Chaplin, Luke was a character that belonged to that category.*[9]

As long as Chaplin continued to hold the franchise on his Tramp character, a cheap imitation like Lonesome Luke ultimately had nowhere to go, and Harold knew it. However, Harold also knew that Lonesome Luke was a moneymaker and should not be lightly discarded, and Pathé and Roach were committed to making as many Lonesome Luke comedies as possible. But Harold was determined to make subtler comedies.

The last Lonesome Luke comedy, *We Never Sleep*, was released on December 2, 1917. The Lonesome Luke films were later withdrawn from distribution; in February 1934, Harold purchased the rights to and prints of all his films from distributor Pathé Exchange. Unfortunately, in August 1943 a vault fire at Greenacres destroyed the nitrate film negatives and prints of nearly all the Lonesome Luke comedies. The loss of the majority of these films hinders the study of the development of Lloyd's career; however, Harold himself had a low opinion of the Lonesome Luke comedies, and it is unlikely that he would have made these films available, even if material had existed. Today, only about twelve of the nearly seventy Lonesome Luke films are known to survive.

The Glass Character

Harold persuaded Hal Roach to let him try a persona he called the "Glass Character," a bespectacled, earnest, ordinary young man with a straw boater hat, whose studious appearance completely belies his actions. By 1918, the Glass Character would be Lloyd's signature to such a great extent that it became synonymous with the actor who portrayed him.

Harold's own remembrances of the genesis of the character are somewhat muddled. The best evidence suggests that he came upon the idea partly from Earl Mohan, a Rolin stock company player, who appeared in many of the Lonesome Luke comedies and frequently wore horn-rimmed glasses in the films. It was Mohan who inspired Harold's wearing the spectacles. However, it was Harold's seeing the dramatic film *When Paris Green Saw Red* (1918), about a mild-mannered, bespectacled parson who when riled reveals his tough side in a fight sequence, that further inspired the glasses characterization.[10] Harold explained:

> *While my character was not a comic character in appearance I donned the glasses to make him instantly recognizable. They were not just a gimmick. They were a trademark the same as Chaplin's derby and cane. But my glasses gave a character besides. Someone with glasses is generally thought to be studious and an erudite person to a degree, a kind of person who doesn't fight or engage in violence, but I did, so my glasses belied my appearance. The audience could put me in a situation in their mind, but I could be just the opposite to what was supposed. So the glasses not only had an identifying characteristic but also a comedy characteristic.*[11]

Harold experimented with different styles and sizes of glasses before deciding on tortoiseshell horn-rims. As mostly young men of the period wore tortoiseshell plastic frames, Harold chose them because they symbolized youth. Harold found the first pair he liked in a little shop on Spring Street in downtown Los Angeles. He wore the pair exclusively with great care for a year and a half, until he was no longer able to repair them. They were then sent to Optical Products Corporation, an optical supply manufacturer in New York, for duplication. The company sent back twenty pair at no charge; the popularity he had given to horn-rims left them indebted to him.[12] What separated Harold's spectacles from those of the person on the street was that Harold's frames were lensless; the absence of lenses eliminated any reflection from the sun or studio lights. There was one instance when Harold actually lost the only frames he had left, and production was held up until a new shipment was received. Optical Products would thereafter replace Harold's frames six at a time.

Harold never allowed his gagmen to create gags about his glasses:

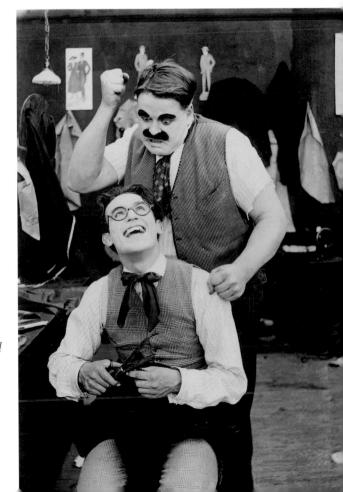

> *I never used my glasses to draw special attention to them. They were like my nose, my mouth, my eyes. They were something that was part of me. I never took my glasses off. I don't think my audiences ever saw a picture of Harold Lloyd without his glasses. If I was to play a Civil War soldier [Grandma's Boy], I had my glasses adapted to give the feeling of a century ago. So, when I played football, people didn't give a thought to it that I wore my glasses. Even when I went in swimming, I had my glasses on. When I was in bed, I had them on too. People accepted the glasses as part of my screwball type of character. There was a scene in one of my pictures [The Freshman] where people were stepping on my face, and generally giving me a going over. The audience didn't stop and think, "Oh, his glasses will be broken!" They just didn't think of my glasses as separate from my own personality.[13]*

Above:
Harold takes shelter from a
spilled bottle during a brawl at
the Howling Poodle Tango Bar
in *Two-Gun Gussie* (1918).

Above right:
Harold is a substitute photogra-
pher amused with the dark-
room misfortunes of Snub
Pollard in *Look Pleasant
Please* (1918).

Right:
As a flirtatious soda fountain
clerk, Harold shares some ice
cream with Bebe Daniels in
Let's Go (1918).

Harold in drag at a dinner party in *Kicked Out* (1918). Snub Pollard is enacting a Cinderella moment with Harold's slipper.

Without the glasses, Lloyd was no longer Harold Lloyd the screen comedian. "There is more magic in a pair of horn-rimmed glasses than the opticians dreamed of," according to Harold in his autobiography. "With them, I am Harold Lloyd; without them a private citizen. I can stroll unrecognized down any street in the land at any time without the glasses, a boon granted no other picture actor and one which some of them would pay well for."[14]

With the Glass Character, Harold came back to his roots and found his soul. The genius of the character was not that it was extraordinary, but that it was so ordinary, so normal — a store clerk, a fellow next door, a cousin, a brother. As Harold wrote, "funnier things happen in life to an ordinary boy than to a Lonesome Luke."[15] Whereas none had Keaton's granite stare or Chaplin's balletic grace, Lloyd was Everyman, the earnest, young, go-getter from humble Nebraska roots whose sole mission was "to make good." In short, Harold found success by playing himself, and his optimism and relentless pursuit of success delighted audiences who were familiar with the Horatio Alger myth.[16] Soon, Harold Lloyd would be as American as mother and apple pie.

Pathé agreed to let Harold try his new character, but not at the immediate demise of Lonesome Luke. The Lonesome Luke comedies continued, with the last Lonesome Luke two-reelers alternating with the first Glass Character one-reelers. Lloyd initially opted to make one-reelers with the Glass Character instead of two-reelers so that the character was on the screen in a new comedy every week, and if he made a bad one, it was quickly forgotten.

Lloyd felt that the proper start of his film career occurred with the advent of the Glass Character, who came into being in the baseball comedy *Over the Fence* (1917). (Lloyd, who was always superstitious, had started Lonesome Luke with a baseball comedy, *Spit-Ball Sadie*). *Over the Fence* is amusing (particularly

Right:
Harold happily accommodates some schoolgirls shopping for corsets in *Here Come the Girls* (1918).

Below:
Harold anticipates trouble from guest Helen Gilmore as an employee of the Punkville Hotel in *The City Slicker* (1918).

Opposite:
Harold and Snub Pollard enter the world of seer Professor Goulash to escape the police in *Are Crooks Dishonest?* (1918). Behind them are William Blaidsell as the professor and Bebe Daniels as his daughter.

Harold—called "Ginger" in the film—on the pitcher's mound), but nothing exceptional. The early Glass Character films were like the Lonesome Lukes—with glasses. Although the glasses made him look sympathetic, he was as aggressive as his earlier characterizations. Many of the films were heavily influenced by the Chaplin comedies made for the Mutual Film Corporation between 1916–17. It took Harold a while to change from the resourceful but callously aggressive Luke to the gentler, cleverer, and kinder Glass Character, whose personality eventually caused romance to become a part of the films. A series of knockabout situations evolved into comedies with an expanded story; the girl became a wonderful foil for his developing screen persona. Over time this began to enhance the reality of Lloyd's films.

Ask Father (1919), directed by Hal Roach, is perhaps the finest of the one-reel comedies for its construction and clever gags. Plucky Harold tries numerous ways—including scaling the side of a building (which is not played for "thrills"), firing off pistols, and wearing a suit of armor—to see an inaccessible businessman for his daughter's hand in marriage. Every time he tries to get into the office to "ask father," he is kicked out. Bebe Daniels plays the businessman's stenographer, who is sympathetic to Harold's plight and manages to toss her pillow right where Harold falls. When the girl announces she has married someone else, Harold turns his attention to Bebe and a happy ending.

One of the most original of the early one-reel Glass Character comedies is *Look Out Below* (1919), the first Lloyd "thrill picture." It was directed by Hal Roach, who came across the idea for these "high and dizzy"-type sequences when he was filming a scene of two people on the terrace above the Hill Street tunnel in downtown Los Angeles. The cameraman neglected to include the balustrade in the shot and it appeared as if the two people were suspended high in the air. In *Look Out Below* Harold and Bebe sit on a girder that—unbeknownst to them—slowly rises to the top of a building under construction. The film climaxes with Harold clinging to the swinging girder. Although Roach and Lloyd did not invent the genre of "high and dizzy" film comedies, they undisputably made the best of them, and other comedians borrowed from their work.

By the end of 1919, Harold had produced eighty one-reel comedies—an extraordinary quantity—and his popularity nearly matched that of Chaplin and Arbuckle.

Harold Lloyd's films benefitted from a talented, creative team: Walter Lundin was his first cameraman (with Henry Kohler in the position of second cameraman during most of the silent film period); Fred Guiol and later William MacDonald were Harold's technical directors, responsible for set construction and the mechanical planning of special stunts and effects; Jack Murphy was the production manager; Harley M. "Beany" Walker and later Tommy Gray were the title writers; Joe Reddy was the press agent; and Thomas Crizer was the film editor (and later a gagman).

Hal Roach, Gilbert Pratt, and Alf Goulding were Lloyd's principal directors. Roach was increasingly required to give his attention outside the Lloyd comedies, and for a time he worked to develop a clown named Toto while Pratt and Goulding alternated the direction of the Lloyd comedies. Pratt had begun his screen career as an actor with the Kalem Film Company, and had been with Rolin since 1915. Goulding, an Australian with much stage experience, was a friend of Snub Pollard and had worked at Fox. Both men acted

Opposite top:
Harold and Snub are rival suitors who find themselves submerged in paint in *She Loves Me Not* (1918), with Wallace Howe between them.

Opposite below:
Harold was not required to serve in the armed forces during World War I, as authorities decided that his appearances in films like *Kicking the Germ Out of Germany* (1918) would better serve the war effort than his participation in the military.

Below:
Filming *Look Out Below* (1919), Harold's first "thrill" picture, on top of the Hill Street tunnel in downtown Los Angeles. The illusion of danger was created by photographing the action at such an angle that the balustrade is left out of the shot to give the impression that Harold and Bebe are on a girder suspended in the air. On the left is director Hal Roach, and Snub Pollard is at center.

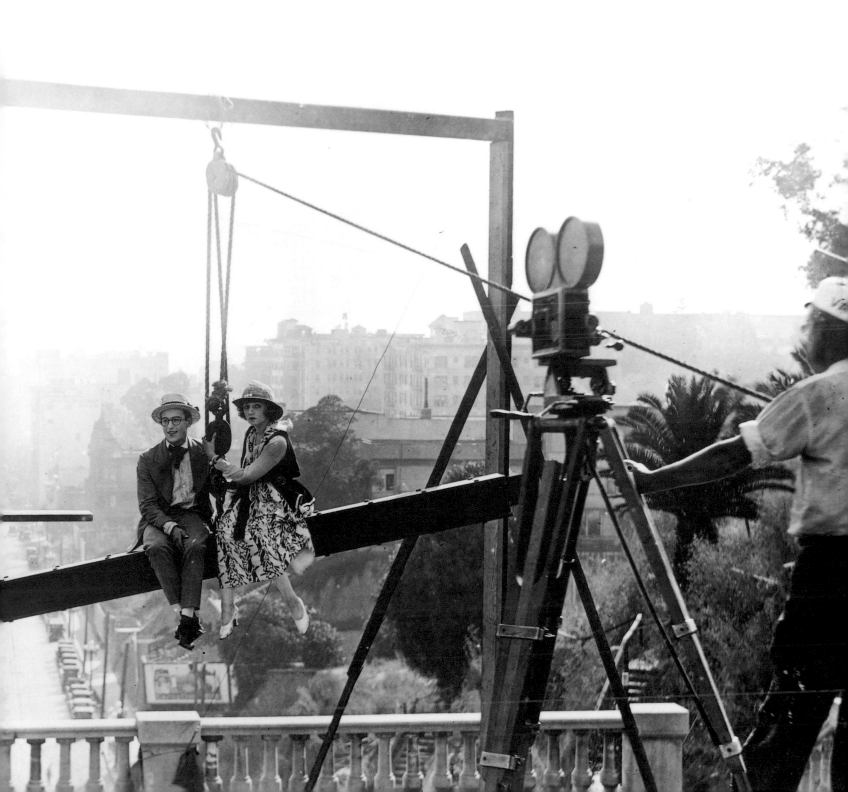

Harold and Bebe Daniels as a young married couple in *Bride and Gloom* (1918). Snub Pollard (left) is disguised as a blind man, and Sammy Brooks is seated on the right. Note the blackface caricature that was typical of Hollywood films of the period.

as director and gagman. Since Lloyd made one film per week, a system was devised for filming: one director shot a film with Lloyd while the other prepared the next.

Frank Terry (an Englishman whose real name was Nat Clifford) joined Rolin in early 1919 as a gagman for Harold. Terry had been with the Fred Karno Company in England, where he worked with Chaplin; he was invaluable to the Lloyd comedies; his nimble mind held a vast treasury of comedy routines. Terry's influence can be easily seen in *Billy Blazes, Esq.* (1919), directed by Hal Roach and arguably the funniest of the Lloyd one-reelers. A parody of William S. Hart westerns, Harold is first seen from behind. When he turns around, he is revealed with his glasses framed in a ten-gallon cowboy hat. The film has a wonderful sequence in which Harold is able to draw aim with his six-shooter before his enemy (played by Noah Young) can flinch. Terry was a good gagman and greatly helped the Lloyd one-reel films, but he left the studio in 1920 (he returned briefly to work with Harold on *Movie Crazy*), and was replaced by gagmen Sam Taylor and Jean Havez.

Bebe Daniels continued as the leading lady of the one-reel Glass Character shorts and the first of the two-reel Glass Character comedies. Harold and Bebe had fallen in love soon after she had joined Rolin in 1915 and were inseparable. By all accounts, they made a marvelous couple and were known around Los Angeles for their fantastic dancing; they entered dance competitions once a week and frequently won. But Bebe wanted to become a dramatic actress. In 1919 she left Roach when her contract came to an end and joined Cecil B. DeMille at Paramount to become a star in her own right. Bebe's move to DeMille was also a push for Harold to marry her, as she was more anxious to settle down than he. Harold, however, felt they were

too young and that his career was at a critical stage. He wanted to postpone marriage; she wanted to force it. She eventually married actor Ben Lyon and relocated to England where the couple appeared on radio and television in the series *Life with the Lyons*. However, Harold and Bebe remained very good friends. The fact that for the rest of his life Harold wore a pair of cufflinks Bebe gave him during their time together at Rolin attests to the value he placed on their relationship. Bebe Daniels died eight days after Harold passed away, on March 16, 1971.

Graduating to the production of two-reel comedies with the Glass Character afforded Lloyd the opportunity to explore more complex character development and comedic situations. The films were immediately successful with the release of the first in the series, *Bumping into Broadway* (1919). These comedies were marketed as "The New Million Dollar Two-Reel Comedies," indicating the enormous amount of money put into them for the time (and imitating First National's advertising campaign of Chaplin's "million dollar comedies" for that company). An April 12, 1919, contract between the Rolin Film Company and Pathé Exchange called for nine two-reel comedies that were made over an eighteen-month period. Harold's agreement allotted him half of Rolin's profits from the Lloyd comedies. In the case of *Bumping into Broadway*, which had cost $17,274 to produce, Rolin made a net profit of $63,987 in its first three years of distribution. Harold, therefore, received half ($31,993). As each succeeding two-reeler (released one per month) made progressively more money than the earlier Lloyd films, Harold's income grew considerably. He was soon one of the wealthiest actors in Hollywood.

Harold cleans up the town in one of his best one-reel comedies, *Billy Blazes, Esq.* (1919), a parody of William S. Hart westerns. Harold is able to produce a pointed gun at the flinch of his enemies, even when it appears he is not looking. Bebe Daniels is the object of Harold's affection. Noah Young is the moustached villian on the right.

Left:
Harold, Snub Pollard, and Bebe Daniels are in front of the camera in this behind-the-scenes still from *Just Neighbors* (1919). Fred Guiol is the cameraman. Observing the action is Paul Brunet (vice president and general manager of Pathé) and his sons.

Top:
Harold does not care for monkey business in *The Rajah* (1919), a one-reel comedy with a plot similar to Lloyd's first feature, *A Sailor-Made Man* (1921).

Above:
Harold and canine friend in *Count Your Change* (1919), in a still inspired by Charles Chaplin's *A Dog's Life* (1918).

Right:
Harold only has eyes for stenographer Bebe Daniels at the conclusion of *Ask Father* (1919), arguably the best of the Lloyd one-reel comedies. Bud Jamison (with clenched fist), Noah Young, Snub Pollard, Dee Lampton, and Sammy Brooks comprise some of the disgruntled onlookers.

Below:
Harold's fez-wearing days as a Shriner are anticipated when he goes through the initiation rites of the Ancient Order of Simps, Young Turks Lodge No. 13 in *Pay Your Dues* (1919). Signaling with him is Bebe Daniels.

Below right:
Harold in his office signing autographs, 1918.

Harold was preparing the fifth in the series of two-reel comedies, *Haunted Spooks* (1920), when an accident occurred that nearly killed him. On Sunday, August 24, 1919, in what was the most tragic moment in his life, Harold was holding what he believed to be a prop bomb for publicity photographs at the Witzel Studios when it accidentally exploded in his hand, burning his face and blowing the thumb and forefinger off his right hand. However, Harold was extremely lucky: had he not lowered the bomb from his face at the instant it went off, he would have been killed. He was near death for four days, suffering severe burns to his face and body. He later developed rashes and other skin complaints as a reaction to the antiseptic used to prevent gangrene. After eight months, during which Harold was unsure whether he would lose his right eye — let alone have a career before the camera — he recovered, and resumed his work in films using a specially designed prosthetic glove. Inside the glove was a false finger and thumb; when the second finger moved, the false first finger appeared to move normally with it. The leather glove was stretched tightly over the hand; high on his forearm Harold wore a rubber garter with elastic bands that ran to the top of the glove to keep it in place when performing his highly physical comedy. Film producer Samuel Goldwyn, who was once a glove merchant, recommended to Roach and Lloyd a firm that would manufacture the special glove. Harold would wear the glove only for

Bumping into Broadway (1919), Harold's first two-reel comedy with the Glass Character, culminates in a wild police raid on a gambling house.

Harold dreams of being captured by a bevy of pretty female pirates in *Captain Kidd's Kids* (1919). Lloyd thought the film to be one of his weakest two-reel comedies.

filming. For the rest of his life, Harold never publicly discussed the loss of his right thumb and index finger. He did not want audiences to be distracted by, or view him with, pity or curiosity because of his accident.

Harold was lucky to be alive. His ability to return to work after the accident and the commercial success of his subsequent work motivated him to want to make better films and resulted in his being more critical of his work. He also resolved to never forget his good fortune.

As the films of Harold Lloyd grew more and more popular, greater care and expense were given to their creation. Originally, directors of the one-reel comedies filmed each shot of a scene only once; soon the company was filming as many as ten takes of a scene, varying the action in each take. The best take was chosen after previewing a rough cut of the film to an unsuspecting audience and observing their reaction. In this way, Harold and his team could determine what worked and what needed to be reshot or refined. Harold relied

heavily on this practice, occasionally previewing a film as many as seven times. His impeccable timing and pacing came about in large measure thanks to the fine-tuning that resulted from the previews. Lloyd explained:

Harold saves a waif (Peggy Cartwright) and a dog from starvation and the cops in From Hand to Mouth *(1919), his most Chaplinesque film.*

> *They weren't just previews that were made to satisfy yourself and then send it on. Our previews—we started our picture with the idea that we were going to preview to let the audience actually tell us whether we were on the right track or not, whether the sequences that we were making were funny or not. And in that way we made the picture and then went back and took out parts that we felt were not funny enough or that didn't have the right interest and either made them over or bridged them around another way, or embellished them. And in that way it was tremendously helpful to keep right in tune with what the audiences liked or didn't like.*[17]

An example of how a film was developed by the preview is *I Do* (1921), which was previewed in three reels, and it was a disappointment. The first reel depicted Harold and his girl eloping (with the girl's parents secretly helping them, as they liked Harold and approved of the marriage). It was funny, but it did not seem to work in the first preview. Harold and his team eliminated all of the first reel, filmed a short introduction to the remaining two reels, and previewed it again. It emerged as one of the most popular of Lloyd's two-reel comedies.

Above:
Harold recovering from the explosion that resulted in the loss of his right thumb and fore-finger, 1919. With him outside his home, located at 369 South Hoover Street in Los Angeles, is an unidentified nurse and his father, Foxy.

Below:
Charles Pathé (seated), Hal Roach, Harold, and Paul Brunet (vice president and general manager of Pathé) negotiate a new contract for the Harold Lloyd comedies in Pathé's New York offices, November 1919.

Lloyd has frequently been credited as one of the earliest filmmakers to use previewing to the extent that he did. As a filmmaker, Lloyd understood that audiences were an integral part of the making of films, and Harold knew his audience better than anyone.

The creative force behind Harold's superb team was Harold. The gagmen would suggest ideas, and Harold would choose what he liked and what he did not, what he called "picking the wheat out of the chaff," thereby assembling the material into a coherent story. Harold knew his character better than anyone and knew what the character would be able to work with best.

Harold's character did not function on a single note; they were significantly varied. Although the horn-rimmed glasses remained the same, the man behind the glasses was different from one film to the next. Indeed, the Glass Character was less a character than it was a comic attitude; no matter how varied the role he played—the coward of *Grandma's Boy*, the determined young man of *Safety Last!*, the hypochondriac of *Why Worry?*, the callow newcomer of *The Freshman*, the self-absorbed millionaire of *For Heaven's Sake*, the shy mountain boy of *The Kid Brother*, the brash young man of *Speedy*—the essence of Harold's screen person—determination, optimism, ambition, and ingenuity—was always evident.

Harold demanded and received salary increases with Roach as the Lloyd comedies grew in popularity. By his November 1921 contract, Harold received a base salary of $1,000 per week and an 80 percent share of the profits received by Rolin. At this rate, Harold was earning nearly a quarter of a million dollars a year. Harold saved most of his money; his future plans did not involve working for anyone but himself. By the end of the silent-film era, Lloyd was the biggest box-office draw in films. When *Variety* ranked the twenty wealthiest members of the entertainment industry in 1927, Lloyd was the only performer/filmmaker who made the list. His estimated net worth at the time was fifteen million dollars.

By the time of his last short comedy, *Never Weaken* (1921), and after all the work he had gone through—in repertory companies, as an extra, as Willie Work, as Lonesome Luke, and in the one-reel Glass Character pictures—Lloyd had finally found a characterization and had developed it. The silent feature films that followed would constitute his finest work.

Left:
The prosthetic glove on Harold's right hand—used to conceal his impairment—is clearly visible in this still from *Haunted Spooks* (1920). With him is Ernest "Sunshine Sammy" Morrison.

Overleaf:
Harold and Hal Roach photographed on the first day of filming at the new Hal Roach Studios in Culver City, March 1920, during production of *An Eastern Westerner* (1920).

Top right:
An Eastern Westerner (1920), one of Harold's best two-reelers, is a fast and furious parody of westerns.

Bottom right:
Harold is first seen in a reflective moment in *Among Those Present* (1921).

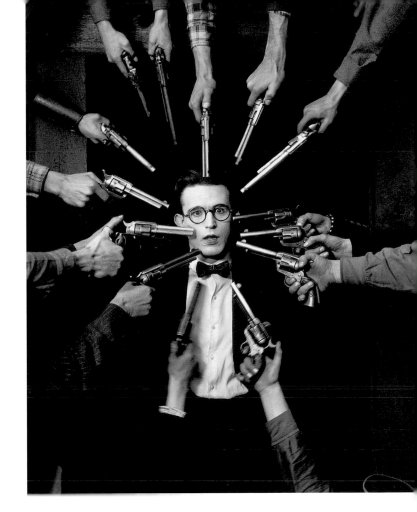

Opposite:
Harold filming *Number, Please?* (1920) on location in Ocean Park, near Santa Monica, California.

Left:
Harold is no match for boxing champ Jack Dempsey in a gag photo taken around the time Dempsey made his first film for Pathé, c. 1920.

Below:
Get Out and Get Under (1920), titled after a popular song of the period, features Harold's misadventures with his Model T Ford.

Right:
Harold on location for *Now or Never* (1921) his first three-reel comedy. Unlike most of Lloyd's stunts, several sequences in *Now or Never* involving Harold riding under and running on top of a train car were not achieved authentically, but staged against a rolling cyclorama.

Below:
Harold poses for the camera during production of *Never Weaken* (1921), one of his most brilliant films. Lloyd considered it to be his best three-reel comedy.

Harold is a would-be suicide who finds himself on an uncompleted skyscraper in *Never Weaken* (1921), his third "thrill" picture and the last of his short comedies.

Mildred Davis and Family Life

Harold first saw Mildred Davis on a projection room screen. He and Hal Roach were searching for a new leading lady after Bebe Daniels left the company to join Cecil B. DeMille, and both agreed that the next leading lady must bear a sharp contrast to Bebe in every way so that the individuality of her replacement would be even more pronounced. They found the girl they were searching for in Mildred Davis. Harold thought she looked like "a big French doll."[18]

Mildred Hillary Davis was born February 22, 1901, in Philadelphia, Pennsylvania, to Howard and Caroline Davis, and was raised a Quaker. Howard relocated his family to Tacoma, Washington, and became a prominent newspaperman. While Mildred was on an extended vacation to Hollywood, her wholesome, all-American-girl looks landed her a role in the Bryant Washburn film *All Wrong* (1919). By the time Roach and Lloyd had seen the film and began tracking her down, Mildred had become discouraged with Hollywood—casting directors thought she was too young for parts other than children's roles—and returned home to Tacoma with her mother to finish high school.

Harold and Roach finally found her in Tacoma and wired her to come back to Los Angeles for an interview. They were expecting to meet the unsophisticated little girl from *All Wrong*; instead they were introduced to a beautifully dressed, sophisticated young woman. Mildred's hair was in a pompadour; she wore a large black hat adorned with several plumes, a long gray dress, a black fur collar, and high heels. Mildred, in her effort to appear more worldly, nearly lost her opportunity. Harold, however, was captivated by the youthful, peaches-and-cream girlishness he had seen on screen, and knew that with a change in wardrobe it could instantly be restored.

Although Mr. and Mrs. Davis were not particularly happy (like many small-town people of the time, Hollywood was not something good people did), Mildred signed a contract to appear in the Lloyd comedies. Her first film with Harold was *From Hand to Mouth* (1919). Although a limited actress, she was charming, pretty, and did not detract from Harold, who at that time did not have important roles for his leading ladies. Harold was instantly drawn to her good humor and her enjoyment of his practical jokes. However, more than a year passed before Harold started to date her.

It was during the production of *A Sailor-Made Man* that Harold started to seriously date Mid, as she was called. Mid enjoyed dancing, and they would frequently go dancing or to the theater. Upon the expiration of her contract with the completion of *Safety Last!* she was planning to embark on a dramatic career and had already signed to make a film. It was at that point that Harold began to think seriously about his relationship with Mildred. According to Harold:

> *I knew by that time I really loved Mildred and I was sure she loved me. We were always so happy together and we liked the same things. And*

though she never said "yes" when we talked about marriage, I was pretty sure in her heart she intend-
ed to marry me some day.

I knew if she left our quiet little studio and got to playing in other pictures, she'd change. And I
decided, since I wanted a wife who loved her home and husband and wanted a family, that we'd better
marry right away before she got into a lot of other interests.

So I asked her—and told her how I felt. Up to that time
she had never been willing to leave the screen. But I told her
how I was sure it was the only way we could be happy, and at
last she consented.[19]

Harold and Mildred were married at a small private wedding
at St. John's Episcopal Church in Los Angeles on February 10,
1923, with Harold's brother, Gaylord, as best man and Mid's friend,
Jane Thompson, as maid of honor. They enjoyed a short honeymoon in San Diego, returning to Los Angeles ten days later to
a rented bungalow at the Ambassador Hotel. They then lived in
Harold's house at 369 South Hoover Street with Foxy and Gaylord
and his wife for two years before taking up residence at 502 South
Irving Boulevard in the Hancock Park area of Los Angeles, where
they continued to live until they moved into Greenacres in 1929.

Mildred's demure sweetness complemented Harold's domi-
nating personality. One discordant note to their marital harmony
was Harold's mother, Elizabeth. Elizabeth was always very jealous
of Mildred; if Harold bought Mildred some jewelry or other valuables, and the imperious Elizabeth found out
about it, she would demand that Harold buy the exact same gift for her. Harold would usually give in and pur-
chase a duplicate gift. He and Mildred soon learned to hide the fact that Harold gave Mildred anything.

At one point after the marriage, Mildred wanted to resume her career. She had wanted to play the role of
Alice in an independent film production of *Alice in Wonderland* but was too old, and the part went to
another actress. Mildred's final films were two cheaply made pictures, *Temporary Marriage* (1923) and
Condemned (1923), and *Too Many Crooks* (1927), a production of a much higher quality produced by
Harold Lloyd and distributed by Paramount. However, the giddy young girl with Mary Pickford-type curls was
becoming passé in 1923 when she made her last film with Harold, and her screen persona was obsolete by the
time she made her last film in 1927. Mildred realized this and permanently retired from the screen.

Mildred gave birth to their first child, Mildred Gloria Lloyd (called Gloria), on May 21, 1924. The proud
parents devoted much of their private lives to the little girl. By 1930, Harold and Mildred had made several
attempts to have another child, but were unsuccessful; Mildred suffered several miscarriages. They decided
to adopt a sister for their daughter, and on September 2, 1930 Gloria Gabrielle Freeman (born April 15, 1925
in Hermosa Beach, California) became a member of the Lloyd family, was renamed Marjorie Elizabeth
Lloyd and nicknamed Peggy. The adoption became legal on December 5, 1930. At about the same time, quite
unexpectedly, Mildred became pregnant again and on January 25, 1931, Harold Lloyd, Jr. was born, two
months premature. He was placed in an incubator, where he stayed for two months. From infancy he was
called Brother and was later given the nickname Duke. The family was complete.

Virtually a member of the family was Roy Brooks, an openly homosexual friend of Mildred's from
Tacoma, who had appeared in some of Harold's films—most memorably as Harold's inebriated friend in
High and Dizzy (1920). Roy eventually had an apartment at Greenacres, where he served as Harold's
secretary and a companion for Mildred. He lived on the estate for forty years.

Above:
Harold, Peggy, Harold, Jr.,
Mildred, and Gloria at
Greenacres, c. 1945.

Opposite:
Harold and Mildred in the
domestic comedy *I Do* (1921),
one of Lloyd's most successful
two-reel comedies. The film's
first big laugh-provoking
sequence is a topical gag (the
film was made during Prohibi-
tion). In the pram, hidden
under a blanket, is a bottle of
bootleg liquor.

The marriage of Harold and Mildred was held up as a Hollywood model. It was, in fact, a typical Hollywood marriage. Harold had an affair with leading lady Jobyna Ralston and numerous other infidelities, particularly with many of the young models who posed nude for him for his 3-D photographs. Mildred was aware of this, and along with keeping Mid company, Roy tried to see that she was exposed to as little of this as possible. As active as Harold's sex life appears to have been, it was still tame compared to the sexual exploits of others in Hollywood. That fact, however, was small consolation to Mid. Harold was a ladies' man.

By today's standards, Mildred did not live a very stimulating life after she retired from films. Yet her life was typical of a woman of her time and station. Mid and Harold spent much of their time together playing games or participating in one of his hobbies, but when he was making a film or away on business, Mid would enjoy the company of her close friends Marion Davies, Frances Marion, Mary Pickford, Colleen Moore, and Roy Brooks. She also enjoyed needlepoint (which she would do with Colleen Moore). Warm, fun, and very girlish even in her later years, Mid was a joy to be around.

Above:
Harold and Mildred, c. 1930.

Below left:
Proud parents Harold and Mildred with baby Mildred Gloria, May 1924.

Right:
Harold and Mildred at the time of their marriage, 1923.

Opposite:
Harold poses as Prince Razzamatazz and proposes to Princess Florelle (Mildred Davis) in *His Royal Slyness* (1920).

However, life was sometimes lonely for Mildred; for many years Harold would be either planning his next motion picture or in the throes of filming it. Sometime after Harold, Jr.'s birth, Mid became an alcoholic. Her drinking was unpredictable; after a long period of abstinence she would quietly drink heavily in her bedroom. In later years she also would also take pills that were prescribed by her younger brother, Jack, one of the original members of Our Gang (Hal Roach's series of children's comedies), who became a prominent Beverly Hills physician. Harold, who never smoked or drank, could not understand these addictions. Fortunately, Mid's drinking periods were short-lived.

Despite the frictions caused by Harold's infidelities and Mid's drinking, they were a wonderful team; their mutual love and respect were apparent to all who knew them. Harold and Mildred were married forty-six years, until her death on August 18, 1969, following a heart attack and second stroke at the age of sixty-eight.

Greenacres

In 1923, on the advice of his business manager, uncle William Fraser, Harold purchased ten acres of what was considered remote property in Beverly Hills for $60,000 as an investment. The property was formerly owned by Colonel Benedict, for whom Benedict Canyon is named. The old Benedict home on the property was remodeled for Harold's mother, and over the next two years Harold would frequently visit her on the property. Although initially he did not like the country, he grew to love the area. His mother kept urging him to move her to another part of Beverly Hills and to build on the land; that is what he eventually did. Harold acquired an additional six acres of adjacent property from the Thomas H. Ince estate, and built his dream home, Greenacres.

Harold hired the architectural firm Webber, Staunton, and Spaulding, of Pasadena, to design the house. He had definite ideas for an Italian Renaissance villa, and he gave the house the same exacting attention that he gave to his films, insisting on the same type of changes and retakes. When the architects first presented their plans, he wrote them a check for $25,000 and said, "Take it away, boys. I want a home, not a museum."[20]

Opposite:
Harold strikes a pose on the fountain that dominated the forecourt of Greenacres, c. 1930. Known for his modesty, Harold's nomadic and poverty-stricken childhood perhaps best explains why he built the forty-four-room Italian Renaissance mansion. As an adult, he had an over-whelming desire for domestic permanence.

Above left:
View of Greenacres from the Formal Garden

Above right:
Groundbreaking day for Greenacres in 1926. With Harold, Mildred, and Gloria are the architectural team of Webber, Staunton, and Spaulding.

The revised plan perfectly blended simplicity with splendor: a livable showplace that was both grand and accessible.

The groundbreaking took place in 1926, and the first structure built on the estate was a playhouse for Gloria. It was a miniature Tudor cottage with an adjacent French barn so that she would have somewhere to play while Harold and Mildred supervised the construction of the main house. The playhouse was fitted with complete furnishings scaled down to children's size, hot and cold running water, electric lights, and heating. Adjoining the buildings were an aviary and monkey cage.

In August 1929, the Lloyd family moved into Greenacres. Built at a cost of over $2 million, it was the most expensive movie star estate constructed at the time. The main house has forty-four rooms in 32,000 square feet. Greenacres is impressive by any standard. The entrance hall has a sixteen-foot ceiling and a solid oak grand stairway leading to the second floor. The first floor contains a formal dining room, a music room, a library, a L'Orangerie (also known as the sunroom, hand-painted with flowers and plants indigenous to California), and a fifty-foot sunken living room (featuring a gold-leaf ceiling, intricate paneling, a hidden projection booth, and a 33-rank Aeolian theater pipe organ for accompanying silent films). The six bedroom suites on the second floor all have their own bathrooms; there are twenty-six bathrooms in the entire house and grounds. No expense was spared; Harold allowed only custom-made furniture for the house, even having all of the Oriental rugs woven to his specifications.

A statue of Peter Pan in the central courtyard was one of Mildred's contributions. The house had been designed with an underground tunnel that led from the main house under the formal lawn to a game room and bar. Harold had originally planned to install a bowling alley in this long passageway, but Mildred had other ideas.

In 1937, Mildred and her good friend Marion Davies planned to line the tunnel walls with Harold's already significant collection of signed photographs of politicians and other famous people that he had been collecting since 1927. The idea was to augment this collection with newly acquired photographs of film stars, friends, scientists, politicians, and athletes of the day. This was to be Mildred's Christmas present to Harold, and in preparing it Mildred sent out letters to a wide array of Harold's friends requesting their signed photos, with a personal inscription to Harold. The response was overwhelming; more than three hundred such photos were received. Lloyd delighted in showing off this collection to visitors at Greenacres, and it served as a time capsule of the popular personalities of the late 1920s and 1930s. Among the people who provided their signed photographs were Thomas A. Edison, Helen Keller, Amelia Earhart, Calvin Coolidge, Babe Ruth, Clarence Darrow, Charles Chaplin, and Cecil B. DeMille (who wrote "To Harold Lloyd, hoping that my spectacles never get as many laughs as yours"). The passageway soon earned the nickname The Rogues Gallery.

An aerial view of Greenacres, located at 1225 Benedict Canyon Drive (present-day 1740 Greenacres Place), Beverly Hills, reflects the emphasis on nature and landscaping. The plush, green acres gave the estate its name.

The landscape architect was A. E. Hanson who, at Harold's request, utilized natural features as much as possible, reflecting Harold's midwestern roots. The grounds boasted seven formal gardens and twelve fountains. The Cascade Garden was copied from the Villa d'Este in Rome. Hanson was sent to Europe twice to lay out the plans for Greenacres. One fountain could reach a spray height of twenty-five feet, and the overflow was recycled to the waterfall that dropped one hundred feet to the canoe run and Harold's "Safety Last!" nine-hole golf course. Since Harold's estate adjoined that of Jack Warner, who had built his own nine-hole golf course, it was possible for guests to play eighteen holes thanks to the course's ingenious Alister MacKenzie design. Greenacres was the site of a number of tournaments in which top golfers of the world participated.

An Olympic-size swimming pool, eighty-five feet long and forty feet wide, containing 250,000 gallons of water, featured underwater windows in a tunnel running completely around the pool so that one could see or photograph those under water. The pool pavilion had its own bandstand and kitchen grill facilities for entertaining, and it was in this pool that Buster Crabbe taught the Lloyd children how to swim.

The property had its own private well (the only one in Beverly Hills) that supplied the fountains and other water demands. In the 1930s, Lloyd hired sixteen full-time gardeners and two men to maintain the tennis court and swimming pool. The household staff consisted of two chauffeurs, two cooks, two butlers, two governesses, three maids, and three secretaries, all under the supervision of the chief housekeeper.

Harold and Mildred also maintained a retreat in Santa Monica, a two-story, fourteen-room beach house at 443 Palisades Beach Road (later renamed Pacific Coast Highway), which they built in 1931 for $14,000.

Although Harold had wanted Greenacres to become a museum where public tours would be given along with showings of his films, the house is now privately owned. However, Greenacres continues to be a glorious symbol of the film industry and the taste of Hollywood in the 1920s.

Left:
At Greenacres, c. 1928. Harold's Great Dane, Prince, Harold, daughter Gloria, mother Elizabeth, and elder brother Gaylord. Elizabeth lived in a house Harold bought for her at 623 North Roxbury Drive in Beverly Hills. A leader of both civic and social activities in her beloved Beverly Hills, she at one time served on the California State Industrial Welfare Commission. She died in 1941, at the age of 72. Gaylord began as an actor but soon became a casting director and an assistant director for the Harold Lloyd Corporation. He died in 1943 at just fifty-five years of age from a coronary thrombosis.

Below:
Harold, Mildred, Peggy, Gloria, and Harold, Jr. on the playhouse slide at Greenacres, 1935.

GREENACRES C. 1932:

Above left: The dramatic entrance hall with its sixteen-foot high ceilings and grand stairwell.

Above right: The sunroom sans Christmas tree. Harold took considerable pride in the hand-painted vines and leaves that ornamented the walls and ceiling. The room took a long time to finish—too long for Harold and Mildred. After waiting years for completion of the artwork, Harold finally gave the artist an ultimatum to finish the room in three weeks—which explains why the tiny leaves expand to nearly ten times their size on the far end of the room.

Opposite upper left: The fifty-foot-long sunken living room featured a gold-leaf coffered ceiling, detailed paneling, stone fire place, 35mm projection equipment, and pipe organ. In the 1950s Harold installed high-fidelity equipment with twenty-four speakers for playing music. He would sometimes play music so loud that flakes of the ceiling's gold leaf would fall onto the floor.

Opposite upper right: Harold's study.

Opposite below: Harold with his Great Dane Prince at the beach in Santa Monica, c. 1927. In the late 1920s, Harold bred Great Danes and Saint Bernards at a kennel located on property he owned in Westwood. Later in life, he preferred cocker spaniels and miniature poodles as pets.

Harold's transition to feature-length films was a natural evolution and not the result of any systematic plan. His first feature, A *Sailor-Made Man*, might, at best, be called an accidental feature. The film was intended to be a two-reeler, but Harold and his gagmen believed they had developed so much good comedy material that they expanded the film to four reels. Although more an expanded short comedy than a feature-length film, A *Sailor-Made Man* nevertheless was an advance over Harold's two-reel comedy shorts. In retrospect, Harold liked to think of the film as his last short work. However, the film established Harold as a star who was able to carry a feature-length comedy.

Harold is introduced as "The Boy — Idle heir to twenty millions — And a nerve that would blunt the edge on forked lightning." At the country club, he gets the attention of a popular girl (Mildred Davis) by saying, "It's too hot to play croquet; let's get married." When she tells Harold he must first ask her father, the father tells Harold that he will not allow her to marry him until he makes something of himself; so Harold joins the navy in order to impress the girl and her father.

Harold and Mildred Davis share a hookah in *A Sailor-Made Man*.

Stationed in the fictitious kingdom of Khairpura-Bhandanna, he rescues Davis (whose yacht has also arrived there) from a villainous maharajah (Dick Sutherland) and his army of sword-wielding warriors in the film's frantic climax. Safely back aboard their respective ship and yacht, Harold proposes to his girl using semaphore, and she accepts.

A *Sailor-Made Man* has a lavish look. The Beverly Hills Hotel was used for the magnificent gardens of the summer resort; Hal Roach was able to acquire a filming permit to shoot the ship sequences aboard the U.S.S. *Frederick* (using actual sailors as extras); and the elaborate sets of the maharajah's Black Castle were built in Roach's Culver City studio.

The rescue of the girl involves a series of wonderful, fast-moving chases through the maharajah's palace. Harold ingeniously disguises himself in various ways and hides in a pool, using a hookah for air. When he finally gets the key to the room in which his girl has been locked, another chase ensues as Harold and the girl must dash through a marketplace to safety. For this film, Harold wanted more than just a series of chases. He was seeking a strong central idea for the

The rich young idler deigns to enlist in the navy in *A Sailor-Made Man*. Charles Stevenson is the recruiting officer. Doing double duty are assistant director Robert "Red" Golden and technical director Fred Guiol as the enlistees second and third in line.

Above:
Harold posing with a toy molded figure of himself during production of A *Sailor-Made Man.*

Right:
Rough-House O'Rafferty (Noah Young) is startled when he believes a monkey in the frame of a mirror to be the reflection of himself in A *Sailor-Made Man.* Only Harold and the monkey know that the mischievous simian had caused the glass to drop out while Rough-House was sharpening his razor.

story, something heretofore missing from his comedies. The presence of a central theme brought about the outpouring of gags and situations. Harold recalled:

> *I played a rich young fellow who thought he could have and could do anything he wanted. Through a sequence of incidents he enlists in the navy and, much against his will, goes to sea. His shipmates make a man out of him before they get through. So you see that the central idea was a real one; that hard knocks will bring out a man's mettle, if he has any.* [21]

Harold also began to take greater care to build each comic incident. Jobyna Ralston, Harold's future leading lady, had a small role in the film and recalled in a 1926 interview his efforts to make each comic moment as perfect as he could.

> In A Sailor-Made Man, *for example, do you remember the scene where Harold sat himself down on top of a heap of unconscious opponents and nonchalantly lighted a cigarette? That one simple little scene, over in seconds on the screen, required over five hours in the filming! Harold tried piling the men this way; then that way, then still another way. He held his cigaret [sic] in his right hand, then tried it in his left. He struck a match on a convenient foot in the pile, then on a shaven head. He*

Harold strikes a nonchalant pose with a cigarette and takes half the credit for knocking out a group of local merchants who were pummeled entirely by his pal, Rough-House O'Rafferty, in *A Sailor-Made Man*.

69

tried every possible angle to get the best possible laugh out of the "gag." And all the time the cameras were grinding away, taking the footage from which the one short scene would finally be selected in the studio projection room.

It is the same in all the Lloyd comedies. If genius is really an infinite capacity for taking pains, then Harold Lloyd amply rates the title of genius.[22]

Although Lloyd was the third of the top silent comedians to make feature films, he was in fact the leader in the production of feature-length comedy. Roscoe "Fatty" Arbuckle first appeared in feature films beginning in 1920 with *The Round-Up* (1920). However, *The Round-Up* was a drama, and his other features fell into the light comedy genre rather than gag comedy. Charles Chaplin, who had appeared opposite Marie Dressler and Mabel Normand in the first feature-length comedy, Mack Sennett's *Tillie's Punctured Romance* (1914) made his own first feature film with *The Kid* (1921). Buster Keaton did not excercise any creative control over the first feature-film in which he appeared (*The Saphead* [1920], based on a popular stage play). His first feature-length comedy was *Three Ages* (1923). Lloyd's *A Sailor-Made Man* and *Grandma's Boy* were the first comedy features created in the gag-oriented manner of the two- and three-reel comedies, blazing the trail Chaplin, and particularly Keaton, would follow.

Although Lloyd's contract with Pathé was only for two-reel comedies, the company agreed that *A Sailor-Made Man* should not be cut, and paid more for the film as well as for his next feature film, *Grandma's Boy*. Everyone involved in *A Sailor-Made Man* was generously rewarded for keeping the film at its expanded length; the film had a production cost of $77,315, yet grossed an impressive $485,285.

Harold said of this film's effect on his career, "I felt that at last I had arrived somewhere."[23] The lessons learned and care spent on *A Sailor-Made Man* showed Harold that he could make feature-length comedies of a very high quality. His next film, a true feature and a Lloyd classic, was *Grandma's Boy*.

Above:
Harold takes refuge in a harem pool while trying to rescue his girl (Mildred Davis) who has been abducted by the villainous maharajah (Dick Sutherland) in *A Sailor-Made Man*.

Right:
A Sailor-Made Man boasted lavish sets such as the Black Castle of the maharajah, populated with a large harem of pretty girls reminiscent of Mack Sennett's bathing beauties.

***Grandma's Boy* was one of the most important films** to Harold's development as a screen artist. A well-constructed and wonderfully executed film, it laid the groundwork for Harold's other character comedies, particularly *The Freshman* and *The Kid Brother*. The history of the film's production makes one fully appreciate Harold Lloyd's evolution as a filmmaker.

Grandma's Boy is essentially a five-reel morality play that tells the story of a cowardly young man who runs to his grandmother (Anna Townsend) out of fear when he is asked to participate in the manhunt for a tramp (Dick Sutherland) who has killed a man. The boy finds the courage only after his wise granny gives him a magic talisman that she tells him had helped his equally timid grandfather become a hero in the Civil War. Only after Harold single-handedly captures the killer does his grandmother tell him the truth — the talisman was a fake, nothing more than an old umbrella handle. Harold always had the courage inside him; he just had to find it for himself — a classic Lloyd lesson. The film ends with Harold ridding himself of a bully (Charles Stevenson) and proposing to his girl (Mildred Davis).

Like A *Sailor-Made Man*, *Grandma's Boy* began as a two-reeler and grew into a feature. The film drew upon the mind-over-matter theme Harold had wanted to use for several years, yet was heavily influenced by Chaplin's *The Kid*, a six-reel feature-length comedy that contained dramatic scenes. *The Kid* served as the prototype for *Grandma's Boy* and other silent comedies that contained dramatic content. Harold, wanting to make a comedy that contained several dramatic sequences, made *Grandma's Boy* his first film in which story and character took precedence over gags.

The gags and sequences in *Grandma's Boy*, therefore, were structured more for telling a story and developing the weakling character than creating lengthy comic situations. Indeed, the film had a complex story that could very well have succeeded as a drama, and the comedy was more gentle and human and less of the pure slapstick variety. The film was considered exceptionally well constructed in its time, containing the love story of Harold and the rival (Charles Stevenson) competing for the girl, the tramp terrorizing the town, and the psychological elements

75

of self-doubt and cowardice Harold feels. However, initial previews of *Grandma's Boy* failed until Hal Roach persuaded Lloyd to introduce more gags into the film. Harold later remembered the first preview, held in Pasadena:

Our first preview was a great disappointment. It was good, but not good enough. I remember Roach and I had brought our families, so we left the girls in one car and Hal and I went and sat in the other one to fight this out. We were there almost an hour in his car, with the girls not being happy at all.

Hal said, "Look, Harold, we are making comedies. We are doing things to make people laugh. Let's get back to the kind of picture we should make."

I said, "Hal, this has got heart. It's different from what we've done before. It's much finer. It's really got feeling."

"But it hasn't got any laughs," he said.

"Hal, you're absolutely right. Maybe we'd better go back and build a lot more laughs into this picture."

"I'd say we'd better," he said.

We put in about twenty gags—sorted them all through the picture. Then we spent a lot of money on a little cartoon character called Icky, representing the boy's good and bad spirit. We previewed again. We found little Icky didn't help us at all. But oh, my, the gags helped! We went back and shot still more gags, but we never lost any of our theme. I wouldn't let go one inch of it.[24]

Harold and director Fred Newmeyer spent nearly six months on *Grandma's Boy*; one month was spent solely with the gagmen creating comedy business. Filming began in October 1921, and was completed in March 1922. Amazingly, the film's editing betrays nothing of the patchwork method employed to put in more gags after the first cut. The gags come naturally out of the story rather than merely being injected into it.

It was a common practice for comedians of the time to make a comic treatment of dramatic material. Although he never acknowledged the fact, Harold was influenced by *Tol'able David* (1921) (which he would virtually remake as *The Kid Brother*) and three Charles Ray films: *The Coward* (1915), *The Sheriff's Son* (1919), and *Hay Foot, Straw Foot* (1919). Both *Tol'able David* and *Grandma's Boy* have a tender young man who must prove himself as protagonist in a rural setting. *The Coward* was a popular Civil War drama in which a cowardly young man (played by Charles Ray) deserts from the army, and his old father takes his place at the battlefront to save the family's honor. *The Sheriff's Son* was the story of a timid young man (Ray) who overcomes a gang of outlaws despite his reputation for cowardliness. *Hay Foot, Straw Foot* was the story of a young man (Ray) called to military service, whose grandfather had served with General Ulysses S. Grant in the Civil War. The

Above:
During the production of *Grandma's Boy.* From left: assistant director Robert "Red" Golden, director Fred Newmeyer, (kneeling directly in front of Harold), Harold (costumed as Granddaddy), cameraman Walter Lundin, second cameraman Henry Kohler, technical director Fred Guiol, and gagmen Jean Havez and Sam Taylor. The back of the Hal Roach Studios's main building (just visible) in Culver City was redressed and used for the exterior shots of the southern mansion in the film's Civil War flashback.

Right:
Portrait of Harold, 1922. Out of costume, Lloyd looked more like a leading man than a comedian.

Upper left:
Harold with Mildred Davis in *Grandma's Boy*. His grand-mother had shined his shoes with goose grease, causing them to be a favorite with Mildred's kittens. Harold, dressed "strictly up to date for the spring of 1862," wears a suit once owned by his grandfather that is laden with mothballs. His attempts to conceal this fact result in one of Harold's finest scenes of comedy embarrassment.

Left:
Harold, empowered by the talisman his grandmother has given him, single-handedly goes after the outlaw tramp (Dick Sutherland). His confi-dence, however, is momentarily broken by a black cat crossing in front of him.

Harold — in the Civil War flashback as his own grandfather and sporting rectangular glasses — is decorated for his heroism as a Confederate soldier.

film contains flashbacks to the Civil War. With the creation of *Grandma's Boy*, Harold produced a Charles Ray-type film in a comic manner.[25] Harold was also filling a niche recently left vacant by Douglas Fairbanks, who, after *The Nut* (1921), abandoned his early screen characterization of a brash, optimistic young man who finds within himself the courage and physical ability needed to succeed, in favor of the swashbuckling costume films for which he is best known. The light comedies of Douglas Fairbanks were unquestionably a strong influence on Lloyd's work.

Grandma's Boy is one of Harold's most successful films. A dramatic situation imbued with a strong central theme as the basis for a feature-length comedy gave Harold's characterization an added depth. Combined with exemplary direction, acting, and editing, *Grandma's Boy* resulted in a tremendous hit with the critics, the public, and the motion picture community; it also influenced the genteel comedy and well-harmonized plot and gags Chaplin gave to *The Pilgrim* (1923) and Keaton to his films beginning with *Our*

Harold becomes the town hero in *Grandma's Boy*.

Hospitality (1923). Upon its release, Chaplin called it "one of the best-constructed screenplays I have ever seen."[26] Buster Keaton also admired the film,[27] and elements of *Grandma's Boy* can be seen in Keaton's *The General* (1926). In fact, many comedies imitated its structure and its handling of gags; comedies with loose and episodic structures diminished in favor of those with solidly integrated plots and gags. The film was so finely crafted that even Erich von Stroheim praised it, and it was included in the book *The Best Moving Pictures of 1922–1923*. *Grandma's Boy* cost $94,412 and grossed an astounding ten times that amount, $975,623, an enormous sum at the time.

The successful integration of slapstick comedy and the genteel comedy traditions that Harold achieved in *Grandma's Boy* is arguably his greatest contribution to the development of motion picture comedy. Harold was always very proud of his work in *Grandma's Boy*, and regarded the film as his favorite amongst his own work until *The Kid Brother* supplanted it in his last years.

Harold Lloyd divided his silent feature films into two categories: character comedies and gag comedies. Not wanting to immediately attempt to recapture the enormous success of *Grandma's Boy* with another character comedy, he instead made the pure gag comedy *Dr. Jack*. As with *Grandma's Boy*, mind over matter is again the central theme. Harold plays a doctor who believes that joy can often be the best medicine, a belief Harold himself held in real life. Indeed, Harold's optimism and positive attitude were never more evident than in *Dr. Jack*. The film also shows the influence of the middle-class, midwestern, Christian Science upbringing of Harold's childhood (many thought the film was advocating Christian Science, which Harold insisted was not true). *Dr. Jack* is simply a gag comedy designed to make people laugh.

Harold plays Dr. Jackson (Dr. Jack, for short), a small-town doctor who is a friend to everyone and eager to help all. His methods are common sense and the belief that many illnesses are psychosomatic and can be cured if one puts one's mind to it. He is first seen receiving an emergency telephone call from a little girl. "Come quick, Dr. Jack. Mary is dying!" reads the intertitle. After

Dr. Jack rescues "Mary," a
little girl's doll that has fallen
down a well.

he speeds down the road to make the house call, the patient turns out to be the little girl's rag
doll. He obligingly rescues the doll from a well, gives it artificial resuscitation, and makes the little
girl happy. Later, Dr. Jack diagnoses an elderly lady's (Anna Townsend) only illness as loneliness,
and arranges for her son to spend more time with her. Dr. Jack approaches the healing of his
patients through psychology and the nontraditional means of joy and excitement rather than
medicine.

The film's thin plot involves the Sick-Little-Well-Girl (Mildred Davis) who is deliberately
coddled by her quack doctor, Dr. Ludwig von Saulsbourg (Eric Mayne), so that he can continue
to collect enormous fees from her wealthy father. As the consulting physician, Dr. Jack comes to
the rescue when he gives her the excitement she craves—he disguises himself as an escaped
lunatic and runs through the house in the middle of the night. Dr. Jack also participates with the
household in his capture (which has Harold doing some wonderfully adroit costume changes).
He rids the house of both imaginary illnesses and of the quack doctor.

he speeds down the road to make the house call, the patient turns out to be the little girl's rag doll. He obligingly rescues the doll from a well, gives it artificial resuscitation, and makes the little girl happy. Later, Dr. Jack diagnoses an elderly lady's (Anna Townsend) only illness as loneliness, and arranges for her son to spend more time with her. Dr. Jack approaches the healing of his patients through psychology and the nontraditional means of joy and excitement rather than medicine.

The film's thin plot involves the Sick-Little-Well-Girl (Mildred Davis) who is deliberately coddled by her quack doctor, Dr. Ludwig von Saulsbourg (Eric Mayne), so that he can continue to collect enormous fees from her wealthy father. As the consulting physician, Dr. Jack comes to the rescue when he gives her the excitement she craves — he disguises himself as an escaped lunatic and runs through the house in the middle of the night. Dr. Jack also participates with the household in his capture (which has Harold doing some wonderfully adroit costume changes). He rids the house of both imaginary illnesses and of the quack doctor.

Dr. Jack rescues "Mary," a little girl's doll that has fallen down a well.

Filming the race to the rescue of a sick child (which turns out to be a little girl's doll) in *Dr. Jack*. Cameraman Walter Lundin is standing on the platform behind the camera, with director Fred Newmeyer sitting beside him. Harold goes from car to motorcycle to bicycle in a scene that anticipates the race-to-the-rescue chase created for *Girl Shy* two years later.

With the working title *Doctor's Orders*, production on *Dr. Jack* began in March 1922 and ended in July 1922. In January of the same year, Harold signed a new contract with Pathé for six pictures of five reels or more. *Dr. Jack*, the first film of that contract, was also the first Lloyd film conceived and designed as a feature. As *Dr. Jack* was the first intended feature, it exhibits a strained story and an episodic structure. A problem with the film—which it shares with the later *Hot Water*—is that Harold's characterization is established in the opening scene, and no character development follows; he has no obstacles to surmount as he always does in his best feature films. The character development is focused on the Sick-Little-Well-Girl and her parents as Dr. Jack tries to remove the influence of the quack.

As arguably one of the weaker and more mechanical of the silent Lloyd features, *Dr. Jack* is the film that perhaps comes closest to deserving the dreadful little stricture that critic of American popular culture Gilbert Seldes wrote of Harold:

> *Harold Lloyd [is] a man of no tenderness, of no philosophy, the embodiment of American cheek and indefatigable energy. His movements are all direct, straight; the shortest distance between two points he will traverse impudently and persistently, even if he is knocked down at the end of each trip; there is no poetry in him, his whole utterance being epigrammatic, without overtone or image.*[28]

Above:
Dr. Jack is immediately suspicious of Dr. Ludwig von Saulsbourg's (Eric Mayne) diagnosis of the Sick-Little-Well-Girl (Mildred Davis) in *Dr. Jack.*

Opposite:
Dr. Jack's bedside manner convinces Sonny (Mickey Daniels), a potential truant, that he should be in school. The son of Lloyd character actor Richard Daniels, Mickey was one of the original children of Hal Roach's Our Gang comedies, and also appeared in *Safety Last!* and *Girl Shy.*

In prescribing "excitement" to cure the Sick-Little-Well-Girl, Dr. Jack disguises himself as an escaped lunatic and manages to scare the entire household (including the butler and family dog) in the frantic haunted-house comedy scene that concludes *Dr. Jack*.

Disturbed by this criticism — particularly as it was written after *Grandma's Boy* — Harold would flatly disprove Seldes's assertions with his first independent production, *Girl Shy*.

However, *Dr. Jack* does have some wonderful moments, culminating in an elaborate and ingenious haunted house sequence, which Harold derived from his earlier films such as *Haunted Spooks* and *I Do*. Harold was virtually alone (with the exception of Buster Keaton's 1921 two-reeler *The Haunted House* and the opening scene of Keaton's 1922 two-reeler *The Balloonatic*) in making this kind of haunted house sequence (he had been influenced by the stage success of *The Bat*), and his success with this kind of material no doubt piqued the interest of director D. W. Griffith to make *One Exciting Night* (1922), which was released in the same year as *Dr. Jack*. However, *One Exciting Night* was an artistic failure. Not even the great D. W. Griffith was as adept in constructing this type of material as Harold Lloyd.

Delightfully upbeat with ingenuity and a healthy dose of fast-paced action, *Dr. Jack* is still very entertaining, despite being a minor Harold Lloyd film. Although the critics noted the film was not as strong or as innovative as *Grandma's Boy*, it nevertheless fared better at the box office. *Dr. Jack*, with a production cost of $113,440, grossed $1,275,423, making it one of the ten top-grossing films of 1922.

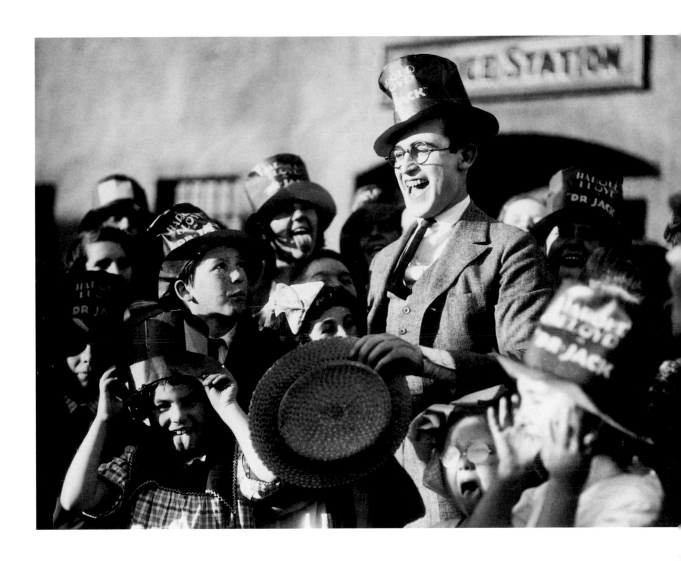

Above:
Harold, publicizing *Dr. Jack*, with some of his young fans whom he has encouraged to stick out their tongues and say "Aah." A party was arranged for local orphaned children by the Hal Roach Studios and the Los Angeles *Examiner* where Harold entertained the children at the studio after a screening of *Dr. Jack*.

Left:
Dr. Jack and the Sick-Little-Well-Girl are instantly smitten.

Safety Last! is the film for which Harold Lloyd will always be remembered,
and it is because of a single image. Even people who have never seen a Harold Lloyd film are familiar with the image of a bespectacled young man hanging off the hands of a collapsing clock on the side of a skyscraper high above teeming city streets. It is one of the most iconic images of the silent-film era.

However, beyond that image, *Safety Last!* deserves to be remembered for the brilliant film that it is. Harold's scaling of the building is a classic sequence in which comedy at its most inspired and suspense at its most excruciating are ingeniously interwoven to perfection—and the climb is the grand finale to the superb gags that precede it. Beautifully structured, expertly photographed, and containing a plausible story to support the film's thrills, *Safety Last!* deserves the icon status it still enjoys.

Safety Last! was Harold's fourth and most complex "thrill" picture. He came upon the idea for the film after watching a so-called human fly climb up the side of a tall building—a typical

spectacle in the stunt-crazed America of the 1920s. Harold sought to capitalize upon its popularity. He later remembered:

I was in Los Angeles walking up Seventh Street and I saw this tremendous crowd gathered around a building, the Brockman Building. Upon inquiring I found out that a "human spider" was going to scale the side of that building. That naturally intrigues anyone, to see a feat like that kind performed. So I stayed around for awhile and pretty soon a rather young fellow came out and was introduced and there was a certain amount of commercialism attached to it at first. Without too much ado he started at the bottom of the building and started to climb up the side of this building. Well, it had such a terrific impact on me that when he got to about the third or fourth floor I couldn't watch him anymore. My heart was in my throat and so I started

The opening scene of *Safety Last!* shows what appears to be Harold at the gallows. As the camera pulls back, the location is revealed to be an ordinary railroad station where friends and his girl (Mildred Davis) gather to say farewell to the city-bound Harold. This famous opening scene is an expansion of the opening gag from Buster Keaton's two-reel comedy *Cops* (1922) where Buster, behind bars, appears to be in prison. The reverse angle reveals that the bars are to the gate of his sweetheart's home and he is actually locked out, not locked in.

walking on up the street. I walked about a block up the street; but, of course, I kept looking back all the time to see if he was still there. Finally, I went around the corner. Silly as it is, I stood around the corner so I wouldn't watch him all the time, but every once in a while I'd stick my head around the corner and see how he was progressing. I just couldn't believe that he could make that whole climb, but he did . . . So I went back, went into the building, got up on the roof and met the yong man, gave him my address and I told him to come out and visit Hal Roach and myself. His name was Bill Strother.[29]

Roach and Harold put Bill Strother under contract and then devised a rough idea of a story that would involve a daredevil climb. The film in fact was constructed around this comedy faction (a term used by silent comedians of the 1920s to define a sequence within a picture), and introductory material was later built around it. In fact, the skyscraper sequence was shot first. As Harold climbs higher and higher, more complex obstacles confront him, from a flock of pigeons, to entanglement in a net, to a painter's trestle, to a swinging window, to the clock itself. As Harold navigates these travails, the audience's hysteria escalates. It was not uncommon for 1920s spectators to hide their eyes or even faint when watching these portions of the film. Many theaters actually hired a nurse or kept ambulances on call outside.

The plot of the film has Harold as a country boy who sets out from his hometown of Great Bend to make good in the big city. His sweetheart (Mildred Davis) promises to marry him once he is a success. Harold is only able to get a position as a sales clerk in a department store, although he writes his girl at home telling her he is one of the executives and it will only be a matter of time before he will send for her. When his girl impatiently decides to pay him a surprise visit, he manages to give the impression that he is the manager of the department store. Harold's last hope to make good comes when he overhears the general manager pledge to pay $1,000 to anyone who can draw a large crowd to the store. Harold successfully proposes that the general manager hire Bill (Bill Strother), his roommate who works as a steeplejack, to be a human fly and climb the side of the department store building. He makes a deal with Bill to split the $1,000 fee, and Bill readily

Harold and Mildred at the railroad station in *Safety Last!*. The film was Mildred's last for Harold—her contract expired upon completion of the film, and Lloyd proposed a marriage contract rather than another film contract.

accepts. But on the day of the publicity stunt, Bill is forced to dodge a disgruntled policeman (Noah Young) who has been after him, and Harold has to make the climb himself.

Harold never revealed exactly how his most famous sequence was filmed. He and his crew—Walter Lundin, Fred Guiol, C. W. Christensen, and Jack Murphy—were highly skilled cinema craftsmen who believed that the illusion that Harold was up there just as high as one sees him in the film had to be maintained so that audiences could fully enjoy the film. Today interviews, still photographs from the other Lloyd "thrill" comedies (no behind-the-scenes photographs survive from *Safety Last!*), and Los Angeles topography reveal how the feat on the clock was accomplished. Few special effects were available at the time, and the techniques that could be employed—such as mirrors, double exposure, glass shots, or miniatures—were not utilized. The crew worked from three different buildings at various stages of the climb, and angles that could accomplish an overemphasis of perspective and distance were carefully worked out for the placement of the cameras. Harold was a good athlete and did many of the climb shots himself, but there were limits. His insurance company would not allow him to do the entire sequence. An injury to the star could shut down the entire production and cripple the company. Another reason was that Harold had only one complete hand. The long shots of Harold climbing the building were not Harold but Bill Strother (who climbed the International Bank Building in Los Angeles on Sunday, September 17, 1922 with four cameras, under the direction of Roach). For a few additional moments (such as the long shots when Harold swings the length of the building by a rope), a stunt double was used. Audiences always assumed that Harold was actually hanging off the clock hands many stories above the street, and they were correct. However, Harold was actually hanging on a clock built on a platform near the edge on top of a tall building at 908–910 Broadway in downtown Los Angeles. Again, Harold's crew used camera tricks designed to hide the platform, which was about fifteen feet below, out of frame, and utilized perspective to make the clock appear on the side—not on top—of the building. To this day, the effect is remarkable. Although many techniques of early cinema seem dated, the climb is still completely convincing. The clock sequence remains one of the most effective and thrilling comic moments in film comedy.

Late for work, the resourceful Harold manages to sneak into the store by disguising himself as a dress mannequin and gets carried inside, where he readjusts the time clock and punches in, unseen by the supervisor.

Harold uses a yardstick as a sword to fend off the overly zealous bargain seekers while working the service counter in the store's fabric department in *Safety Last!*. Some of the interiors were filmed after hours at Bernal Dyas's Ville de Paris department store in downtown Los Angeles.

Harold thought he had something special from his earlier "thrill" pictures, and he was right. *Safety Last!* had cost $120,963 and grossed $1,588,545, making the film a tremendous commercial as well as critical success. Even ailing President Warren G. Harding saw the film at a special screening at the White House and declared: "Loved it!"[30] His audiences hereafter would look to every subsequent Lloyd film to top the thrills and laughter of this picture. Harold may have equaled this film in laughs with *The Freshman*, but would never surpass the brilliance of *Safety Last!*. The film remains a visual metaphor for the upwardly mobile American of the 1920s and the extent to which he would climb to achieve success and the American Dream.

Despite the fact that Harold made only five "thrill" pictures in a career that encompassed over 200 films, he is often thought of as a thrill comedian. This characterization upset Harold, who rightfully thought himself more versatile than that reductive label suggests. However, Harold understood that he was best known for his "thrill" comedy because he did it better than anyone else.

Safety Last! exceeded the thrills of *Look Out Below, High and Dizzy*, and *Never Weaken*. More than just improving upon the earlier films, *Safety Last!* was innovative for its integration of this type of comedy into a feature-length narrative. The excellence of *Safety Last!* was not merely the climb; the five reels that lead to the climb provide the necessary narrative and thematic context for the climb. Chaplin would use thrill comedy in *The Gold Rush* (1925), *The Circus* (1928), and *Modern Times* (1936), and Keaton would use it in several of his feature-length comedies of the 1920s, particularly *Our Hospitality* (1923).

One of the many admirers of Harold Lloyd and *Safety Last!* was Orson Welles, who told director Peter Bogdanovich in a 1969 interview:

> *Harold Lloyd—he's surely the most underrated [comedian] of them all. The intellectuals don't like the Harold Lloyd character—that middle-class, middle-American, all-American college boy. There's no obvious poetry to it, and—they miss that incredibly technical brilliance. The construction of Safety Last!, for instance—I saw it again only a few years ago. As a piece of comic architecture it's impeccable. Feydeau never topped it for sheer construction. He was, almost entirely, his own gag man. Really a writer who acted, if you know what I mean. To the silents, what Fred Allen was to radio. Someday he'll get his proper place—which is very high. . . . I got to know Lloyd through magic—we were both members of the same magical fraternity. What a lovely man!*[31]

Safety Last! is a superb example of Harold Lloyd's comedy. Seen today under the right conditions—a large audience and live orchestral accompaniment—the film retains all its power to thrill and amuse. Millions of dollars' worth of digital visual effects will never buy the quality of laughter that one still achieves from *Safety Last!*. The superlative gags, structure, rhythm, and integrity of the film can be enjoyed by anyone and everyone. Harold still dangles over all who attempt to fuse comedy and thrills.

Harold's social climb becomes manifest when he is forced to scale the building himself, instead of his friend, at the last minute in *Safety Last!*. This scene was filmed at the studio using a replica of the bottom of the building to avoid filming in crowded streets. William Gillespie is on the far left and Noah Young is the cop on the far right.

Harold clings to the hands of
the clock face in *Safety Last!*,
his most famous sequence. He
hated heights himself and made
his "thrill" pictures because he
rightly believed that audiences
would find them just as terrifying as he did. Although he was
just as high as he seemed, he
was actually clinging to a two-
story set mounted on the roof
of the building from which he
appears to be hanging. Perfect
alignment of the perspective of
the set with the buildings visible
in the background, along with
ingeniously selected camera
angles, contributes to the illusion. Nevertheless, there was
still an element of risk: the set
was dangerously close to the
edge of the roof, and Harold
had only one complete hand.
The scene was also arduous to
perform; Harold's right shoulder
was eventually thrown out of
its socket while he was holding
onto the clock hands during
one of the many takes in an
effort to make the scene as
perfect as possible.

Why Worry? is one of Harold's funniest comedies. It was the last Lloyd film produced by Hal Roach; the two men decided to end their nearly ten-year partnership on a high note by lavishing the picture with the best production values money could buy (making it the most expensive Lloyd film up until that time) and incorporating the highest number of gags of any Lloyd picture, played in breathless succession.

According to Harold, the original idea of *Why Worry?* was suggested by the popularity of Dr. Emile Coué, the French psychotherapist who maintained that autosuggestion was able to effect cures in all cases.[32] The interest in Coué and the emphasis on mental attitude gave Harold the idea that his next characterization should be a mental case. He decided to play a wealthy young hypochondriac, a completely different characterization from that of the poor country boy seeking his fortune in the city of the previous film.

Harold's hypochondriac, Harold van Pelham, travels with his private nurse (Jobyna Ralston) to the fictitious island of Paradiso to live blissfully in a warm climate in order to regain his health. In Paradiso, he finds himself in the middle of a revolution, which Harold assumes is being staged as an entertainment for his amusement. Even when a man is shot by

Why Worry? marks the first appearance of Harold's new leading lady Jobyna Ralston.

revolutionary forces and falls forward over a nearby horserail, Harold believes the man is merely bowing to him. When Harold is thrown into prison with a toothache-suffering giant hermit named Colosso (Johan Aasen), the pill-popping patient organizes their escape. After helping the giant extract his ailing molar, the odd couple rescues Harold's nurse, crushes the rebellion, and provides an American renegade (James Mason) responsible for the unrest with his just punishment. The excitement cures Harold of his imagined ailments, and he returns home. In an epilogue, Harold is married to his nurse (with a baby just born to them), and the giant is happily situated as a traffic cop in downtown Los Angeles.

Harold shines as the rich hypochondriac and is much more likable than the brash, wealthy idler of A *Sailor-Made Man*. The direction by Fred Newmeyer and Sam Taylor is superb. *Why Worry?* was the second film for which Taylor received directing credit, and he brings a more nuanced approach to the chracterization. Moments such as Harold's gradual change in expression while his nurse tells him off made the character more emotionally believable. The film also has a strong and distinct visual flair in such moments as the shot of renegade Jim Blake's hand—with the townspeople superimposed in his palm—that

introduces the character and his desire for power. However, it is the wide array of abundant gags that makes the film a Lloyd classic. The most memorable gag sequences include Harold attempting to extract a tooth from Colosso and the final battle of the counterrevolution, where Harold, his nurse, and Colosso — alone behind a wall — make the revolutionary forces think there is a whole army behind the wall with them.

Once the basic scenario of Harold and the giant had been established for the film, Harold and producer Hal Roach began a casting search for a giant. George Auger, a circus attraction who stood over eight feet tall, was hired. Harold began to film the early scenes without Auger while Auger fulfilled his prior commitment to two months of engagements with Ringling Brothers. Just prior to his departure for Los Angeles to start the film, Auger died suddenly in New York. A national publicity campaign was implemented to find a replacement. Ultimately, Harold chose twenty-four-year-old Johan Aasen from Minneapolis who was working for the C. A. Wortham shows. He was eight feet nine and a quarter inches tall and weighed over 500 pounds. Harold was startled when he met Aasen, as his voice was soft and high-pitched — the voice of a small person and hardly what one would expect. Aasen was an inspired casting choice; his shaggy behemoth Colosso combines a wonderful childlike innocence and a doglike faithfulness that is very endearing.

The film marked the beginning of two partnerships and the ending of another. It was during the production of *Why Worry?* that Harold and Mildred Davis were married, and Jobyna Ralston, who had been working in one-reel comedies for Roach, became Harold's new leading lady. Ralston, who would appear with Harold in his next six films, brought a dimension of genuine emotion to his films that neither Bebe Daniels nor Mildred Davis was able to provide. As a result, the importance of his leading lady began to increase in Harold's story ideas, and his films developed a greater maturity.

In addition, *Why Worry?* marked the end of the partnership between Harold and Hal Roach. By 1923, Roach was producing not only the Lloyd films but also the Our Gang comedies, the Will Rogers comedies, the Stan Laurel comedies, and the Dippy Doo-Dads series. Harold, who by contract had the exclusive use of the big stage at the Roach studio at Culver City and first call to everything on the lot, including Roach's time, believed Roach was contributing too much time and gag ideas to his other units on the remaining stages and

Harold poses with 8 foot 7 ½-inch-tall George Auger, 29-inch-tall "Princess Wee Wee," and an unidentified three-legged performer, all from the Ringling Brothers circus, on the set of *Safety Last!* (the department store exterior is just visible to the right of Harold). The part of Colosso the giant in *Why Worry?* was originally intended for Auger, who died suddenly the day before he was to leave New York to begin work on the film in Los Angeles. He was replaced by Johan Aasen.

not enough time to him. The parting was Roach's idea, and Harold always maintained it was "the friendliest possible severance after nearly ten years of teamwork."[33] Roach released the entire Lloyd production team so that they could continue making films of the same high caliber with Harold.

Why Worry? was seven months in the making; production began in December 1922 and was completed in June 1923 at a cost of $220,626. The film grossed $1,476,254, making it one of the largest box-office attractions of 1923. Now on his own for the first time, Harold rented space at the Metropolitan Studios located at 1040 Las Palmas Boulevard in Hollywood and through the Harold Lloyd Corporation (which he had formed on April 24, 1922) embarked as his own producer on the films that are generally considered among his greatest achievements.

Filming the tooth-pulling sequence from *Why Worry?*, in which Harold acts as a living counterweight in order to extract the giant's ailing molar. Director Fred Newmeyer is directly in front of Johan Aasen. Gagman Ted Wilde is the man fully visible pulling the rope.

Above:
Harold and Colosso (Johan Aasen) are a two-man counter-revolutionary army in *Why Worry?*.

Below:
Harold offers one of his pills to cure Colosso's giant-sized toothache.

107

Girl Shy was Harold's first independent production and contains arguably the greatest race-to-the-rescue sequence of the entire silent cinema. Lloyd was justifiably proud of the elaborate and brilliantly executed chase — he actually decided to make the film because of it — but he was not satisfied with the film as a whole. Harold felt uncomfortable about his stutter character in later years, and believed the chase sequence — which he loved — overwhelmed everything that preceded it. Modern viewers do not share Harold's reservations. *Girl Shy* contains some wonderful comedy, a well-developed and moving relationship between Harold and leading lady Jobyna Ralston, and the precision pacing of the very best Lloyd features.

Harold plays Harold Meadows, a shy tailor's apprentice who has a pronounced stutter and is afraid of girls. He spends his lonely evenings writing a guidebook called *The Secret of Love Making*, which he claims is based on his own experiences, but in fact Harold has had no experience with girls. When Harold ventures to the city with his manuscript to seek a publisher, he is seated next to Mary Buckingham (Jobyna Ralston), an heiress forced to take the train when her car breaks down. Harold and Mary bond while hiding her small dog from the train conductor who will not allow pets on the train. During the journey, Mary's interest in Harold makes him less shy. When they part, a grateful Mary kisses him good-

bye. She keeps the box of Cracker Jack he has purchased for her on the train, and he retains a packet of dog biscuits as a remembrance of her. Harold now knows something of love.

As the days go by, Mary is pursued romantically by the cad Ronald DeVore (Carlton Griffin), but she can think only of Harold. While driving with DeVore she asks to be taken to Harold's hometown of Little Bend where fate brings Harold and Mary together again. While passing through Little Bend, DeVore accidentally drives the car off the road. When he goes to get help in town, Mary strolls onto a nearby rustic bridge, under which Harold happens to be sitting in a rowboat; he sees her image in the water, but thinks it is only his imagination. Later, she steps onto a raft that drifts off and bumps into him, and she falls into his boat. Astonishment and delight register on his face, but his stutter prevents him from speaking. When both realize they are each still carrying as treasured tokens the Cracker Jack box and dog biscuit packet, their feelings for each other are instantly communicated.

The meeting is short-lived. DeVore returns and takes Mary away, but not before she makes a date to meet Harold in the city. On the appointed day, Harold finds that his book has been rejected and he has become the laughingstock of the publisher's office. Realizing that his book

Harold encounters Mary Buckingham (Jobyna Ralston) aboard a train in *Girl Shy*.

109

Above:
In a scene borrowed from
Henry King's silent-film drama
Tol'able David (1921), Harold,
too shy to join in at a dance
across the street, wistfully
dances a few steps on his
own in *Girl Shy*.

Right:
Harold's "My Flapper" fantasy
from *Girl Shy*. "In the case
of flapper, I apply my caveman
methods," writes Harold,
whereby he takes her shoe
and gives her a spanking.

will not make him the success he has bragged about to Mary, he is unable to tell her the truth about what has happened. He instead tells her that all of his actions toward her have been false. "You didn't believe all I said to you, did you? I tell that to all my girls. I was just experimenting, getting ideas." As Harold has developed a stronger love story in *Girl Shy* than in any of his previous films, the rejection scene is quite moving. Her rejection by Harold results in Mary's agreement to marry DeVore. Harold reads the announcement in the newspaper and is disconsolate. However, events quickly change in Harold's favor: the publisher has decided to publish his book after all as a comic novel; a spoof of lovemaking manuals retitled *The Boob's Diary*, for which he will be paid handsomely. On the day of Mary's wedding, Harold discovers that DeVore is already married and has abandoned his wife. Harold must immediately set out to stop the girl he loves from marrying the wrong man.

What follows is an exemplary race-to-the-rescue chase sequence in which Harold commandeers anything that moves. It starts with Harold missing his train. He next tries to flag down a car. When that fails, he takes a car, going through two of them before he happens upon a horse. He next chases after a fire engine, and commandeers a streetcar, a motorcycle, and finally a two-horse cart. The scene keeps building, one gag after the other, faster and faster, with intercuts to the solemn wedding that Harold is attempting to stop. As *Variety* said in its review of the film, "What he goes through to get there is beyond the mere power of a type-writer to describe. It is a chase that caps anything else that has ever been done on the screen."[34]

A third fantasy sequence was filmed for *Girl Shy* depicting Harold as a rich sportsman and demonstrating his lovemaking technique with an old-fashioned Mary Pickford-type girl. The sequence was discarded after a preview.

Harold's "My Vampire" fantasy from *Girl Shy*. Attired as a Beau Brummel, Harold pays a visit to the vamp's chambers, where his indifference to the Barbara La Marr look-alike wins her over.

The chase was filmed on location primarily in downtown Los Angeles. Harold did most of his own stunts, including hanging by the electrical connective wire of the streetcar. However, in more complicated and dangerous sequences involving horses and the buckboard, a rodeo stunt driver was hired. Performing his own stunts was not without its perils. While grabbing the hose nozzle on the back of the fire truck in the streets of Culver City, Harold was involved in an accident. He later remembered:

Above:
Harold gets the bird when he rides a motorcycle through an open market in the spectacular race-to-the-rescue chase from *Girl Shy.*

Once I caught on the backend of a fire engine and it had this hose and the business was that the hose was loose and, as I grabbed a hold of the nozzle, the hose started to unwind and I began pulling it and, of course, I began to lose out in the struggle and finally I was practically parallel with the street still hanging onto this hose, which was supposed to be fastened on at the end and holding me. But something went askew, and it came off and hit me in the head, the big brass nozzle, and off I went—I was unconscious for about five minutes. Somebody asked me if I was all right and I said, "Well, I could have got along without that!"[35]

Below:
Harold hangs from the electrical connective pole of the streetcar he has commandeered in the race-to-the-rescue chase from *Girl Shy.*

Incredibly, with a big bump on his head, he went right back to work shooting the same gag.

Not only was the action in *Girl Shy* well conceived, it was breathtakingly photographed by cameraman Walter Lundin. It is a testament to Lundin's superlative work that his best effects—such as mounting the camera in a manhole on Grand Avenue in Los Angeles for the shot of the chase at street level with Harold driving two horses that gallop over the viewers' heads—were seen and copied by B. Reeves Eason, second unit director of the M-G-M epic *Ben-Hur: A Tale of the Christ* (1925), who largely directed the film's chariot race scenes.

Left:
The climax of *Girl Shy* has
Harold stopping the wedding
and running off with Mary
Buckingham (Jobyna Ralston).
The sequence inspired the end-
ing of *The Graduate* (1967).

Below:
Harold's marriage proposal gets
an emphatic "YES!" from Mary
(Jobyna Ralston) at the conclusion of *Girl Shy*.

Girl Shy also inspired later filmmakers. In a scene that anticipates the ending of *The Graduate* (1967) over forty years later, Harold runs to the minister and tries to explain that DeVore is a bigamist. His stutter prevents him from getting past the first word, so he throws Mary over his shoulder and runs up the stairs, kicking DeVore back down the stairs when he attempts to stop him. Outside, Harold's stutter prevents him from asking Mary to marry him. She manages to get him to pose the question, to which she replies in an intertitle in large lettering: "YES!"[37]

Girl Shy cost an estimated $400,000 and grossed $1,729,636, making the film a tremendous box-office success. The love story in *Girl Shy* was the start of Lloyd's maturity as a filmmaker, which would reach its peak with *The Kid Brother*, and the film remains one of his most endearing achievements.

Below:
Harold and father Foxy reading fan mail received by the Harold Lloyd Corporation offices in Hollywood, c. 1924. The feckless Foxy was much loved by Harold, who made him vice president and treasurer of the Harold Lloyd Corporation from 1922 until his death in 1947 at the age of eighty-three. His principal responsibility was putting Harold's signature on photographs mailed to fans.

Right:
Filming the stopping of the wedding from *Girl Shy*. Note the musicians in the foreground, used to create mood music for the actors.

In alternating character comedies with gag comedies, Harold followed up the character comedy *Girl Shy*—which some film exhibitors had deemed overlong, with an overabundance of plot—with *Hot Water*, a simple gag comedy made purely for laughs. Although he achieved greater personal satisfaction from creating character comedies (which placed an emphasis on developing character and story) than gag pictures, he was forever mindful of the public, who foremost went to see him to laugh.

Hot Water opens with the title, "Married life is like dandruff—it falls heavily upon your shouders—you get a lot of free advice about it—but up to date nothing has been found to cure it." A bridegroom is seen running to his wedding, with Harold, as best man, keeping pace with him. "Believe me, I'll never give up my freedom for a pair of soft-boiled eyes," Harold says in an intertitle. He literally runs into Jobyna Ralston and is immediately taken by her soft-boiled eyes (shown in a close-up); next seen is the title "Followed moonlight walks and tender talks—a honeymoon—then rent to pay."

The rest of the film is divided into three episodes of similar length. The first part involves Harold (called Hubby) struggling with an abundance of bundled groceries his wife has asked him to pick up from the market. He reluctantly accepts a live turkey he has won in the grocery store's raffle, which

burdens him with the task of carrying all the bundles and a live turkey home on a crowded street-car. Harold's plight creates chaos on the streetcar: bundles fall to the ground, the unruly turkey escapes from him and hides under seats and a woman's skirt, and two mischievous boys let loose a small crab that manages to crawl inside Harold's trousers. The passengers and streetcar conductor become increasingly agitated by his presence, and Harold is ejected from the streetcar—with his bundles and feathered charge. He resourcefully improvises his necktie as a gobbler leash for the walk home.

In the second part, Harold arrives home to find Wifey's (Jobyna Ralston) family visiting. The awful brood consists of her mother (Josephine Crowell), described with the intertitle, "with the nerve of a book agent, the disposition of a dyspeptic landlord, and the heart of a traffic cop," brother Charley (Charles Stevenson), "so lazy he gets up at four o'clock every morning so he'll have a longer day to loaf," and little brother Bobby (Mickey McBan), "a child with a skin you love to touch—with a strap." Harold has them all in his new automobile—named Butterfly Six—in a brilliantly executed action sequence that ends with the beautiful new car being completely destroyed.

As best man on his way to his friend's wedding, Harold declares never to "fall for a pair of soft-boiled eyes" until he encounters Jobyna Ralston in *Hot Water*.

Harold struggles with an irritable turkey and the disapproving looks of his fellow passengers aboard a streetcar in *Hot Water*.

The third part has Harold getting the impression that he has accidentally murdered his mother-in-law during the course of the evening when she decides to spend the night at his home. The episode — the weakest of the three — is reminiscent of the haunted-house-type thrills Harold had created in *Haunted Spooks, I Do*, and *Dr. Jack*. The film concludes with the in-laws fleeing from Harold's home, leaving a relieved Hubby and Wifey.

Of the three episodes, Harold's favorite was bringing home the turkey on the streetcar. He would later use the sequence in his compilation *Harold Lloyd's World of Comedy* (1962).

As with all his feature films, *Hot Water* had some gags that were filmed but later cut out prior to release because they did not work when shown to preview audiences. Harold later remembered:

Generally, you can analyze why an audience doesn't laugh at a piece of business, but occasionally you can't. I had one failure that no one ever figured out. I was carrying a group of bundles — it was a marital story called Hot Water *— and I was bringing home a turkey that I'd won in a raffle. I had taken my tie off and had tied it around the turkey's neck so I could lead it like a dog and carry my bundles at the same time. My shoe was untied so I set all of them down on one of these big mailboxes — you know, where you pile the mail packages on top — and as I sat down on the curb to tie my shoe, the postman came and picked up all my bundles with the mail, and I looked up just in time to* *see him starting to drive off with them. We always thought that was a funny piece of business, it was a funny situation, but it never got a laugh. Oh, it got a titter, but not enough for the amount of footage we gave to it. I never, to this day, have been able to figure out why that wasn't funny.*[38]

Another sequence, also cut after a preview, involved Harold's attempt to kill the turkey. According to Harold:

I told the bird it wasn't going to hurt, told it how nice it was to have a head chopped off by an ax. Even offered to blindfold it before I severed its neck. I coaxed it to come on and get killed, but it wouldn't listen. I put some grains of corn on a newspaper to tempt it. They happened to be directly over a picture of my mother-in-law, and when the turkey ate the corn, it looked as if the fowl was pecking at mother.

 "You're my pal!" I cried joyously.

 "Too far-fetched!" said the bunch.

 "Oh, no, it isn't!" I urged. "We'll do that by all means!"

 And we did. Then we previewed the picture and that scene was a complete dud. Not a giggle. Barely a smile. We cut it out entirely.[39]

This sequence, in which Harold is unable to kill the turkey (named Genevieve), was filmed but later deleted from the final picture.

HL-70

Harold is tormented by little
Bobby (Mickey McBan) while
his mother-in-law (Josephine
Crowell) looks on approvingly
in *Hot Water*.

Left:
Harold believes that his sleep-walking mother-in-law (Josephine Crowell) is a ghost that has come back to haunt him in *Hot Water.*

Below:
Harold's new car is destroyed on its maiden voyage in *Hot Water.*

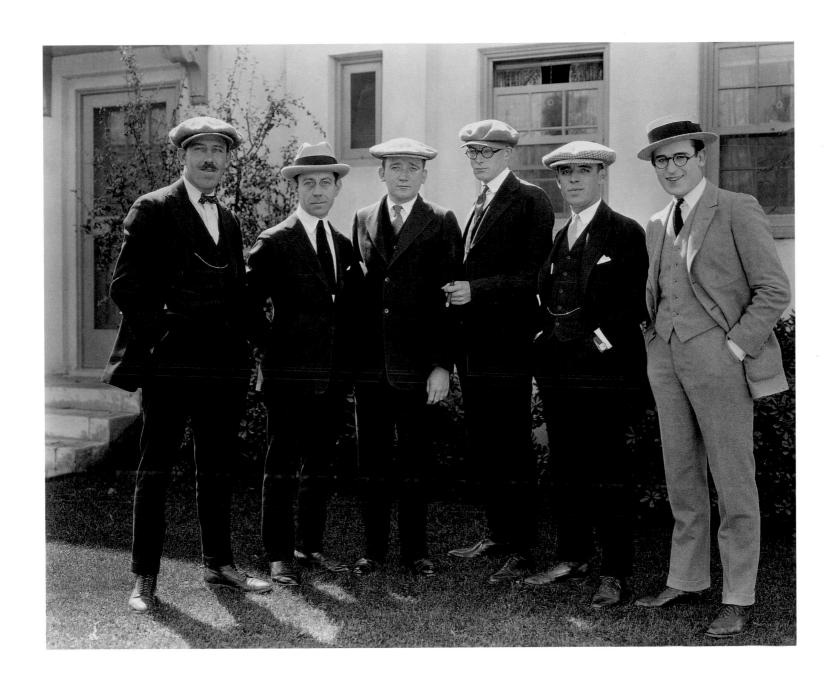

Although the characterizations in *Hot Water* are one-dimensional, they are exceptionally well acted; the most memorable performance is Josephine Crowell as the mother-in-law. Crowell, best known as a character actress in the D. W. Griffith films *The Birth of a Nation* (1915), *Intolerance* (1916), and Mary Pickford's *Rebecca of Sunnybrook Farm* (1917), would later appear briefly in Harold's last silent film, *Speedy*.

Hot Water fared well with the critics, although none thought the film ranked with his best work. The film was a commercial success, grossing $1,730,324, but Harold did not think highly of it. Only four years after it was released, he dismissed it in his autobiography, stating, "*Hot Water* ran only five reels, and, coming as it did between two longer, better films, it is little remembered."[40] Harold was perhaps too harsh — although one of his lesser silent features, it nevertheless contains sequences that stand with his very best work. The turkey on the streetcar, in particular, is brilliant in its construction and execution and is one of Harold's finest studies of the comedy of embarrassment. An unpretentious effort, *Hot Water* nevertheless still has the power to make audiences roar with laughter.

Above:
Harold's gagmen assemble for a group photograph during the production of *Hot Water*. Left to right: Fred Newmeyer, John Grey, Thomas Gray, Sam Taylor, Tim Whelan, and Harold. By this point in his career, Harold was employing more gagmen than any other comedian in Hollywood.

Opposite:
Harold poses for the still photographer during a rain delay while filming *Hot Water*.

The Freshman is widely regarded as Harold's finest film. It is arguably his funniest, and was his most commercially successful silent comedy feature. Harold had contemplated doing a college-boy character as early as 1915, when he was first considering a character other than Lonesome Luke, but felt such a character might be too limiting in scope over an extended number of comedy shorts, so the idea was discarded. The notion of a college theme stayed with him, however, and when he finally chose to do one his timing was perfect. Harold wisely tapped into the college craze of the 1920s by telling a classic Lloyd tale in a university setting.

As he did with the building climb sequence in *Safety Last!*, Harold decided to film the concluding scene, the football game sequence, first. Harold later recalled:

> *We tried to do the same thing [as* Safety Last!*] with* The Freshman. *We went out to Pasadena, where all the Rose Bowl football games are held. That's where we did the football game, out there. And I think we worked for about two days. . . . And just somehow the business or the spirit wouldn't come. And finally I came to the boys and I said, "Fellows, let's call it off. We can't do this picture that way. I've got to know the character, I've got to feel it, or we're not*

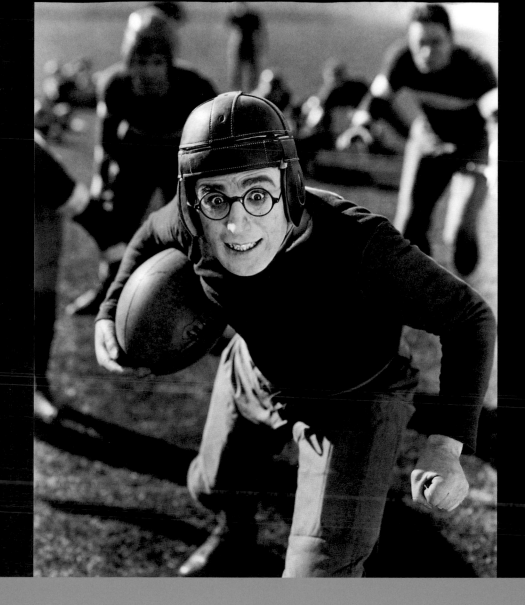

Harold is determined to transform himself from college jeers to college cheers in the last moments of the big football game in *The Freshman*.

going to get out of it what we think we've got here." So we scrapped what we'd shot there and went back . . . and we did The Freshman *right from the beginning. We started at the beginning and did it right in continuity all the way through. And as I look back, it's a good thing we did, because the whole thing is a characterization of this boy and his great desire to win popularity.*[41]

Harold quickly realized that *The Freshman* should be a character picture rather than a gag picture like *Safety Last!* and therefore needed a carefully constructed characterization, plot, and theme. Harold later remembered:

The Freshman, *for instance, there is only one theme in that: the boy wants to go to college and be the most popular of all, but he goes about it in the wrong way and gets the wrong impression of how he should do it, taking an actor's idea from a play* [sic] *he saw, which of course can only lead to trouble. His father says they are going to break his heart or his neck, and they do both. That was all the theme we had in that.*[42]

Opposite:
Clad in his letterman sweater and having perfected his "college yell," Harold Lamb is determined to be the Big Man on Campus in *The Freshman*.

Left:
Harold meets and is instantly taken by Peggy (Jobyna Ralston), an old-fashioned girl aboard the train on his journey to college in *The Freshman*.

Below:
Harold introduces himself with a ridiculous jig and greeting, "I'm just a regular fellow! Step right up and call me 'Speedy!'" in *The Freshman*. Charles Farrell, who would later become a popular leading man in such films as *7th Heaven* (1927) with Janet Gaynor, is to the right of Harold.

Right:
Harold receives a loving lick from Pete the dog between takes of *The Freshman*. Pete (called "Mike" in the film) terrorizes Harold in the film, but this photo indicates a different relationship off-camera. Pete was the son of the original Our Gang mascot.

Below:
Harold mistakes the severed leg of the tackling dummy for his own in *The Freshman*.

Opposite top:
Harold and Jobyna Ralston between takes during the production of *The Freshman*.

Opposite bottom:
In one of Harold's finest comedy sequences, his unfinished tuxedo, hastily basted together for the annual Fall Frolic dance, comes undone under the social strains in *The Freshman*.

Harold plays the appropriately named Harold Lamb, a college-bound boy who longs to be the Big Man on Campus. Like the real Harold, Harold Lamb works relentlessly to succeed, practicing over and over the handshake jig and catchphrase from a movie, "The College Hero," that has made an impression on him. "I'm just a regular fellow. Step right up and call me 'Speedy.'" He begins his journey to college on a train, where he is instantly smitten by Peggy (Jobyna Ralston), an engaging but shy, old-fashioned girl with long curls who is outnumbered on campus by flapper coeds. Harold soon becomes the butt of the popular crowd's jokes, embarrasses himself before the entire student body, and loses his college savings. Tate College is described in an intertitle as a "large football stadium with a college attached," so Harold determines that the key to his success is to become a member of the football team. He is used as a tackling dummy — literally — by the football team and led to believe he is on the team when he is really only the water boy. After the humiliation of the Fall Frolic, where Harold struggles to be popular and finally loses his tuxedo because of his tailor's weak stitching, Peggy tells him: "Stop pretending, Harold — be yourself! Get out and make them like you for what you really are and what you can do!" Harold finally gets his chance to prove himself at the big football game, where he transforms himself from the college's biggest zero to its greatest hero; Harold wins the big game and the girl after a hilarious romp on the field.

If *Safety Last!* is the ultimate comedy of thrills, *The Freshman* is the ultimate comedy of embarrassment, exemplified by the Fall Frolic sequence. Harold finances the Fall Frolic, the annual college ball. He has ordered a new tuxedo, but the tailor who is making it is slow and subject to dizzy spells that can be cured only by alcohol. By the day of the frolic, Harold is forced to wear a suit that is only lightly stitched together. As he plays the host, the suit slowly falls apart. Harold later remembered:

> *I wanted to be not too old-fashioned and I didn't want to pull my pants off. I said, "Everybody pulls their pants off in a scene. Let's not do that old, corny, lose-your-pants situation." So the first two previews I never lost my pants, but there was always something wrong with that section. One of the fellows said, "Harold, you've got to lose your pants." So I did and from then on it went fine. The audience loved that section. I had lost everything else and they wanted me to lose my pants.*[43]

The hilarity of the basted suit sequence has lost a bit of its punch; the violation of "correct" behavior of the 1920s does not translate well to modern audiences. However, audiences of any generation can relate to Harold Lamb's struggle for self-respect, success, and acceptance.

The football game sequence was partially filmed during an actual college game in November 1924 between the University of California–Berkeley and Stanford. Harold's company was forced to work quickly before the game and in between halves. The climactic touchdown race was filmed at the Rose Bowl in Pasadena when the arena was empty.

There had been college films prior to *The Freshman*, but after its enormous success, the number of college films jumped considerably. Seen today, *The Freshman* may in fact be a victim of its own success. There have been so many last-minute-touchdown comedies since then that some of the film's impact is blunted. The film was so successful that Buster Keaton produced his own film entitled *College* (1927). *The Freshman* was second only to Chaplin's *The Gold Rush* as the most successful feature-length comedy of

Harold cries in Peggy's lap when he realizes that he is perceived by others as a laughingstock in *The Freshman*. Harold would cut this poignant scene from his subsequent reissues of the film, believing that modern audiences would find it to be excessively emotional.

the entire silent era. It grossed $2,651,000 on a production cost of $301,681. However, a lawsuit that went on for over seven years consumed some of the film's earnings.

H. C. Witwer was a well-known short story writer and a friend of Harold's. Upon hearing that he was working on a college film, Witwer related to Harold and William Fraser over lunch the plot of his story "The Emancipation of Rodney," originally published by *Popular Magazine* in 1915. Harold and his gagmen were not interested in "The Emancipation of Rodney," as they had their own plot and gag ideas. However, when *The Freshman* became a huge commercial success, Witwer filed suit claiming copyright infringement, but the suit was dismissed. In 1929, he again attempted to sue the Harold Lloyd Corporation. Witwer died soon thereafter, and a decision was granted in his widow's favor in 1930. The Harold Lloyd Corporation won the case on appeal in 1933, but the litigation was an expensive ordeal.[44] Thereafter Harold was extremely careful when dealing with unsolicited scenarios and gag ideas.

An unusual portrait of Harold in straw boater hat sans glasses, 1925. Although his character frequently wore a boater hat, Harold himself never wore one offscreen.

The Freshman was the last Lloyd film to be distributed by Pathé, which had been distributing his films from the very first Lonesome Luke comedy in 1915. Pathé could not match the terms Harold wanted and was offered by Paramount: 77½ percent of the domestic gross and 90 percent of the foreign gross — incredible terms. So Harold signed a new distribution contract with the latter.

Unlike Harold's other films, *The Freshman* has been the one Harold Lloyd silent feature film that has been available — at least in part — for many years. A portion of the climactic football sequence was incorporated into the beginning of *The Sin of Harold Diddlebock* (1947). Of all his silent comedy features, Harold believed *The Freshman* to be the one film that would be best received by new audiences; this belief was based in part on the enormous popularity the film had enjoyed in the 1920s and the continuing popularity of college football. Editing out moments that he felt were dated or he no longer liked (such as references to radio operators and the scene of Harold crying in Peggy's lap), Harold attempted a reissue of the film in 1953. This reissue was not the success he had hoped for, and he quickly withdrew it. He reedited the film in 1959 and incorporated this edit into the compilation *Harold Lloyd's Funny Side of Life* (1963). Harold was persuaded by the distributor Janus Films in the late 1960s to travel with *Harold Lloyd's Funny Side of Life* to several Big Ten university campuses, as the film is partly a satire of college life. Harold took great satisfaction in the tremendous enthusiasm the film invariably received; he felt the college students of the 1960s responded to the film as enthusiastically, if not more so, than audiences had in the 1920s.

Filming the big football game in *The Freshman* at the Rose Bowl in Pasadena, California.

Harold followed up the character comedy *The Freshman* with a gag picture, *For Heaven's Sake*. It was his first film to be distributed by Paramount. The film gave Harold many problems, and he was never satisfied with it as a whole. However, the film does not betray any of the difficulties Harold had making it. Indeed, *For Heaven's Sake* is a delightful, well-made, and fast-moving comedy.

For Heaven's Sake was originally conceived with gangsters and political corruption central to the story. However, most of that storyline was soon discarded and would later become part of *Speedy* as Harold and director Sam Taylor developed with their gagmen a gag picture with a very thin story. Harold plays J. Harold Manners, a millionaire who inadvertently contributes to a mission in skid row (which is then named in his honor). He meets and falls in love with Hope (Jobyna Ralston), the mission pastor's daughter, when he visits the mission to protest his name being used. Under her influence, Manners makes parishioners out of all the seedy characters and tough men of the neighborhood. When his idle club friends abduct him on his wedding day (believing they are preventing him from making a foolish mistake), Harold must race back to the mission so as not to miss his own wedding.

Harold's character of the rich man is similar to the wealthy young men he played in *A Sailor-Made Man* and *Why Worry?*. It would be the last time he would play a rich man. Manners is the kind of reckless millionaire who buys a white car to match his trousers and when he wrecks it, walks into an automobile showroom, seats himself in the top-of-the-line model, writes a check for the full amount, and drives off. This gag was inspired somewhat by an incident from Harold's own life. In 1916, he celebrated the completion of his first year of appearing in Lonesome Luke comedies by buying a new car for $1250. The very day he purchased the car, he ran it up a tree and destroyed it and sold it the same day for scrap for $100.

The race-to-the-rescue sequence in *For Heaven's Sake* on the double-decker open-top bus is one of the film's most memorable moments. Harold is late for his wedding to Hope. To complicate matters, Harold must also chaperone his inebriated groomsmen back to the mission. At one point, they take possession of a runaway double-decker bus. Lloyd later remembered:

That whole bus was on a truck, but on rockers. It was terrifying up there because it felt like the bus was really going over. As it tipped, we all went over the edge; it gave the perfect illusion of the bus cornering on two wheels.

Harold had a difficult time making *For Heaven's Sake*. Many photographs like this one survive depicting entire sequences that were later discarded.

137

Right:
In the opening gag of *For Heaven's Sake*, Harold is unfazed by the destruction of his new car, while his chauffeur (Oscar Smith) is aghast.

Below:
Harold presents director Sam Taylor with a special megaphone to commemorate their fifth feature film together, *For Heaven's Sake*. Lloyd had the highest regard for Taylor's talents as a gagman and director.

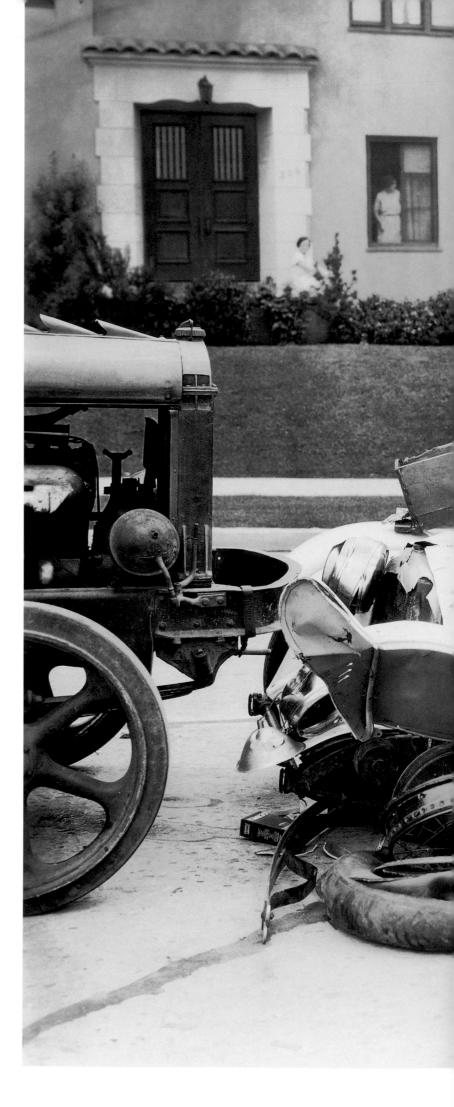

The tightrope walker was done by a brace, an iron brace that came up one leg and fitted to his body. It was up to him to bend his body, and his loose leg, so that you couldn't tell it was completely stiff. Oh, we did things quite elaborately, believe me!

A scene like that would take two weeks. We would get a whole cordon of police and rope off probably three blocks. We used all our own traffic and all our own pedestrians. All those people that we run through there are our own people, being paid.[45]

Harold borrows heavily from his earlier films in *For Heaven's Sake.* A brilliantly executed gag where Harold innocently eats a powder puff thinking it is a cookie is similar to the gag in *Grandma's Boy* where Harold eats a mothball thinking it is a piece of candy. The sequence in which Harold goads an entire neighborhood of gangsters in order to make them chase him into the mission is a reworking of the police chase in *From Hand to Mouth* (including the earlier film's superb long tracking shots). In addition, the race-to-the-mission climax is similar to the race to the church in *Girl Shy.*

Harold previewed *For Heaven's Sake* five times (he spent $150,000 after its first preview alone, correcting mistakes in judgment) and felt the final film was somewhat repetitive. He reluctantly gave the film to Paramount for distribution against his better judgment, as he believed it still required more work. Photographs survive showing that actors were replaced, scenes shifted, and relationships altered as the film developed. Originally it was seven reels, but Lloyd cut one reel out of the film prior to its release, making the six-reel film his last short comedy feature (running under an hour in length).

Even giving the film its title proved difficult. It eventually came about when after one of many days of discussions, an exhausted gagman started to blurt out, "Oh, for heaven's sake!" Harold interrupted him and said, "You've got it!" It was a coincidence that "for heaven's sake" happened to be an expression Harold used throughout his life.

Despite the difficulties, *For Heaven's Sake* nearly equaled *The Freshman* as a commercial success, grossing $2,591,460 and placing the film as one of the ten most popular films in America in 1926. Undoubtedly, the gross earnings reflect that Paramount was a much more effective distributor than Pathé. One admirer of the film was Pulitzer Prize-winning poet Carl Sandburg, who wrote of the race to the rescue on top of the double-decker bus: "the stuntiest that Harold has had since he hung by his eye-winkers from the skyscraper in *Safety Last!* It keeps him in his unique place on the screen, not so important an actor as Charles Spencer Chaplin by any stretch of the imagination, but the best showman the comic spirit has had to date on the screen."[46]

Although *For Heaven's Sake* does not have the pathos and plot construction of *The Freshman*, the gags are nonstop and superbly executed. Yet Harold was so disappointed by this film that he considered paying Paramount to keep it on the shelf and not release it. Although not as strong as the Lloyd films that surround it, *For Heaven's Sake* is delightful and remains a spectacular crowd-pleaser.

143

Harold's penultimate silent film, *The Kid Brother*, is his masterpiece; a near-perfect balance of story, character development, and ingenious gags. *The Kid Brother* also boasts the distinction of being Harold's personal favorite of all his films.

Lloyd plays Harold Hickory in this backwoods tale, beautifully photographed by Walter Lundin. Harold's father (Walter James), the town sheriff, and his two elder brothers (Leo Willis and Olin Francis) are strapping men who dismiss Harold as a worthless weakling, and treat him as the Ugly Sisters treat Cinderella. However, an inventive mind works behind those horn-rimmed glasses. He whisks the family laundry in a butter churn and dries it on a clothesline fastened to a kite. Using a fish net, he washes dishes without getting his hands wet and allows a warm stove to do the drying. Harold Hickory is very much like the clever boy from Nebraska that Harold Lloyd had been.

Harold uses the same ingenuity to defeat the villainous medicine show strongman Sandoni (Constantine Romanoff), to whom Harold has inadvertently given permission to perform in town during his father's absence. Harold wins the love of medicine show performer Mary Powers (Jobyna Ralston) and recovers the money for a dam entrusted to his father as sheriff, stolen by

Harold extends a cup of water
to a grateful Mary Powers
(Jobyna Ralston) in *The Kid
Brother*. The film was the last
to feature his finest leading lady,
Jobyna Ralston. Ralston left
Lloyd to play Richard Arlen's
sweetheart in *Wings* (1927),
and subsequently married Arlen
in real life.

the strongman, in a fight in the hull of an abandoned ship. Harold wins the respect and admiration of his family and the town when he triumphantly returns with the money and the culprit.

Although *The Kid Brother* shares a similar plot to *The White Sheep*, produced by Hal Roach and starring Glenn Tryon,[47] the film was truly inspired by Henry King's silent drama *Tol'able David* (1921), in which a kid brother (Richard Barthelmess) fights against overwhelming odds to recover the United States mail and struggles back triumphant. Harold adored *Tol'able David*; it was one of his favorite films — he even cast one of the actors who played an outlaw in *Tol'able David*, Ralph Yearsley, in *The Kid Brother* as Hank Hooper, Harold Hickory's archenemy.[48]

The film, under the working title *The Mountain Boy*, was in production for over six months. Production began with Lewis Milestone (who would later make *All Quiet on the Western Front* [1930]) as director, but contractual difficulties with Warner Bros. forced him to withdraw from the film. Harold replaced him with gagman Ted Wilde, who remained with the production until November 1926, when he caught pneumonia and was replaced by gagman Lex Neal (a boyhood friend of Buster Keaton) and J. A. "Kit" Howe. It was Harold himself, of course,

who was solely responsible for making all of the creative decisions and who held the film together artistically through all of the changes.

The Kid Brother was mainly photographed on location at the Providencia Ranch, near Burbank, California, where Forest Lawn Memorial Park–Hollywood Hills is now located. The village scenes were filmed in Placentia, near present-day California State University–Fullerton. The ship exteriors were filmed off Catalina Island.

The film is technically the most polished Lloyd production. One of its most memorable moments is a vertical traveling shot that moves up with Harold in the farewell scene as he climbs a tree to keep Mary in view as she walks away. As Harold keeps climbing higher and higher, the camera climbs with him. The feat was accomplished by using a huge, specially constructed tower containing an elevator, built alongside the tree, which allowed the camera to track all the way to the top of the tree.

Harold calls out to her, "What's your name?"

"Mary!" she replies.

As she disappears into the distant valley, Harold climbs still higher and calls out to her again to find out where she lives. The film cuts back to her and in an intertitle she responds, "With the Medicine Show — down by the river."

"Goodbye," says Harold, climbing still higher to keep her in view, reluctant to let her go.

An intertitle with tiny letters gives her response, "GOODBYE!"

Harold waves, loses his balance, falls from the tree, and when he lands on the ground, instantly sees a flower and picks its petals — she loves me, she loves me not, she loves me — as the scene fades out.

Like Buster Keaton's *The General* (1926), *The Kid Brother* contains many elements not usually associated with film comedy, such as the lynch mob that accuses Harold's father of stealing the money for the dam,

Above:
Harold dons his father's hat, vest, badge, and gun and imagines himself the sheriff in *The Kid Brother.*

Right:
Harold's breakfast in bed is short-lived when his brothers (Olin Francis and Leo Willis) discover him and not Mary behind a blanket curtain he has rigged in *The Kid Brother.*

Above left:
Harold defends Mary (Jobyna Ralston) from the advances of medicine show strongman Sandoni (Constantine Romanoff), not realizing there is a snake wrapped around the stick he is using to protect her. Sandoni, terrified by the snake, runs away.

Above:
Harold hides from the evil strongman Sandoni (Constantine Romanoff) in *The Kid Brother*.

and the dramatic fight between Harold and Sandoni in the hull of an abandoned ship. Harold plays the scene with a determination and ruthlessness uncommon in film comedy. The sequence, however, contains one of his best gags. Harold later remembered:

We had one piece of business that was always what we called "sure-fire"—a piece of comedy business that anybody can do and get big laughs. This particular one was down in the hold of a ship. This big fellow—we were having a fight—he was trying to kill me and nearing that objective. He threw me up against the side of the hold and came over and picked up a big iron belaying pin and took ahold of me and hit me over the head with this big iron—which should have crushed my skull. All I did was blink my eyes and, of course, he was amazed and so naturally he struck me again, but with the same result. The third time he hit me, he even bent the bar. Then he was so flabbergasted he let go of me, and as I ran away, you see that when I was thrown against the wall, there was a bracket, an iron bracket that fitted over my head. He was hitting the iron bracket, of course, and his weapon wasn't touching me at all, but you can't see that in the picture until we're ready to let you see it. That's very "sure fire." Now we shot that scene two ways. We thought it would be good to let the audience know that the iron bracket was there. And the funny thing is, they laughed both ways. We had a hard time figuring out which was better. We finally left it a surprise. I think surprise has a sharper laugh to it.[49]

Left:
Harold clinging to the gunwale of an abandoned ship in *The Kid Brother*, a scene reminiscent of his earlier "thrill" pictures. Lloyd intended *The Kid Brother* to be composed of equal parts of the character comedy of *Grandma's Boy* and the gag comedy of *Safety Last!*.

Below:
A behind-the-scenes photograph showing the filming of Harold's climb onto the abandoned ship to confront the crooks in *The Kid Brother*. The scenes aboard ship were influenced by Buster Keaton's exploits on a derilict vessel in *The Navigator* (1924).

Opposite:
Harold directs his director Lewis Milestone (right of Harold) and camermen Walter Lundin and Henry Kohler (in hole) while preparing to shoot a fishing sequence filmed on location in Placentia, California. Gagman Ted Wilde (who would replace Milestone as director) is at right in swimsuit and bandana. Assistant director Robert "Red" Golden is at left. This scene was later discarded from the film.

149

Harold with Chicago the monkey in a gag still from *The Kid Brother*. The talented simian helped Lloyd achieve the film's most brilliant comedy sequence.

The derelict ship also contains one of the most brilliant Lloyd comedy sequences, involving a little monkey (named Chicago)[50] that Harold enlists to throw Sandoni off his tracks. Harold places a pair of big boots on the little simian, and Sandoni chases the boots all over the boat, believing it is Harold walking on the deck of the deserted ship. Harold would later recall that the monkey was the hardest part to cast in the entire film. He found a great monkey in Chicago who really helped make *The Kid Brother* special.

The Kid Brother was a commercial and critical success. However, with a gross of $2,403,130, it made slightly less money than the film that preceded it, *For Heaven's Sake*. This disappointed Harold greatly because he had worked so hard to make *The Kid Brother* his very best film; he had twice as many gags and sequences worked out and photographed as actually used in his quest for perfection. After its initial release, *The Kid Brother* remained unseen for over thirty years until Harold himself—when selecting clips for his compilation films—realized what an exceptional film it is. He allowed theater organist Chauncey Haines to tour with the film in the mid-1960s, followed by a few public screenings with his favorite theater organist, Gaylord Carter. The film was later featured under the auspices of the American Film Institute as the retrospective choice of the 1969 New York Film Festival. He also showed the film at a few universities in 1970, the year before his death. In October 1970 *The Kid Brother* was shown as part of the Cinema City exhibition held to celebrate the seventy-fifth anniversary of motion pictures at the Round House in London, where it was hailed as a masterpiece and a major rediscovery. People who associated Lloyd's films with stunts on tall buildings were taken by *The Kid Brother*'s visual beauty, inventiveness, and style. The film is an exemplary marriage of all the best Lloyd elements of comedy and storytelling, refined into one exceptionally accomplished film.

Left:
Harold applying his makeup on location for *The Kid Brother.*

Below:
Harold resting between takes during the filming of the fight scene on the set of the hull of a derelict ship from *The Kid Brother.*

***Speedy,* Lloyd's last silent film,** is a superb valedictory to the silent era. "Speedy" was Harold's real-life nickname (given to him by his father), and the film is appropriately fast-paced. It is one of his most stylish films, filled with brilliant comedy, thrills, and surprises, climaxing with a wild chase scene in downtown Manhattan, where Harold must hurtle a horse-drawn streetcar pell-mell through chaotic city traffic.

In *Speedy*, Lloyd plays Harold "Speedy" Swift, a baseball-crazy young man who cannot hold a job. His employment misadventures include work as a soda jerk and a cab driver. Harold's girlfriend, Jane (Ann Christy), lives with her grandfather, "Pop" Dillon (Bert Woodruff), who owns New York's last horse-drawn streetcar. The horse and streetcar are stolen by a gang hired by a railroad monopoly. By stopping Pop Dillon's streetcar from operating for more than twenty-four hours, the rail monopoly hopes to steal away his franchise. Speedy ultimately finds the car and manages to get it back on track in time to make the daily run, saving Pop's old franchise.

Harold's original idea of *Speedy* was a tale of political corruption and underworld dealings. According to Harold:

Harold and Jane (Ann Christy) having fun on a Luna Park, Coney Island attraction in *Speedy.*

There is almost no vestige left in Speedy *of the original idea—an underworld story. Its origins date back before* For Heaven's Sake; *we wanted a big-city picture as a change, and began with a plot of New York politics, gangsters and such. It called for a girl who should live with a grandfather or an uncle. . . . Someone suggested that the grandfather drive a horse car. A horse car is quaint, has been little used in pictures, and provokes comedy of itself. There had been a horse-car line in New York until recently, operated to hold a franchise. This suggested a plot to steal the franchise from the old man, permitting me to step in, thwart the conspiracy and win the girl, after the usual misadventures. The franchise plot grew until it crowded out the original underworld story.*[51]

153

Speedy was filmed partly on location in New York City. The film begins with a montage of the city that is reminiscent of the montage that begins King Vidor's great silent drama *The Crowd* (1928). The film has an extended cameo appearance by Babe Ruth and a spectacular race to the rescue through the streets of Manhattan. Evocative scenes of the rides and arcades of Luna Park at Coney Island comprises the bulk of the New York material, although Lloyd also filmed at the Plaza Hotel, the Queensboro Bridge, Wall Street, Times Square, Yankee Stadium, the Brooklyn Bridge, Greenwich Village, and Central Park. Glimpses of some of this footage can be seen in the film, providing an invaluable record of New York in the 1920s. The New York crowds caused delays to such an extent that an intended four-week shooting schedule turned into twelve weeks. Occasionally, the company would hide the cameras and shoot a scene furtively and quickly (particularly the Coney Island scenes), but for the most part the filming was watched by thousands of New Yorkers. Harold would eventually create a street set at a cost of $80,000 on property he owned in Westwood, California, replicating the Lower West Side, for some scenes — such as the big fight sequence — to complete the film. Nevertheless, few films of the period had ventured as bravely — and succeeded — in using New York City locations to the extent that *Speedy* did. Buster Keaton would try with *The Cameraman* (1928), but ultimately he and his crew returned to M-G-M's Culver City studio after failing to get the scenes they needed because of the disruptions caused by the crowds that formed as soon as Keaton was recognized.

Harold was virtually unrecognizable without his trademark horn-rimmed glasses and, owing to his average American man screen persona, was better able to stroll through a crowd unnoticed than Keaton. In fact, Harold bet director Ted Wilde he could walk down any two blocks of Fifth Avenue in daylight and no makeup and go unrecognized. Wilde chose the most difficult stretch of Fifth Avenue — 41st to 43rd streets — but Lloyd nevertheless won the bet. He later admitted that two tricks aided him considerably: he lowered his eyes to avoid eye contact with anyone and the appointed time of the bet (four p.m.) prevented few casual strollers; everyone is bound somewhere in a hurry and preoccupied with their business.

Harold carefully prepared the material he filmed on location in New York. However, two unexpected things happened, one good and one bad. An accident (in which no one was injured) created a wonderful gag. During the filming of the dramatic race to the rescue, in which Harold drives the horsecar through

New York City traffic, the horsecar was at full speed going down Third Avenue when it still had the El (an elevated subway). The stunt driver (Harold did not drive for these shots — one of the few things he was unable to do) did not make a wide enough turn, and the car hit one of the massive El posts, throwing the driver from the cab. Miraculously, neither the driver nor the horses were injured, and the accident provided such wonderful footage that Harold reworked the scenario to incorporate the sequence in which the wheel of the car breaks and Speedy commandeers a manhole cover, quickly improvising by using it as a wheel. One can never overstate how much grueling work went into filming these silent feature-length comedies, and must marvel at the quick minds involved that could turn a mistake on location into a great comedy sequence.

Above:
Harold and Jane (Ann Christy) enjoy a Luna Park, Coney Island, attraction in *Speedy*.

Opposite:
Harold and Jane (Ann Christy) endure a crowded New York City subway ride to Coney Island in *Speedy*.

Harold and Jane (with King Tut the dog) make themselves comfortable and contemplate a domestic life in the back of a moving van (by setting up the furniture and creating a make-shift home while getting a lift back from Coney Island) in *Speedy*. This charming scene, which helps establish the rela-tionship between the two char-acters, was inspired by a similar sequence in Mary Pickford's *My Best Girl* (1927).

The bad situation, which was not planned, was the realization in the editing room after they returned to Los Angeles that they needed some pickup insert shots of Harold in medium closeup driving the streetcar during the final chase. The cost of returning to New York for what would end up being less than one minute of film was prohibitive. Harold instead opted to use the newly introduced Williams process, a traveling matte visual effect showing him driving the horsecar at a frantic speed through the streets of New York. Harold had never used rear-screen projection before because it was not previously available. Unfortunately, the technical primitiveness of this technique is apparent to modern eyes and detracts slightly from what is otherwise a bril-liantly executed chase.

For his leading lady, Harold replaced Jobyna Ralston (whose contract had expired with *The Kid Brother*) with Ann Christy. She had previously appeared in Christie Comedies (produced by Al Christie — no relation to Ann), which were released by Paramount, where she was seen by Harold. Lloyd thought Ann Christy looked like a modern New York girl. Although she has many charming scenes with Harold — particu-larly in the Coney Island sequences — she showed little of the depth that Ralston had been able to bring to the previous Lloyd films.

George Herman "Babe" Ruth, the best-known baseball player of his time, appears in a cameo role as himself. He is first seen giving away baseballs to children at the city orphan asylum on First Avenue when he hails Speedy's cab. Starstruck Speedy can only watch his idol Babe in the back seat and not the road ahead, and his worshipful awe results in a comedy-of-thrills cab ride through the traffic to Yankee Stadium. Babe Ruth agreed to appear in the film in part because Ted Wilde, the film's director, had just directed a film with Ruth called *Babe Comes Home* (1927).

Speedy was the only Harold Lloyd film to receive an Academy Award nomination. Ted Wilde was nomi-nated for Best Comedy Director, a category eliminated by the Academy of Motion Picture Arts and Sciences

Left:
Harold is a soda jerk in one of his short-lived jobs in *Speedy*.

Below:
Harold endures an unwanted dental exam in a sequence filmed but later abandoned from *Speedy*. W. S. Wilton (Byron Douglas), the man behind the railroad monopoly, is on the left wearing the pince-nez.

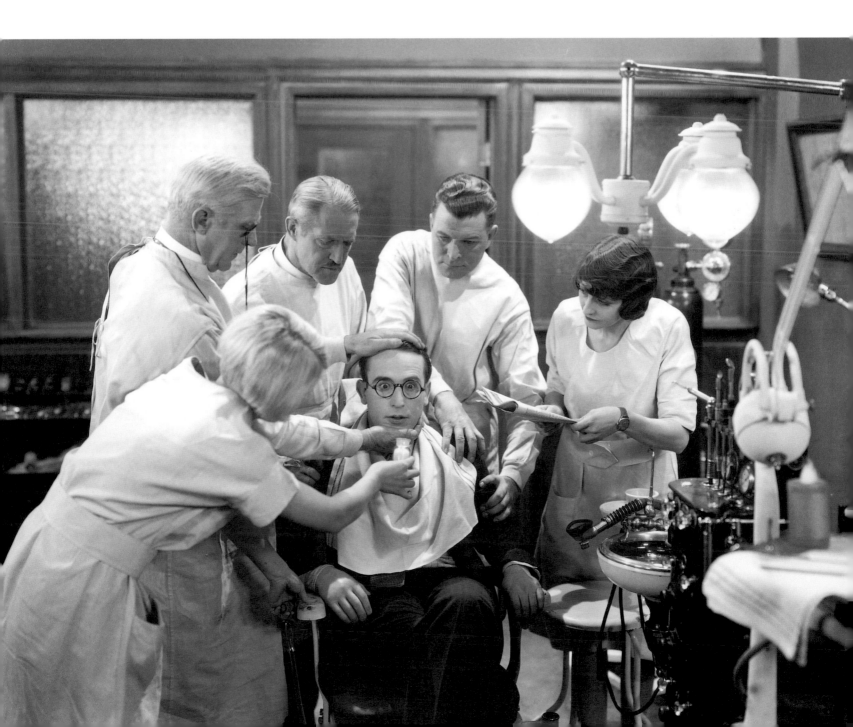

Harold rallies the elderly trades-men in the neighborhood to fight off the racketeers sent by the traction magnates to steal the city's last horse-drawn streetcar in *Speedy*. Hank Knight (just visible on the far left), the last of the six Wells Fargo horse stage drivers, appeared at the age of eighty-two as one of the tradesmen.

after the first Academy Awards ceremony. Harold, one of the founding members of the actor's branch of the Academy, would eventually receive an honorary Oscar in 1953.

Whereas his typical features went through five or six preview screenings, Harold only found it necessary to have three previews before he was convinced *Speedy* was finished. The film was appropriately premiered in New York City—a first for a Lloyd feature—to a clamor of critical applause and tremendous popularity with the public. However, with a gross of $2,287,798 (the film had cost nearly $750,000), it made slightly less than *The Kid Brother*.

Speedy has the distinction of having been shown on a Ford Trimotor airplane at 5,000 feet in September 1928. In the era of highly flammable nitrate film, the potential consequences should have made such a public-ity stunt prohibitive.

In the same year that *Speedy* was released, Harold published his autobiography, titled *An American Comedy* (a play on the title of Theodore Dreiser's 1925 novel, *An American Tragedy*). Written in collabora-tion with Wesley W. Stout during the making of *Speedy*, the book provides a good account of Lloyd's work-ing method of story and gag construction while making the film.

In his autobiography as well as in his films, Harold had both reflected and shaped the idealism of 1920s America. *Speedy*, Harold's last film of the Jazz Age before the Great Depression brought it to a close, was also his last silent film and the last great film he ever made.

Left:
Filming *Speedy* with Harold as the taxi driver for the "Only One" cab company. Director Ted Wilde is on the far right.

Below left:
Harold with his three-year-old daughter, Gloria, costumed as a pirate for a children's Halloween party at the Lloyd home at 502 South Irving Boulevard in the Hancock Park area of Los Angeles, during production of *Speedy* in 1927.

Below:
Harold with baseball great Babe Ruth during the production of *Speedy* in New York City. Ruth appears in a delightful cameo role as himself.

The talkie revolution had overtaken Hollywood when *Welcome Danger* began production in August 1928 as a silent film. Director Ted Wilde became ill (he died the following year from pneumonia) and was replaced by Mal St. Clair, who had worked with Buster Keaton and made the sophisticated screen comedies *Are Parents People?* (1925) and *The Grand Duchess and the Waiter* (1926). *Welcome Danger* was in the editing stages — the first cut was an inordinately long seventeen reels and had been previewed twice and pared down to twelve reels — when Harold boldly decided it needed to be remade into a talking film. Lloyd's first talkie, *Welcome Danger* was an enormous box-office success as a result of the novelty of sound. Although the film was a huge commercial success — more popular than anything Lloyd had done since *The Freshman* — artistically, it was one of his worst films.

Harold was extremely audience-conscious, as his intensive use of previews shows. It was when Harold heard roars of laughter while passing Sid Grauman's Million Dollar Theater in downtown Los Angeles that a sudden desire to remake the film in sound came upon him. When he went into the theater to find out what was being shown that caused all the laughs, he discovered it was a short subject depicting the sounds of everyday objects such as frying eggs

or ice clicking in a glass. Harold realized that if everyday sounds could cause such laughter, he could provide a guaranteed laugh riot by remaking his current picture with sound. Harold later recalled:

Gags and comedy "business" we wouldn't think of using were getting laughs because it was a different medium now. I said to my associates, "I think we've missed the boat on this. Maybe we ought to make this over." They thought I was out of my mind. We had already made the picture and it had cost me five or six hundred thousand dollars, my own money, too, but I insisted we should find out how we could put sound to it. It was dubbing of course, and we didn't know anything about dubbing in those days, but that is what we did and it cost me another four hundred thousand to do that. But it was worth that; it probably made more money than any picture that might have been my first talking picture. Yet I kept the same pace in there, the same technique as I would have done in a silent picture.[52]

In *Welcome Danger*, a woman of ill repute drops her handkerchief in front of Harold to get his attention. Without missing a beat, Harold picks up the handkerchief with his toe and drops it in her lap. Harold liked this little comic moment so much that he later had actor Edmond O'Brien recreate it in *A Girl, a Guy and a Gob* (1941), a film Harold produced but in which he did not appear.

Harold hired Clyde Bruckman to helm the sound version of the film. Bruckman had previously worked with Lloyd as a gagman and had worked in this capacity as well as in the role of director for Buster Keaton and Laurel and Hardy. Approximately half of the silent film was dubbed over and retained, while the other half was conceived as a talkie and refilmed over a period of two months. This resulted in a hybrid film that Harold then believed was a successful blend of silent-film action with dialogue.

Harold plays botanist Harold Bledsoe, who is summoned to San Francisco, where his late father had once been chief of police. His father's colleagues desperately hope he is a chip off the old block and take the extreme measure of making him chief of police to thwart the flourishing crime of the Chinatown underground led by the Dragon (Charles Middleton), overlord of the city's underworld. Fascinated to the point of preoccupation with the affinity of botany and police fingerprinting, and further distracted by the pretty Billie Lee (Barbara Kent), Harold nevertheless corners the Dragon at his home and forces him to confess his crimes in front of the entire police force.

Welcome Danger, at 112 minutes, is unusually long for a comedy film of this period; most comedies ran under an hour and a half. The film went through more than ten previews—each eliciting further cuts—before Lloyd was satisfied. Harold Bledsoe is not at all like the previous Lloyd characters; he is completely charmless—a strange mixture of prissiness, obnoxiousness, and aggressiveness. The first two-thirds of the film are cumbersome and suffer from many of the pitfalls associated with early talking films—a lot of stilted dialogue and sound at the expense of action. Poor dubbing further hampers the film. It is only in the last third of the film, set in San Francisco's Chinatown, that the action and comedy of the old Lloyd manner are seen in flashes. Despite its numerous drawbacks, *Welcome Danger* was well made for its time; the silent sections that were dubbed gave it more action than most films made in 1929. Indeed, in one sequence, Harold and policeman Noah Young are left in total darkness when the lights go out in intervals, leaving a completely black screen. Having dialogue and sound effects carry the action in this manner was an experimental and novel use of the medium. In later years, Harold felt uneasy about the film as a whole and believed it should have been cut by at least another two

Right:
Harold with Noah Young in *Welcome Danger*. Young had been an actor at the Rolin Company, where he first worked with Harold in his early one-reel Glass Character comedies.

Below:
Harold struggles with the evil John Thorne (Charles Middleton) and his henchmen in the climax of *Welcome Danger*.

The film had a new leading lady, Canadian-born Barbara Kent. She had previously appeared in such notable films as Clarence Brown's *Flesh and the Devil* (1927) and Paul Fejos's *Lonesome* (1928). She brought little of the talent she displayed in these earlier films to the role of Billie. Charles Middleton, however, was very effective in the role of John Thorne (the Dragon). He would go on to play Emperor Ming in the three Universal *Flash Gordon* science fiction serials starring Buster Crabbe, the part for which he is best remembered.

The final production cost of *Welcome Danger* was $979,828 and it grossed nearly $3,000,000. It was Lloyd's highest-grossing film; for audiences of its time, the novelty of sound outweighed its artistic failure. In a common practice of the time to accommodate theaters that had not yet converted to sound, *Welcome Danger* was also released as a silent film that was principally adapted from the talkie version. However, more of the original silent version was retained, resulting in cast variations (Edgar Kennedy appears only in the sound version), a few differing scenes, and alternate credits (Ted Wilde and Clyde Bruckman both are credited as directors, but inexplicably not Mal St. Clair). Unfortunately, the complete, original silent version of *Welcome Danger* no longer exists.

Harold on location for the silent version of *Welcome Danger*. Walter Lundin is at the camera. Mal St. Clair (the film's original director) is behind him. From left: Wallace Howe, Gaylord Lloyd (just visible on extreme left), Jimmy Anderson, head electrician "Bard" Bardwell, Jake Jacobs (Harold's double) holding the slate board, and leading lady Barbara Kent.

Feet First was Lloyd's fifth and final "thrill" picture. Harold had deliberated for nine months before deciding he wanted to duplicate the thrills of his best-remembered film, *Safety Last!*, by reworking the silent film's climb sequence to include sound. Despite his efforts, Harold and director Clyde Bruckman were unable to recapture the thrills of *Safety Last!* because of the film's weak story and its overabundance of dialogue, which disrupted the comedy sequences.

Harold plays Harold Horne, an ambitious shoe clerk in Honolulu determined to make his way into the ranks of high society. He crashes a formal party where he meets Barbara (Barbara Kent), a girl with whom he had had a previous brief encounter and of whom he has become enamored. He wrongly believes she is the daughter of the wealthy Mr. Tanner (Robert McWade), the owner of the store where he works, whose favor he seeks. (She is actually Mr. Tanner's secretary.) To impress her, Harold pretends to be a wealthy young busness-man. The subterfuge eventually forces him to become a stowaway—without a cabin, clothes, or money—on board the ship on which Barbara and Tanner are traveling en route to

California in order to keep up his masquerade as a successful businessman. Hiding in a mailbag, he is flown ashore by seaplane, from which the bag is accidentally dropped on a painter's scaffold that starts ascending the facade of a downtown Los Angeles office building. The mailbag gets caught on an awning hook, which leaves it — and Harold — suspended several stories above ground. Ignorant of his location, Harold cuts his way out of the mailbag, is horrified to discover his predicament, and is forced to climb the building. After surmounting the comic obstacles placed before him, Harold makes it to the top, wins the girl, and gains the favor of his employer.

As with *Safety Last!*, *Feet First* began with the idea of a thrill sequence without a fully realized plot that would bring the character to that point. However, *Feet First* lacked the motivation for the final thrill sequence that *Safety Last!* had developed. In *Feet First*, the reason for the climb is accidental, and Harold has to make it because of the peril; it is not like *Safety Last!* in which he must climb the building to succeed. Also, the realism of sound in *Feet First* heightens the danger at the expense of the comedy; the cries for help quash the comedy, and the grunts and groans betray the effort and slow down the action.

Opposite:
Harold perilously close to the edge in *Feet First*. Lloyd used the same techniques of illusion that he had used in *Safety Last!*. Long shots were performed by stuntman Harvey Perry.

Below:
A behind-the-scenes photo that reveals the mattressed platform below the parapet.

As with *Welcome Danger*, Lloyd previewed the film at an inordinately long running time; he felt all the material filmed was good and that preview audiences would tell him by their reaction what to cut and what to retain. Lloyd later remembered the first preview:

> *The first time we previewed this picture was here on the coast in San Diego. And I think the climb was about two and a half to three times as long as we intended to leave it. In other words, the climb must have been at least three reels, if you could imagine that. Well, we wore the audience out. They were in a state of horror all the way through. At first they got great fun out of it, but finally they got to the point where they were tired, they couldn't stand any more of it. Of course I groaned. I'd loved to have taken the picture right off at that moment, and taken out a reel or so, but we had to go through with it. Of course, our reason for having done that—and we were a little shortsighted because it didn't accomplish the purpose we wanted—was that we wanted to leave all the scenes that we'd shot in it and pick out the best ones. And the ones that we didn't think were as strong or as funny or as thrilling, we'd eliminate them and make bridges [to connect what remained]. But it didn't tell us that because by the time it was halfway through the audience was tired out, they didn't tell us anything anyway. So we finally cut it down to a length and we previewed it and it has proven to be one of our outstanding sequences.*[53]

The final sequence was ultimately cut to one reel. However, even in 1930, some audiences found the sequence difficult to watch with the added realism of sound. One cinema in Berlin solved the problem by turning off the soundtrack during the climb sequence.

Feet First has less talk than *Welcome Danger*, but the dialogue is awkward and has not aged well. Nor has the weak situation comedy of the opening scenes. Barbara Kent, Harold's leading lady from *Welcome Danger*, was again the leading lady. She is pretty to look at, but her performance is only serviceable; the romance between her and Harold is doltish. Harold was mired with a thin story, awkward dialogue, and an uninspired supporting cast. Moreover, at thirty-seven years of age in 1930, Harold was too old to play this character, and Depression audiences no longer cared to see his 1920s ambitious go-getter.

Feet First had a production cost of $647,353 and grossed $1,589,263, nearly $750,000 less than *Welcome Danger*. It was a severe box-office drop for Lloyd, the first big decline in his career. However, it was a very respectable gross for a Depression-era film, and better than all but a handful of films that year, and the film was generally well-received by critics. In 1953 Lloyd re-edited the film, cutting it from ten reels to eight for television distribution.

Above:
A little boy (Buster Phelps) takes aim when Harold attempts to take his magazine in *Feet First*.

Opposite:
Harold gets the bird when he stows away on a boat in *Feet First*, which was partly filmed on board the S. S. *Malolo* en route to Hawaii in June 1930.

Dissatisfied with the weak story and overabundance of dialogue that had plagued *Feet First*, Harold spent a long time preparing his next project. The tremendous success of Charles Chaplin's *City Lights* (1931), a silent film with a synchronized musical score and sound effects, was the major factor that spurred Harold to put back much of his silent technique into *Movie Crazy*. The resulting film greatly pleased Harold, who rightly believed it to be his most successful integration of silent-film comedy technique and dialogue.

Harold portrays Harold Hill, a rube from Littleton, Kansas, who dreams of making it in the movies. In response to a fan magazine article, he writes a letter with his photograph enclosed to Mr. O'Brien of Planet Studios. However, Harold's father accidentally replaces his photograph with that of a man much better-looking than Harold. The mistake elicits a favorable response from the studio and an invitation to come to Hollywood for a screen test; Harold at last has his big break into the movies.

Upon his arrival in Hollywood, Harold manages to wreak havoc as soon as he steps off the train. He falls in love with a beautiful Spanish actress, failing to recognize that she is the same

girl, without makeup and wig, who later gives him a ride home in the rain. Mary Sears (Constance Cummings) keeps the two identities concealed from Harold and has him act the role Harold plays best: the fool.

By 1932 the idea of a boob let loose in a motion picture studio appeared hackneyed; this kind of material was originally popularized by the book (1922), the film (1924), and the play (1925) *Merton of the Movies*. Buster Keaton had reworked the same theme for his first talking feature, *Free and Easy* (1930). Harold was determined to have an excellent script prepared prior to filming. He hired Agnes Christine Johnson, Charles Ray's former scenarist, and Broadway playwright Vincent Lawrence to write the script; gagmen Clyde Bruckman and Lex Neal were hired to embellish it with comedy in an effort to combine good dialogue with sight gags.

Despite its overused theme, however, the film, which had the working title *Movie Struck*, succeeds on all levels. The opening gag is one of Harold's best. He appears to be riding along in an expensive convertible listening to a Hollywood program on the car's radio. The car speeds up, Harold lifts his arm from the car, and it is revealed that he is actually on a bicycle peddling along

Harold battles it out with Vance (Kenneth Thomson) in an elaborate fight sequence on the set of a flooding boat in the climax of *Movie Crazy*. It was such an arduous experience to perform that both men had to rest for several days after it was completed before resuming work on the remainder of the film. The scene was shot silent with a silent-film camera; the dialogue and sound effects were dubbed in later in post-production.

Harold shows his father (DeWitt Jennings) and mother (Lucy Beaumont) the letter he has received by mistake inviting him to come to Hollywood for a screen test in *Movie Crazy*.

on the far side of the car. Harold fondly recalled this illusory gag in a 1958 interview:

That was an exceptionally good illusion, because it did look exactly like I was sitting in the car, and, of course, I was riding a bicycle hanging onto the car, and, when we got ready, the car went on and I rode my bicycle up a driveway into the garage. That happened to be my own personal gag.[54]

Not only did he contribute some of the best gags; Harold directed much of the film. Credited director Clyde Bruckman's alcoholism made him increasingly unreliable; Harold had to take an even greater hands-on involvement in production than usual. Harold's extended role may be why the film is such a vast improvement over *Feet First*. Leading lady Constance Cummings confirms this view:

Harold was a very sweet man and was like the character that he played in the film. He was without question the most important person on the set. I believe Harold worked out everything with the director [Clyde Bruckman] before they would shoot a scene. His directors I think mainly remained in the background and made certain the scene was done the way Harold wanted it. That was the case with Movie Crazy.[55]

Constance Cummings, who was loaned out from Columbia to play in the film, is without question the strongest leading lady Harold ever had in his sound films. The love relationship between them is the most complex of any Lloyd film. The strange way Mary Sears both encourages and discourages Harold's attention through her two identities has the effect of making the character appear more complex and oddly modern.

The film's most celebrated sequence is the one in which Harold, wearing a magician's jacket by mistake, is unable to control the menagerie that emerges from his sleeves. Although this gag clearly is reminiscent of the basted tuxedo sequence in *The Freshman*, the scene nevertheless remains one of Harold's funniest celluloid creations. According to Harold:

> *This one sequence had to do with my getting a magician's coat on by mistake, not knowing I had a magician's coat on that was loaded with all his tricks and gimmicks, and of course when I got on the floor to dance with a very important personage, things started to happen. A little child's laundry came out of my sleeve and a pigeon flew out from under my coat and eggs came out of my sleeve and a rabbit was found — and mice — everything happened. Well, it was one of our best sequences I would say.[56]*

Harold behind the camera on location for *Movie Crazy*, which he directed mostly himself when credited director Clyde Bruckman's alcoholism made him increasingly unreliable.

Harold fails to realize that Mary Sears (Constance Cummings) is also the Spanish vamp he met earlier at the studio in *Movie Crazy*.

Another sequence that draws from his previous work is an elaborate fight scene on a ship movie set reminiscent of *The Kid Brother*. Wonderfully clever and utilizing much of the material developed but deleted from the shipboard fight in *The Kid Brother*, the scene is played with no background music of any kind — just natural sounds. The effect is somewhat eerie, and Harold regretted in later years not having music to enhance the scene.

Upon completing *Movie Crazy* in October 1932, Harold and his family went to Europe for six months — the first time Harold had ever been abroad. He was convinced *Movie Crazy* was his best work in sound and would be his greatest success. He returned in March 1933, and discovered that the film had received excellent reviews but disappointing box-office returns. *Movie Crazy* had a production cost of $675,353 and, unlike his silent features, grossed only twice that amount — $1,439,182. Harold blamed Paramount's distribution, but the coming of the Great Depression and his two-year absence from the screen had affected his popularity. Harold had successfully translated his silent-film technique into a sound film, yet had produced a relative failure. He realized that if the public did not want the old Harold Lloyd, his next film would have to be entirely different.

Harold makes every possible blunder in his screen test in *Movie Crazy*. The scene is a parody of the ridiculously serious acting style adopted by many dramatic films during the early talkie period. With him are Harold Goodwin as the disgusted director and Mary Doran as the screen test actress.

In one of his finest sequences, Harold unknowingly wears a magician's coat, causing chaos with a string of miniature laundry that emerges from his sleeve as he dances with Mrs. Kitterman (Louise Closser Hale), the dignified wife of the studio owner, in *Movie Crazy*.

The relative failure of _Movie Crazy_ had proved that Harold's 1920s character of the go-getter who overcomes obstacles with optimism and hard work had become an anachronism with the coming of the Great Depression of the 1930s. Harold bought an original story—the first for a Lloyd feature—as the basis for this film in an effort to try something different. The result, _The Cat's-Paw_, is one of his strangest films and least typical of Lloyd or any other comedian of the early 1930s.

Clarence Budington Kelland had written one chapter of _The Cat's-Paw_ when Harold purchased the property for $25,000, thereafter offering suggestions to Kelland as to how to make the principal character of Ezekiel Cobb more affable and pleasant. There were two ways Harold and director Sam Taylor could do the film: "The old way" with lots of comedy business and gags, or "the new way," the way Kelland had written it, allowing dialogue to take the greatest importance and introducing comedy only when appropriate. Harold later remembered:

> _I did a picture called_ The Cat's-Paw, _a story taken from the_ Saturday Evening Post _which was a very good story; and we didn't know whether or not to do it in my style, because to do it in my style would have meant minimizing the story. So we put two pieces of_

paper in a hat and we wrote on them "the old way" and "the new way" and

we drew out "the new way," and we were a little concerned for the moment.

The Cat's-Paw *didn't have nearly the abundance of comedy "business" we had*

had before, but nevertheless the story was a good one and was liked by a

great many people. I think I would have done it funnier if I had done it in

my usual style.[57]

Clyde Bruckman spent an uncredited twenty-one weeks working on the script adaptation.
Because Harold was dissatisfied with Paramount's distribution of *Movie Crazy*, he instead signed
a distribution agreement with the Fox Film Corporation (which became Twentieth Century-Fox
in 1935) for *The Cat's-Paw*. Filming began in the summer of 1933 at the General Service Studios
in Hollywood, with certain scenes filmed on Harold's Westwood property and the Fox lot.

Harold plays Ezekiel Cobb (Lloyd's first departure from the character name "Harold" in a
feature film), a missionary's son who has been raised in China according to the philosophical
principles of Ling-Po and knows little of modern American life. Upon his arrival in graft-ridden

181

Stockport, California, to find a suitable wife, he is persuaded by Jake Mayo (George Barbier) to run as the reform candidate for mayor. Mayo is in cahoots with some machine politicians who are convinced that Ezekiel will lose and their corrupt administration will continue. By a fluke, this "cat's-paw" (a term to describe someone who is used by others to further their own ends) wins, and when he sees the political corruption he applies his Eastern principles and has the chief of police round up all the gangsters in town and take them to a huge cellar in Chinatown, completely ignoring their constitutional protections. Ezekiel cites the example of Chinese leader Fu Wong, who rid a community of corruption by executing every known criminal and offers his gangsters nearly the same terms: confess or die. It would seem that the "cat's-paw" has indeed become a dictator.

The comedy of the situation is that, after seeing the apparent decapitation of one of the criminals, the gangsters think Ezekiel is a fanatic, when in fact the "beheading" is achieved by a Chinese magician and ketchup, leaving the criminal unconscious but unharmed. As a result of his extreme tactics, the gangsters confess their crimes and are taken to prison. Ezekiel finds a wife in Miss Pet (Una Merkel) and is made a hero by the end of the film.

The film has the controversial message that until people take the law into their own hands, nothing will be done about political corruption. The advocacy of police-state methods — even when Ezekiel's methods turn out to be fake — does not diminish the film's fascist overtones, a trait it shares with Cecil B. DeMille's underworld drama *This Day and Age* (1933). Some film scholars have suggested that *The Cat's-Paw* is actually Lloyd's satirical essay on President Franklin D. Roosevelt's New Deal, particularly the president's National Recovery Administration (NRA).[58] Roosevelt's NRA, which promoted drastic economic controls to spur the country's lagging economy, was later found to be an unconstitutional curb on free enterprise. Like Roosevelt's NRA, Ezekiel Cobb's public safety techniques are drastic and illegal. Lloyd, a businessman himself, most likely resented Roosevelt's attempts to control American industry and longed for the pre-Roosevelt, pre-Depression era of the 1920s, where an enterprising young man was free to make his fortune without any interference from the state, limited only by his own talent, wits, and perseverance. However, some have suggested that Ezekiel Cobb's suspension of the Bill of Rights to further the common good may be viewed as Lloyd's approval of Roosevelt's methods to overcome the Great Depression. Like Cobb, Roosevelt might be considered a benevolent, albeit undemocratic, leader, suspending the law for the betterment of the people. Perhaps Lloyd believed in the notion that the only way to get rid of those who violate the law, like the criminals in *The Cat's-Paw* or the robber barons of the 1930s, is to take the law into your own hands. Although Lloyd never revealed which political message drove the film, Harold was an active Republican who was not only a card-carrying member of the party but served as a Delegate to the 1948 Republican National Convention, representing the state of California.

With an expensive production cost of $617,000 and a domestic gross of only $693,000, *The Cat's-Paw* was Lloyd's first real commercial failure, despite favorable reviews. Harold was attempting to make one of the very first "screwball" comedies — an essentially verbal genre of cynical wisecracking and fast and furious cross talk that dominated comedies in the 1930s. This type of comedy was a specialty of directors Frank Capra and Preston Sturges. However, Lloyd's timing for such a film was not right, and Harold was not the right person to be making this kind of film. *The Cat's-Paw* lacked the visual comedy audiences expected from a Lloyd picture, and the comedy is overly dependent on dialogue and plot devices. Harold later had misgivings about the film, regretting that he had not done it in "the old way," with an emphasis on gags and comedy business.

Harold achieved his greatest critical success in a sound film with *The Milky Way*.

For the first time since 1923, Harold agreed to make a film produced by a company other than his own. Paramount Pictures, his distributor since 1926, made an agreement with Harold to be a salaried actor in the film, for which he was paid $125,000. In addition, the contract specified that the Harold Lloyd Corporation would receive 50 percent of the film's net profits and Leo McCarey would be the film's director. Harold accepted the film in part because the property, a Broadway play by Lynn Root and Harry Clork, was an ideal story for his type of comedy. He also liked the idea of not having to risk financing another film himself after the commercial disappointments of *Feet First*, *Movie Crazy*, and particularly *The Cat's-Paw*.

Harold plays Burleigh Sullivan, a timid Brooklyn milkman. When drunk, middleweight boxing champion Speed McFarland (William Gargan) takes a swing at Burleigh — who is adept at ducking — and knocks himself out. Burleigh is mistakenly credited with knocking out the champ. Through a series of fixed bouts orchestrated by the champ's manager, Gabby Sloan (Adolphe Menjou), he is launched to become a contender for McFarland's title, which he wins at the end of the film.

In director Leo McCarey, Harold found an ideal comedy collaborator. McCarey, a veteran

of silent film comedy, was one of the best comedy directors of the time, and a principal architect

of "screwball" comedy. McCarey began his career as a gagman for Hal Roach and graduated to

director, helming films with Charley Chase and Laurel and Hardy. He went on to direct Eddie

Cantor in *The Kid from Spain* (1932), the Marx Brothers in *Duck Soup* (1933), W. C. Fields

in *Six of a Kind* (1934), and Cary Grant and Irene Dunne in *The Awful Truth* (1937). Today,

McCarey is perhaps best remembered for directing *Going My Way* (1944) and *An Affair to

Remember* (1957). He was known for keeping a piano on the set, for often between scenes —

when he was in need of inspiration — he would go to the piano and improvise. He would then

come back and have a new idea or possibly a totally new interpretation for a scene.

Lloyd appreciated McCarey's easygoing style almost immediately. Harold later recalled:

I hadn't made a picture for about two years, if my memory serves me right. And
well for an actor not to be active in his profession, you get very rusty. . . . So I'd
been working with [Leo] McCarey—the mental end of it was fine—but when
we started working, and it was in about our third or fourth day, by that time I

had got what you call "oiled up" and everything was easy and smooth-running, but the first two days were a tremendous effort. You didn't feel at ease and you didn't do things in the way that you should do them, and Leo came around and he said, "Harold, I can tell from the way we've run this stuff in the projection room, you're not too happy with those first two days are you?" "Oh, no," I said. "They're pretty bad. They're horrible." He said, "Would you like to make them over?" And I said, "Oh boy!"[59]

McCarey's skillful direction successfully integrates Lloyd's physical comedy performance with the fast, verbal wisecracks and crosstalk of the film's exemplary supporting cast which included Adolphe Menjou, Verree Teasdale (Menjou's real-life wife), and Lionel Stander. The film contained some improvisation, a technique from silent comedy in which Harold flourished. One scene in particular—Harold smuggling a newborn colt into the back seat of a taxicab—was not in the script and was entirely improvised. McCarey's only direction to Harold was, "Harold, you work to the colt!" McCarey supplied the whinnies of the colt off-camera, and Harold improvised some wonderful bits as he attempted to muffle the noise from the taxi driver. Everyone believed that the sound of an actual colt whinnying would be dubbed in later; however, McCarey's whinnies proved so effective that they were kept in the finished film.

Harold went into training with a daily regimen of running and swimming to lose fifteen pounds for the boxing scenes. His days as an amateur boxer during his teenage years in Denver helped him tremendously with the sparring scenes. The climactic boxing sequence wherein Burleigh ducks his way to pugilistic victory is amusing, and Harold's technique, which involves sidesteps and a variation of the scissor-legged jig from *The Freshman*, is highly entertaining and memorable.

The Milky Way was released almost at the same time as Chaplin's *Modern Times* (1936)—a silent film with a synchronized musical score, sound effects, and some dialogue—to which it was frequently compared. Despite excellent reviews, *The Milky Way*, which had a final production cost of $1,032,798.21 (the film went over budget in part owing to the illnesses of Menjou, Teasdale, and McCarey during production), grossed $1,179,192 worldwide; the film resulted in a $250,000 loss for Paramount. *Movie Crazy, The Cat's-Paw*, and *The Milky Way* failed to salvage Harold's career in talkies. He was at a loss as to what he could do to rejuvenate his career. Although Harold was satisfied with the film, in later years he felt that the superb ensemble cast led by Adolphe Menjou stole the film from him. *The Milky Way* was remade by producer Samuel Goldwyn as *The Kid from Brooklyn* (1946), starring Danny Kaye and directed by Norman Z. McLeod; the original was withdrawn from circulation and, by terms of the contract, destroyed. Fortunately, Harold's own 35mm nitrate print, which was made directly from the original camera negative, survives virtually complete at the UCLA Film and Television Archive, where all of the archival elements to the Harold Lloyd films have been held on deposit since 1985.

Director Leo McCarey, Harold, fight promoter Lou Darro, and Adolphe Menjou pose on location for *The Milky Way* at the boxing arena at the Olympic Auditorium in Los Angeles. Darro provided expert advice for the film's fight scenes.

The initial critical response to *The Milky Way* enabled Harold to secure financing from Paramount in June 1936 for his last independent production, *Professor Beware*. The agreement called for Paramount to finance the film up to six hundred thousand dollars; after that, Lloyd would assume all production costs. In return, Harold would receive 15 percent of the gross receipts (in lieu of a salary) up to the first one million dollars.

The project Harold was initially developing over several months in 1936 was an entirely different film from *Professor Beware*. The story involved a small-town veterinarian whose offbeat life philosophy is so appealing it galvanizes a king (who meets the veterinarian when traveling incognito) to abdicate his throne in order to fully experience life. With nearly a complete script prepared, the Paramount domestic and foreign departments advised Lloyd to abandon the project for fear it would prove to be unshowable in England and unpopular elsewhere as a result of events unfolding in Great Britain. Paramount was correct; soon thereafter King Edward VIII abdicated the throne prior to his coronation to marry American divorcee Wallis Warfield Simpson, effectively ending the film's potentially comic possibilities at that time.

Lloyd was committed to deliver a film to Paramount and now had no script. He had only a fledgling idea for a professor of archaeology character. An original story was adapted by Jack Cunningham and Clyde Bruckman; Delmer Daves, the future director, wrote the screenplay. However, the development of the screenplay was rushed, and it shows; the story is nothing more than a weakly motivated extended chase with reworkings of several Lloyd silent-film comedy routines.

Lloyd plays Professor Dean Lambert, an archaeologist who is afraid he may fall victim to an ancient Egyptian curse should he become involved with a young actress (Phyllis Welch) he meets in circumstances similar to what is described on the fragment of an ancient Egyptian tablet he has unearthed. The resulting film is one long chase as Lambert travels as a fugitive from the law from Los Angeles to New York in order to be part of an expedition to Egypt. The film contains several moments recycled from earlier Lloyd films; one of the most notable is Harold riding with two travel companions on top of a fast-moving freight train; when they see a low tunnel ahead they frantically run for their lives to the rear of the train. This sequence is

Harold traveling with hobos Raymond Walburn and Lionel Stander on top of a freight train, blissfully unaware of an approaching low clearance tunnel in *Professor Beware*. The sequence was filmed three different ways: on a real train involving an actual tunnel, on a miniature train set built with a treadmill leveled up precisely behind the false train with moving scenery (for long shots), and at the studio on another treadmill utilizing rear-screen projection depicting the tunnel (for close-ups). Portions of all three techniques were unsuccessfully interwoven into the finished sequence. The studio reproductions (as seen in this photo) lack the authenticity of Lloyd's earlier uses of this kind of material, such as in *Now or Never*.

an elaboration on the run along the top of a train in Harold's three-reel comedy *Now or Never*. However, this scene as well as the reworking of a car concealed in a tent and other car gags from *Get Out and Get Under* were the only ones from the film that gave Harold any lasting satisfaction; he would later showcase them in his compilation films *Harold Lloyd's Laugh Parade* (1951) and *Harold Lloyd's World of Comedy* (1962).

Despite budgetary restrictions and a weak story, Harold tried hard to make each scene in the film the very best possible. Not wanting the film to look cheap, he invested some of his own money in *Professor Beware*. He chose Broadway director Eliott Nugent to direct and in his relentless efforts to make the film the best comedy possible would often ask Nugent for additional takes to try a scene differently. Leading lady Phyllis Welch, in her first and only film, admired Harold's efforts:

> He loved making films and he wanted Professor Beware *to be the very best it could be. He was a perfectionist. He was very patient with me. I was a Broadway actress and knew nothing about the making of films. . . I would try and sometimes I would become frustrated and be in tears. I would get so terrified. And Harold was very patient and helpful. He would say, "I think that will be all for now. How about if we go bowling?" And he would take us bowling and we would come back and continue with the film. That helped to put me at ease somewhat. He ran the show and he could do that.*[60]

Despite Harold's work and a good supporting cast, the finished film proved to be uninspired and foolish. Harold invested $220,275 of his own money in the film, bringing the total production cost to $820,275. The film was a complete flop, earning only $796,385—$25,000 less than its production cost. Including distribution costs, Paramount's loss was $250,000. Harold received 15 percent of the gross, $119,400, but he still showed a loss of $100,000. Later television sales recouped his investment, but Harold was shaken by the film's poor results. The fickle film-going public had dismissed him as an anachronism. Harold later recalled:

I was never happy with Professor Beware. *It had a lot of good things in it but it was never really up to the standard of some other pictures that we had made. And I was terribly disappointed in it. And after it was released, I said to the boys, "Now I am not going to start on another picture until we get an idea that I think has real merit behind it." And I looked for about six months very diligently, and I didn't come up with what I considered was a good idea. Then I got doing something else and I stopped looking, and then you'd look again and didn't find it, and so it went on for two years. And after I'd stayed off the screen for about two years, I stopped looking and have been enjoying many other things. A lot of people wondered why I had more or less stopped making pictures. That was really behind it; I got producing. I produced some for RKO—enjoyed that very much—but it wasn't that you decided to quit, you just kind of tapered off.*[61]

Harold stopped looking to star in another film, yet he found some success as a producer. Harold had previously produced a series of two-reel comedies with Edward Everett Horton for distribution through Paramount in the late 1920s and Mildred's last film *Too Many Crooks* (1927). At RKO, he produced films with younger comedians: George Murphy and Lucille Ball in *A Girl, a Guy, and a Gob* (1941) and Kay Kyser in *My Favorite Spy* (1942). It was also during this period that he produced "The Harold Lloyd Comedy Theater" radio series that broadcast on the NBC network from 1944 to 1945.

Only the prospect of working with the successful comedy director Preston Sturges lured Harold back onto the screen. Harold greatly admired Sturges, the writer and director of films such as *The Lady Eve* (1941), *Sullivan's Travels* (1941), and *The Miracle of Morgan's Creek* (1944). Sturges was a fan of *The Freshman*, and he wanted to make a film with Harold as a tribute to the Harold Lloyd comedies. *The Sin of Harold Diddlebock* picks up the story of Harold Lamb of *The Freshman* from the moment after he wins the big game. The film opens with actual footage from *The Freshman*, and Harold Diddlebock (the character's last name was inexplicably changed from Lamb to Diddlebock) is then shown twenty years later as a disillusioned bookkeeper. The film has the lamb turning into a lion in the old Lloyd manner, and Sturges even wrote a thrill sequence, partly inspired by *Safety Last!*. However, filmed at the Goldwyn studios using rear-screen projection, it lacked the authenticity of Harold's own thrill sequences.

The first third of the film is an excellent exploration of what might have happened to his character from *The Freshman* twenty years later. However, Sturges wrote the last two-thirds of the film in about a week during production. Harold and Sturges disagreed on the direction of the story, and the two friends were soon at odds. Harold later recalled:

I didn't agree with how he wanted me to play the character. I had a section in my contract that if I didn't like it, I could play it the way I wanted, but I also had to do it the way he wanted. That meant that in the projection room, we had to argue it out, and we didn't fare any better in the projection room than we had on the set. For about two weeks, we made two versions, two scenes, each way. . . . He didn't want gags to come into it, he wanted this dialogue . . . I came to him with business and he said, "Hell, the business is too good for my dialogue!"

I said, "Preston, this is terrible."

He said, "It'll kill my dialogue."

I said, "Let *it* kill the dialogue, what are we after? We're after entertainment, laughs."

[Preston said,] "Harold I can't do it." So I stopped looking for business. There was the difficulty we had.[62]

Harold gets the attention of banker James R. Smoke (Jack Norton) when he calls with Jackie the lion to promote his year-round circus for children in *The Sin of Harold Diddlebock*. Harold was wary of Jackie and would not rehearse the scene with the lion. His reticence was not unfounded; while filming the scene, Jackie tried to bite Harold's hand— as one can see in the finished film—and thereafter Harold refused to do any more scenes in close proximity to Jackie.

Production began in September 1945 and ended in January 1946. It was scheduled for 64 days, but because of the two men arguing the film took 116 days to complete. Harold was paid $90,000 for his work as the star of the film, plus $50,000 for the use of the clip from *The Freshman*. Produced by Howard Hughes, the film cost $1,712,959 and was given a limited release by United Artists as *The Sin of Harold Diddlebock* (the original title was *The Saga of Harold Diddlebock*, but Sturges changed it to *The Sin* as a parody of the Helen Hayes film *The Sin of Madelon Claudet* [1931]). It was poorly distributed and did not fare well critically or commercially. Hughes quickly pulled the film from distribution, took three years to recut it, changed the ending, retitled the film to *Mad Wednesday* (Hughes believed the word "sin" in the original title might have prevented family audiences), and released it through RKO Radio Pictures in 1950. Again, it was indifferently received. Harold was unhappy with the release. He sued Howard Hughes, California Pictures, and RKO for $750,000, charging that they deliberately attempted to damage his reputation by not giving him top billing on the re-release. Harold accepted a settlement of $30,000. The film proved disappointing for both Sturges and Harold, and Harold never worked in film again.

Harold wrote in his 1928 autobiography, "One, even two pictures, are no criterion [*sic*], but if ever three fail consecutively the handwriting on the wall will need no translating. I can only hope that when the time comes I shall not try to fool either the public or myself, but will bow my way out as gracefully as I can manage and turn to directing, producing or developing a younger actor."[63] Harold retired gracefully from motion pictures as he predicted, to devote himself to his family, hobbies, and other interests.

In typical Harold Lloyd fashion, Harold did not let his career disappointments of the 1930s and 1940s destroy him. Like his screen characters, he remained upbeat and optimistic about his future. Having saved a fortune from his most successful films (as well as an excellent investment portfolio and real estate holdings), Harold was able to pursue his hobbies vigorously, including handball, bowling, microscopy, painting, photography, and magic. The two other interests of his last years were rearing his granddaughter Suzanne and doing his work as a Shriner.

Harold was a prominent member of the Ancient Arabic Order of the Nobles of the Mystic Shrine, the fraternal freemasonry organization of high-level Masons, more widely known as the Shriners. Harold began his indoctrination into the Order with his father in 1925 and was as enthusiastic about it as everything else he pursued. His deep interest in Masonry led him through both the Scottish Rite (becoming a 32nd degree Mason) and the York Rite (becoming a Knight Templar). He was elected to the Temple Divan and in 1949 became Imperial Potentate, the highest-ranking position in the Shrine. Lloyd gave of himself unstintingly to Shrine activities, and felt that the twenty-two Shriners Hospitals were the best explanation for the order's existence. He often said, "You can't help a little crippled child uphill without getting closer to the top yourself." Lloyd served as president and chairman of the Board of Trustees of the

Shriners Hospitals for Crippled Children, and dedicated a good portion of his last years to

their administration. He was made president of the Shriners Hospital Corporation in 1963,

a position he held until his death. His prodigious energies were absorbed by the Shriners

Hospitals—he would spend an hour or more each day just signing checks for the hospitals,

No doubt as a result of his own accident, Lloyd took special care to develop the Shriners

Hospitals burn institutes.

The national attention given to Harold's designation as Imperial Potentate (he was given

the front cover of *Time* magazine to celebrate the event) made him ponder the viability of

reissuing some of his old films. He knew he had lost a generation by staying off of the screen

and not reissuing his old films as Chaplin had. He first reissued a shortened version of *Movie*

Crazy in 1949 and later *The Freshman* in 1953, with disappointing results. *Movie Crazy*

and a shortened version of *Feet First* were also sold to television. However, the compilations

he put together from his old films exclusively for Shrine activities—*Down Memory Lane*

(1949) and later *Harold Lloyd's Laugh Parade* (1951)—were so well received he decided

that if the public were to accept him at all it would best be done through a compilation. He

Harold promoting his compilation film *Harold Lloyd's World of Comedy* (1962).

197

made two more for theatrical distribution — *Harold Lloyd's World of Comedy* (1962), and *Harold Lloyd's Funny Side of Life* (1963).

Harold Lloyd was one of the first filmmakers to fully appreciate the importance of film preservation. Notwithstanding the 1943 nitrate film vault fire at Greenacres, in which Harold lost nearly all of the Lonesome Luke comedies, the Harold Lloyd film library remains one of the best preserved of any silent film-maker. After the fire, he built two concrete vaults at the estate for the remaining films and made dupe negatives from the best surviving prints of the films whose original negatives had been lost. In 1966 Harold met eighteen-year-old Richard Correll. Richard was a child actor and the son of Charles Correll, Andy of *Amos 'n Andy* radio fame (who had been Lloyd's partner in the founding of radio station KPMC in Los Angeles along with Bing Crosby, Freeman Gosden, and Paul Whiteman). He had seen *Harold Lloyd's World of Comedy* and became fascinated by Harold's films. With his friend Dave Nowell, Richard volunteered to help organize Harold's film vaults, which had been in a state of disarray after the production of the compilation

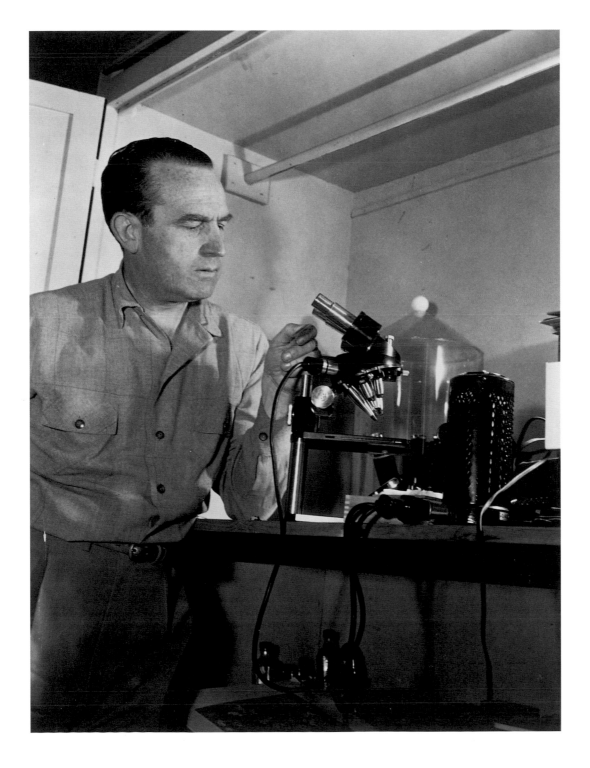

Opposite:
Harold pursuing his interest in painting and color research, c. 1940. Harold took up painting as a result of his interest in color, which grew from his interest in microscopy. A color-maker produced eight standard pigments for him from which he developed his own palette of seventy-two related colors; it was one of the largest private collection of artist's colors in the United States at the time. His painting evolved from scraping samples of these seventy-two colors onto 4x6-inch cards. In 1952, Harold's abstract paintings were exhibited in Beverly Hills and New York City. He called his larger works "fantascopes" and his smaller paintings "imaginettes."

Left:
Harold cultivates his interest in microscopy, c. 1945. "Avocations are things that enrich a person's life," Harold once said, "but to me, hobbies must possess you, in order to really let them do what they can for you."

Harold as Imperial Potentate visiting one of the Shriners Hospitals for crippled children, 1949. As the Shriners's official philanthropy, to this day, the network of hospitals provides expert orthopedic and burn care to children in need at no cost. Harold was instrumental in developing the burn care units, remembering his harrowing ordeal following his 1919 accident.

films. Richard, Dave Nowell, and Harold's friend Richard Simonton encouraged Harold to do further preservation work, which resulted in the Harold Lloyd films being so well protected.

Harold was human and not perfect; his detractors could perhaps label him emotionally immature — a
boyish man with endless games and hobbies. However, he was wonderfully larger than life, a man whose
greatness defined his success and not the other way around. Harold summed up his own success as a combination of luck, hard work, determination, and ultimately comedic skill in this way:

> *The accident of growing up with a new theatrical form, enthusiasm, hard work and business sense*
> *have had much to do with it, but principally I have been an unusually successful*
> *picture comedian, I think, because I have an unusually large comedy*
> *vocabulary.*[64]

Despite his success, some have suggested that Harold Lloyd fails to endure
because he is only a creature of his time, another standard of the roaring 1920s, since
discarded, like bathtub gin and the Charleston. Although Lloyd is certainly emblem-
atic of the Jazz Age, his legacy should not be confined to it. Chaplin and Keaton per-
severe because their characters are aspirational, yet this quality, paradoxically, also
makes them remote. No matter how hard we try, we will never be as clever and
resourceful as Chaplin's Little Tramp, nor will we ever approach impending disaster
with Keaton's stoic reserve. Ultimately, we embrace Lloyd because he is one of us, an
ordinary fellow, dealing with ordinary struggles, losses, and embarrassments. Harold
Lloyd will endure as long as we do.

Below:

The George Eastman House's Second Festival of Film Artists award winners for outstanding contributions to motion pictures during the years 1926–1930, October 26, 1957. Top row from left: Lee Garmes, Frank Borzage, Charles Rosher, Maurice Chevalier. Middle row: Josef von Sternberg, Arthur Edeson, Richard Barthelmess, James Wong Howe, Ramon Novarro, William Daniels. Bottom row: Peverell Marley, Harold, George Folsey, Gloria Swanson, Lillian Gish, Janet Gaynor, and Mary Pickford.

Right:

Harold, Mildred, and granddaughter Suzanne with poodles Pepi (left) and Pierre (right) arrive in New York on March 24, 1962, aboard the S. S. *United States*, having just returned from a European vacation.

Harold, circa 1955.

Harold, Mildred, and Suzanne
in San Francisco for the 92nd
Shriners convention in June 1966.

Opposite:
Harold next to his Christmas
tree, with its 5,000 decorations,
that stood all year round in
L'Orangerie, also called the
sunroom, August 2, 1962. In
1965 — in its final form — three
trees were combined into one
fireproof tree, fourteen feet high,
nine feet wide, and almost thirty
feet in circumference. Harold
had enough decorations left over
to cover two more Christmas
trees of the same size. Each
Christmas he also had an additional white tree set up in the
entry hall.

Harold poses outside the
Cinema City exhibition held at
the Round House in London,
September 1970. His participation at the exhibition's opening
ceremony with a screening of
The Kid Brother was one of
his last public appearances.

Harold examining his auto-
graphed photos in The Rogues
Gallery, accompanied by his
cocker spaniel, Nicki, c. 1955.

One of the biggest events to happen at Greenacres was the marriage of my mother Gloria Lloyd to the dashing playboy William Guasti on September 26, 1950; it was the social event of the year in Beverly Hills. I was the only child of the brief marriage, which ended in divorce in 1954. Not long after I was born my mother suffered a nervous breakdown. She went to Europe to find the cure, and spent much of the next ten years there. As a result, I was put in the care of my doting grandparents Harold and Mildred at Greenacres.

Not many children grow up in a household where Christmas is celebrated 365 days a year. My grandfather loved Christmas, and he had the most magical tree that just kept growing as if it were a Jack-in-the-beanstalk vine. The tree was set up in a corner of the L'Orangerie at Greenacres, and its branches spread out from floor to ceiling, adorned with every imaginable glass ornament collected by my grandfather over years of traveling the world. One of my fondest memories is going with my grandparents around Thanksgiving to the train yards in downtown Los Angeles where the annual shipment of Christmas trees would arrive. Every year the tree grew larger to hold more ornaments; then one year it became a permanent fixture in our home. It was simply too large, too decorated, and too engineered to disassemble. So it was Christmas all year round at the Lloyd home.

I arrived at this home that celebrated Christmas year-round in 1953 at the age of one, and
became the object of Harold and Mildred's affection and the focus of Lloyd family life. I called
Harold "Daddy," and to me he will always be just that—the man who loved me, raised me as his
own daughter, and who introduced me to the most exciting world any child could hope to experience: the world seen through the eyes of Harold Lloyd. I grew up in this most unusual situation
feeling truly loved and cherished. I knew from the first moment of my recollection to the day
that I laid my grandparents to rest that they supported me and loved me unconditionally. Both
Harold and Mildred gave me everything a child needed—most importantly, laughter and joy
that filled our house and instilled in me an optimism that is perhaps the greatest gift in life.

In reflective moments, not without some melancholy, Harold would share with close personal
friends and relatives that he had lost his opportunity to actively raise his own children because of
his film career, and that I was something of a second chance. He now had a chance to raise a
child, and he enjoyed spoiling me rotten. However, he could be very controlling, in a very
Machiavellian way. For example, he allowed me to have wonderful parties at Greenacres, but his
true reason for that was so that he could know where I was on weekends and could watch me.

Wherever he traveled, I would accompany him and my grandmother, Mildred (whom I called "Mimi"). Soon, I was groomed to accompany him to Shriners events, premieres, political meetings, personal engagements, or anything else he had to attend when Mimi could not accompany him.

Harold had many hobbies about which he was passionate. He was a wonderful photographer, and took thousands of 3-D photographs. Harold was also an animal lover; he especially loved dogs, and kept a kennel with more than fifty Great Danes on his Westwood property in the late 1920s. His interest in microscopy gave him a great respect for all creatures, but he could not bear to kill anything—not even an ant, bee, or spider—for use in his microscopes.

Although Harold had always been superstitious—and despite his belief in God and his high intelligence—his superstitions became a major part of his life after his miraculous escape from death the day of the explosion in 1919. For example, he would not step on cracks in a sidewalk. He also believed that he had to leave a building—even his own home—by the door through which he had entered. Whenever Harold went somewhere by car, he had to return by the exact same route. Certain streets—such as Roxbury Drive where his mother had died or Bedford Drive where his brother Gaylord died—were forbidden to him; and he never allowed himself to drive or be driven entirely around the center fountain of the front drive—he would instead back the car around the center fountain. Harold would also hide money in books in the library and throughout the house. When he would later refer to a book and discover the forgotten money, it was placed in the safe in his study. He believed that finding his own money was especially good luck.

Harold was not the same after Mimi died in 1969. I vividly remember him coming home late from the hospital and telling me that she had died. He held out his hand and gave me her wedding ring, telling me: "Honey, Mimi's gone. We wanted you to have this." However, he kept his spirits up by surrounding himself with his young friends. Harold would participate in everything I and my friends did. My grandfather was a man who—even in his late seventies—appeared young. He was always very interested in young people and their ideas. My school friends who were invited to Greenacres affectionately called him "Harry" and interacted with him with an uncommon ease and familiarity.

My first boyfriend Richard Correll and I began to use Greenacres as a playground. Rich would make his own amateur films on the estate, play touch football, tennis, and have movie and swimming parties. He remembers:

> Harold once said to me, "We have a big swimming pool and a tennis court. Come on over and bring your friends." I brought a couple of friends, that became five, became ten, and I remember one time we had over thirty people at Greenacres. It was the greatest playground I've ever been in. We opened up the garage and found a 1924 Silver Ghost Rolls-Royce town car and a 1925 Silver Ghost Rolls-Royce touring car. They were on blocks, and friends who were mechanics got the cars going and we started driving them around. The swimming pool held 250,000 gallons of water; it was probably the biggest pool in Beverly Hills. It was all so much fun. We used to have football games on the back lawn and Harold would come down with potato chips and popcorn and cheer. I think he was delighted that people were using the house again.[65]

Despite the grandeur of life at Greenacres, there was always a down-to-earth sense of the importance of close friendships. The house was usually filled with old friends that had been part of my grandfather's life from his earliest days in the business—Wally Westmore, King Vidor, Colleen Moore, Frances Marion, Mary Pickford, and Adela Rogers St. John.

Harold kept his boundless and enthusiastic spirit until he was told that the prostate cancer he had been battling for two and a half years was a hopeless fight he would lose and that he had only six months to live. My great uncle, Dr. John Davis, told him the news on Valentine's Day. I was completely shattered at the prospect of losing him. Harold retreated to his bedroom and died just three weeks later, on the afternoon of March 8,

1971, at the age of seventy-seven. Harold was never one to waste time. He was entombed in the Great Mausoleum at Forest Lawn Memorial Park–Glendale.

My mother — after a second marriage to John Roberts which ended in divorce — is single and very happy. Today my mother is a painter, creating beautiful works of art in her sun-filled condominium on the Wilshire corridor of Los Angeles. We have a close and loving relationship; our best times together are family gatherings with my two children, Christopher and Jacqueline. We also share an enduring love of our heritage and of our common bond with Harold and Mildred.

Peggy worked as a model and a film stand-in. She married producer Almon Bartlett Ross in 1948 and had a son, David. Peggy divorced Ross in 1953 and married actor Robert Patten in 1956 and had another son, Robert. Her marriage to Patten also ended in divorce. In 1972 Peggy found her birth mother, Dorothy Callison, after a long search, and remained close to her until Peggy's death from lung cancer in 1986 at the age of sixty.

Harold Jr. — known as Duke — was a sergeant in the Air Force, appeared in several low-budget Hollywood films, and pursued a moderately successful career as a nightclub singer. He was homosexual, and despite unconditional support from Harold and the rest of our family, became increasingly unhappy, an alcoholic, and self-destructive. Harold, Jr. died just three months after Harold in 1971, as the result of alcoholism at the age of forty.

Harold and me at the Ice Follies at the Pan-Pacific Auditorium in Los Angeles, c. 1965.

After Harold's death, I tried to have his wish to make Greenacres into a museum become a reality. He left me to oversee and administer a film and memorabilia trust. He also created a foundation so that Greenacres could be preserved as a public museum and park. However, it would not be long before the grand visions would be challenged by harsh reality. On April 20, 1973, Greenacres opened for tours, but this only lasted a year. The costs of maintaining the estate were mounting; the taxes alone were in the six figures, there was a $500,000 mortgage, and back taxes. The hope was to fund the estate through the public tours. I tried to run Greenacres as a museum for three and a half years, but the city of Beverly Hills made it too difficult to continue, and the house had to be sold at public auction on the day before my twenty-third birthday, July 27, 1975. Greenacres — an estate that Harold spent $2 million to build — was sold to Nasrollas Afshani, an Iranian importer of industrial supplies, for $1.6 million. It was probably the worst day of my young life. I felt as if I had failed my grandfather. But I remembered what he always told me: have courage, be strong, and face every challenge with all of the backbone I could muster. He also taught me the lesson of survival with dignity.

In 1984 Greenacres was named to the National Register of Historic Places, which prevents the house from being torn down or removed. Unfortunately, the beautiful grounds around the house were subdivided and developed. However, the proceeds from the sale were used by the Harold Lloyd Foundation to benefit motion picture preservation and for scholarship funds for film students across the country. Today, Greenacres is owned by Ron Burkle, who is committed to restoring the estate to its original splendor. His commitment would have pleased Harold tremendously, and it is considerable consolation to the disappointment that remains with me that Harold's wishes for the house were unable to be fulfilled.

Harold would be proud that his legacy lives on, and that the proceeds from his estate have been used to support the art form he so dearly loved. His glorious body of work helped define motion picture comedy. He was indeed a "master comedian" and remains — to both my mother and me — the finest man we have ever known.

Appendix: The American Film Institute Seminar with Harold Lloyd

Harold Lloyd conducted the inaugural Master Seminar at the American Film Institute's Center for Advanced Film Studies in Los Angeles on September 23, 1969. Following a screening of the compilation film *Harold Lloyd's Funny Side of Life*, AFI founder George Stevens, Jr., film director King Vidor, seminar moderator James R. Sikle, and students in attendance asked Lloyd questions about his films and silent-film comedy technique.

The following is an excerpt of this seminar, published for the first time courtesy of the American Film Institute and Jean Picker Firstenberg. The transcript reveals Lloyd's point of view concerning many aspects of his motion picture work and hints at his tremendous interest in and enthusiasm for young people and their ideas. He also felt a deep sense of responsibility to help encourage and train a new generation of filmmakers.

AFI: (George Stevens, Jr.) I can't think of a nicer way to begin this series. Mr. Lloyd will talk with us for half an hour, and he promises to come back.

HAROLD LLOYD: Thank you. This picture that you've just seen [*The Freshman* as part of *Harold Lloyd's Funny Side of Life*] is what I call a "character comedy." I made two different types of pictures, really—gag comedies and character comedies. *Safety Last!*, where I climbed the outside of a building and hung on a clock, etc., is a gag picture; [*The Freshman*] is more what I call a character comedy, because we start slow, we plant the character very carefully, and let it grow, let the picture gain momentum as it goes through to the end. I think we accomplished that. Now, we took quite a chance with [*Harold Lloyd's Funny Side of Life*]; we put a fast-moving composite on first, which is about half an hour, with mostly comedy business that we call "gags," and then started a picture from scratch, and to condition build the character.

King Vidor asked, "Why didn't you start with *The Freshman*, and put the [composite] afterwards?" Well, he's got a point there, but I don't think there'd be much reason for the composite after we'd started. When we first put it together I talked for half a minute, when they had the glasses rolling. The reason for my wanting to do it—is to kind of condition the audience that we were through with sequences now and that we were going to show more or less a full-length picture.

We made another picture, the first one I did of this type, that we called *Harold Lloyd's World of Comedy*. That picture is purely a composite, very successful. We got a nice break in running it at the Cannes Film Festival. They put us on right after *Mondo Cane* (1962), and I think it was quite a relief. The first two-thirds of the picture was silent, with narration, and the last third went into the talking pictures that I did.

AFI: (King Vidor) Harold, it might be interesting to talk a little about camera speeds. This film that was run tonight was probably twenty-four frames per second?

HL: Yes, they'd have to run at twenty-four because they had dialogue. They were originally run at between sixteen and twenty.

AFI: (KV) I used to hear stories about you and how adroit the cameramen were at slowing down right in the middle of a scene. You had the same cameraman with you all the time?

HL: Yes, Walter Lundin. He was with me for years and years.

AFI: (KV) These were all done with a hand-cranked camera.

HL: That's right.

AFI: (KV) And they developed the sense of slowing down just a little, got to know what would make a fall. I was amazed at the bus running through what seemed to be normal traffic [in *For Heaven's Sake*]. They must have had everything else on the street move at a snail's pace.

HL: No, King. They were actually shot with our own traffic and with, as you know, the car in front or in back with the camera. The camera [operator] was taking every bit as much chance

Harold addressing a university film class, c. 1966, after a screening of *Harold Lloyd's Funny Side of Life*.

as we were. Now, we had that bus, and a lot of that was shot up here on a big, wide street. We put that bus on a cantilever and the bus tipped itself. So as we'd go around the corner, we'd tip it. One thing you had to watch was when you're hanging over the edge—which I was—that you didn't get your leg in between the tip. But we actually did all that stuff and, you see, King, you can't slow your camera down too much because your pedestrians look jerky. They may *be* jerky, but we didn't want them to look that way.

We did that in New York, too. In fact, there was a picture called *Speedy* where I had two horses pulling a horse cart down the street and we'd blocked off about three blocks. We looked like we had the whole police force there with us. Of course, we had a terrible time on that one. One of our own cars got in the way of the horses, and, to keep from running into the car, the man had to pull the horse and go down the subway. It didn't hurt the horse, I'm happy to say, but we never used him again; he was a little shy after that.

AFI: (KV) What would you say the camera speeds ran in that sequence—from what to what?

HL: Oh, they were down around fourteen, I'd say—except in some places they might drop it. As you were saying, the cameraman in those days had a certain technique and an ability to really keep that crank going. They could get it down. I don't think that cameramen today would come close to trying it.

AFI: (KV) I have shot my long chase scenes as low as eight, which at that time was doubling the speed—for an automobile or something.

HL: We had to get an old horse out of a lot one time, and went down to about ten, around there. He sure went out!

AFI: (KV) I think this is a sort of lost art, and I think they'd like to hear about the uses of a cameraman. He had to change his style at the same time, to compensate.

HL: Well, of course, in one way that's sort of a mark against the

picture, to have it go at a slower speed. Now, the funny thing is that it hasn't seemed to be bothering audiences too much; but, as a rule, the majority in the audience think you cranked that way. They think we wanted it to go exceptionally fast, and they accept that as the way we made it. Of course, everyone here knows it's not true, but no matter how many times you tell them it was cranked at a much different speed, and that you had to get a much smaller number of frames through the film than you do now and therefore it's got to go much faster, they don't hear you at all. As much as it's been repeated, I don't think the majority of people have any idea about speed.

AFI: (KV) They're not thinking about it, either.

HL: No, they don't care, really. I guess if they did care, your picture wouldn't be worth a damn.

AFI: (KV) Yes, that's true. I don't think that the public cares, but I think these fellows might.

HL: Oh, these fellows would know the difference. Now, a picture that I was always afraid of was *Safety Last!*, because I had several scenes in there and they moved pretty fast. But I put it in front of an audience and it didn't seem to spoil the laughs any. I showed it to a group of high school students at Hollywood High. It went as well as it ever did with a crowd that I first made it for. So why am I worrying about speed? So I just forgot it.

AFI: (KV) Oh, no, the contrary.

HL: You think it helped?

AFI: (KV) Yes, I do.

HL: Well, in some cases it might, and in other places, no. But I think if your comedy is basic enough in getting home, and they're with you—they're laughing *with* you as well as *at* you—I really don't think it makes too much difference. You all ought to know—you [Vidor] were making pictures back in the same days I did. You made *The Big Parade* the same year that [*The Freshman*] was made.

211

AFI: The theme of the little man who uses his wits to overcome the brawn and strength was a very American theme. This theme came back in *The Kid Brother* also.

HL: Yes, it did. A very similar type theme, but with an entirely different procedure. The stories are nothing alike, not even close, but basically the theme is "brains over brawn"—even more so in *The Kid Brother* than [*The Freshman*]. In *The Kid Brother* I have a father and two older brothers who are behemoths, and I'm the little puny fellow, the boy that thinks and, in the end, outwits the ones that just use their muscles.

AFI: There is also a thematic element in [*The Freshman*], and I'm curious about how it evolved and how you feel about it now: not a goal that Speedy, our hero, tries to attain, but rather—

HL: Well, his goal, of course, was entirely misplaced. His father said in the beginning that if he tries to imitate that stage actor—playing a football hero—they're either going to break his heart or his neck—and they did both in the picture. So it lends itself to "be yourself." "Don't pretend," if you want to take any one theme. In a lot of the pictures, and especially in the character comedies, naturally we wanted laughs because we're supposed to be comics, and the audience came to get a chuckle or two, but we did try to have some kind of hidden theme in there.

AFI: Of course by being himself in this particular film, he happens also to achieve that goal at the last.

HL: Yes. I'd go back to another picture we made that Hal Roach and I had a little contention on—and we were both right, in a way. We made *Grandma's Boy* which had a fine theme of "mind over matter." The boy's a terrific coward, and his grandmother recognizes that. To help him out, she gives him a talisman that she says his grandfather had. His grandfather had been more cowardly than he, and with this talisman he couldn't fail. The boy became a great hero. Of course, he then found out at the end that the talisman was just the handle to her umbrella. It hadn't been a talisman at all—it had been himself. It was probably the best thing we used, but we got carried away a little. We didn't put enough comedy in it. So we previewed it, and it kind of laid there, to a certain degree—the audience didn't laugh as much as they should—and Hal said, "Harold, you're a comic, you've got to get laughs. Let's go back." So we went back and worked for at least a month and just put gags all over the place. The second time we previewed it, it blossomed. It was fine and it's been fine ever since. In fact, the picture probably did as much for us as anyone, because it was the first feature picture we had made. We didn't intend for it to be a feature; we started it as a two-reeler.

In fact, our group—Hal and myself, our staff—we were thoroughly entrenched in making two-reel pictures and doing pretty well with them. But this had such a nice theme that it just kept growing, and we let it grow. But when it came to getting more money for it, the exhibitors were a little loath to pay us more than they had been paying us for two-reelers. They were happy with the two-reelers, so we couldn't get anyplace with it. So we went down to Broadway here, and we took a third-run house that was showing newsreels and we put the picture in there. They thought we were off our rocker, but the picture ran nineteen weeks. It established a tremendous record and from then on we had no trouble. We got the price, from Grauman and his Million Dollar and from the Californian.

We had one funny incident with *Safety Last!*, because in order to [put it in these theaters] they wanted to get a great deal of exploitation. They put some very fine publicists on it. I was on my way to New York and had intended to stop off only between trains, in Chicago. The publicists met me about an hour out of Chicago, with a long list of things that I was to do, which were the usual things: greet the mayor, get the key to the city, etc. But among them, they wanted me to "christen the Wrigley Tower," the clock, because our picture had a clock in it. It's a big, prominent clock, as you know, on the Wrigley Tower in Chicago, where the bridges are, and I didn't quite understand that. They said, "Well, they figured that you'd break a bottle of champagne over it, like christening a ship. It would be the first time it's ever done." I thought, "Well, we can get along without that." I drew a line through that. He said, "I'm afraid it's not as simple as that. The crowd's already waiting there for you—there must be at least ten thousand people there by now." So I was in what you might call a trap. I never saw so many people in my life—on all the bridges around there. We got into the Wrigley building—it's a very high building. At that time, I think it was the highest building in Chicago—up, up, up. And we got up there. Of course, they had figured that I might not do it, so they had hired a steeplejack up there. They figured that when I went in, he would put on my hat and coat and glasses, and he would do it. Well, they were crazy. They had like a boatswain's seat, a board with two holes in it and a rope goes through and underneath—no windlass, just lowering it down over the edge of the building. Well, of course, the steeplejack was a smart cookie and he looked at it. He knew the wind velocity around that building, and he said, "Gentlemen, I need the money but I don't want to commit suicide," and he walked out on them. There was no one to take my place. So they said, "What are you going to do?" It's quite a question. Someone said, "Well, if Harold does that he'll cancel all of his insurance. He's got quite a bit. In pictures, he really tries to protect himself." So I got the idea what I'd do. I knew damn well I wasn't going to be lowered down there and break the bottle over that clock. So I got a megaphone and I went downstairs. I got up on a taxi cab, I got the crowd's attention, and I told them exactly what had happened. I told them that I didn't want to commit suicide. Of course, it became a big joke. We got tremendous play in all the Chicago papers, more than if we had gone through with the stunt.

AFI: Are you planning to rerelease *Grandma's Boy*?

HL: Here's the way I look at it. If I thought there was a demand with the public for the pictures, I would love to release a great many of them. I am loath to release any of them unless I feel they're really wanted and desired. And what I mean by that is that I have stayed off the screen for many, many years, and while I think I'm quite well known with the nostalgia group, I'm known very, very little, if at all, with a great many. That's the reason I took it to Hollywood High down here. Somebody presented the opportunity to me, and I went down there and found that this generation is more "hip," or whatever you want to call it in this day and age. Their whole response was tremendous because they didn't miss a gag; anything that was even a little subtle, they got it right away. There wasn't any question in my mind that it appeals to the high school group. I went around [with *The Freshman*] and did a symposium with about eleven universities, including Purdue, Ohio State, and the University of Illinois, and the picture went about as well there as I've seen it. In my mind, I feel that people would like the picture, but the question is, are they going to come and see it? Now, what's the use of releasing pictures in the theaters if they don't know you and they don't know what they're going to see? They won't come to see it. You put the pictures into a theater, and they come in to pay their two or three bucks, you'd better be known. And that's my situation. Now, I do show them, like Mr. Simonton has done many times, to a large, national, pipe-organ group, and they filled the Wiltern Theater. They know Lloyd, they're coming to see Lloyd—but the general public is different. Mr. Simonton has the nicest theater out there in his home. He has two big pipe organs—an Aeolian Skinner and a Wurlitzer, and he is allowing me to use his theater and to have a wonderful organist, Gaylord Carter, who is going to make as many as he can of the feature pictures with organ scores behind them, so that you gentlemen can run them up here the way you want to, with different kinds of organ scores. I just don't like pictures played with

pianos. We never intended them to be played with pianos. When you see them played with pianos, that's not the way the public saw them. They're being misrepresented. So if I can find a way to actually condition the pictures, then I would like to run *Grandma's Boy*. I took a long way around—by way of Pasadena!—to answer that question.

AFI: I think there's a great demand among 16mm outfits, you know. They would be of great interest because there is Keaton and Chaplin.

HL: I tried that a long time ago and I was very unhappy. It's probably different now, but I just don't want to go that route.

AFI: Why? Because of the quality of the presentation or the mechanics of it?

HL: Many things. You don't control it, for one thing, and they take it into homes. Now, I could go on television very easily if I wanted to come down on the price—I've had many offers. I want $300,000 per picture for two showings. That's a high price, but if I don't get it, I'm not going to show it. They've come close to it, but they haven't come all the way up. A good picture is getting a hell of a lot more than that in television. You know that.

AFI: How did it happen, Mr. Lloyd, that you kept control of your films when so many people didn't?

HL: Well, that was kind of fortunate. I know—because Buster's a very good friend of mine, and I knew Laurel and Hardy very well—that they got in situations where they weren't able to have control of their pictures. First I made pictures for Roach, and he had complete control. Later on, I had three-quarter interest and Hal had a quarter. It was all Hal's idea; he came to me and said, "Harold, you don't need me anymore. I got so many pictures of my own to do, we might as well just go our own way." Which we did, in the most amicable way that any two people could have done. So from that time on, I produced and financed my own pictures. It sounds like bragging, but we didn't borrow from the bank. We kept a certain amount of money aside to finance our own pictures. In a way, that's gambling a little heavier than some people do in Las Vegas, but we got away with it. In one picture we put in almost close to a million dollars. No one wants to lose that much, and you can, very easily, in the picture business. But by doing that I was able to have the pictures. Pathé, who owns so many of the Roach pictures, turned them over to me, and I bought a number of them from Roach. So I either owned them all or controlled practically all of them. There's about four I don't.

AFI: This was a time when the people who were making or appearing in films finished a film and forgot it. That's why so many films have been lost. You seem to have a respect for what you did.

HL: Well, we're going through the throes right now of trying to keep a lot of one-reelers from being lost. Richard Correll and David Nowell are doing a very good job handling nitrates for me. More than half of all the pictures made — more than *half* — have been lost through nitrate negatives because they're very expensive [to maintain]. Nitrate, as you all know, is a very dangerous form of film and very tricky. It turns into jelly and for no reason at all just explodes. It gets to a certain point, activates, and away it goes! And they're such nasty fires because of the fumes and everything. I lost an awful lot of films. They were stored in New Jersey, in a place called Bound Brook. Everybody stored them there. They had a tremendous fire and everything— Lonesome Lukes, etc. — were all lost. And I had a nitrate fire at the house. Fortunately, I didn't have the ones that I treasure the most. They were in another place. So that's where a great many films have been lost, and a lot of them have been lost because no one knew who could preserve them. They didn't think it was valuable. If we had known that they were going to have a certain value afterwards, we'd have saved a lot more. The picture was made, we were happy with it at the time, and we went on to make something else. That was that.

AFI: Why do you think your films have held up so well?

HL: I think that one of the reasons comedies seem to have a better chance today than dramatic pictures of the same era —I'm not talking about *The Big Parade* because I think that's an exception, as a number of them are — is that comedies I made at that time didn't have a local type of humor. It was a basic type, and we did that for certain reasons — not just because we were astute, but because we released them all over the world. We were smart enough to realize that they had to be understood in India or Tokyo or Holland as well as here, so we tried to make what I consider to be a basic type of humor that they would understand, too. It's understood and is fresh today, if the picture's made well and has been tight in its organization. The gags that you will see —the Keatons, the Chaplins, and the Laurel and Hardys — are just as fresh today as you could possibly dig up to put in modern pictures.

AFI: Did you start with a story or did you start with an idea for a gag?

HL: We never had a written script until we made a talking picture —we had a script in our *mind* up to a point. The first thing I wanted to get was a character, and, of course, they used to laugh at me. They said, "You have your character: your glasses, your straw hat." Well, that is so. It was the thing that identified me as Lloyd, the man with the glasses. But

contrary to what most of my contemporaries did—I don't say they did it all the time — but most of them played exactly the same character. Chaplin played his Little Tramp; Keaton was the Stone Face; Laurel and Hardy were practically always the same. But in the pictures that I did I could be an introvert, a little weakling, and another could be an extrovert, the sophisticate, the hypochondriac. They looked alike in appearance, with the glasses, which I guess you'd call a typical American boy. Still, the sophisticate who wrecked his car and went in and bought a new car and it was all shot to pieces thought entirely differently from the character in *Grandma's Boy* or the character in *The Freshman* and is just as different as could be from the character that was in *The Kid Brother*. I wanted to know how the character thought. Then I tried to find a premise.

Now, when we did [*The Freshman*] we were warned not to do an athletic picture. They were dismal failures. Practically all of them had been, whether it was baseball or golf or football. And I just didn't believe that an athletic picture couldn't be made — but you must make it simple enough. Now, we tried to make that picture about as simple as possible, as far as football rules are concerned. Some women in the audience who had never gone to a football game before could get the idea that all he has got to do is carry the ball to the end of the field and they're going to win. That's all you had to know. Now, there's nothing complicated about that. Of course, we treated *The Freshman* as sort of a semi-satire. That was our aim, and titles went along in that direction. Now, the boy gained most of his success on the playing field by being lucky, and that was not good for the finale of the picture. He had to win something on his own merit. That's why we put the final run in: so that to really win the game, even though he had done everything through luck, he accomplished the final bit on his own. So he became popular for a moment, at least, through his own efforts and determination.

AFI: (KV) In the era you made these films —with Sennett, Keaton, and Chaplin —there were a lot of comedies being made and they were right at the top of popularity. Then, all of a sudden, the day came when this type of film wasn't made anymore. I ponder why.

HL: Well, it's a little ambiguous for me to pinpoint. Almost all of the comedians weren't quite equipped for sound. Now, my going into sound was sort of like when we went into features. It was an evolutionary type of thing. It was kind of difficult, to start with — not knowing any more about sound than they did in those early days —to keep the same kind of pace like you did in the silents and still have your sound. Another thing, too, is that everybody went sound-happy. They thought that because you were making a sound picture you had to talk all the time, you had to go verbal, and they were much cheaper to do. You can get verbal gags much easier than you can get sight gags. There you had to pay some nice, handsome prices for your idea men, gagmen as they were called.

Now, in my case, it was kind of a transition. I had completed a silent picture called *Welcome Danger*. When we previewed it for the third time, on the bill was a little one-reel sound comedy and the audience howled at this comedy. They had the punkest gags in it, but it didn't matter—they were laughing. We said, "My God, we worked our hearts out to get laughs with thought-out gags, and look here: just because they've got some sound to it, they're roaring at these things. We missed the boat. Let's get on the ball. Maybe we ought to try and make this a sound picture. Let's see how much we can keep of it and dub and we'll make the rest of it over." That cost me close to a million dollars! So I had silent technique to it, and oh, the dubbing was horrible. We didn't know what we were doing. We had a screen up there and we'd run the picture with "x" marks on it and just try to hit those things. Cutters didn't know too much about cutting them in. It was a horrible thing. Well, as I look at *Welcome Danger* today, and hear the sound on it, I groan. But it worked fine because, gee, they liked the sound gags. So we made a natural transition from silent to sound. It didn't turn out to be one of our best pictures, but it has good points. It also made the most money.

AFI: I notice in [*The Freshman*] that the construction of the gags is very carefully worked out. Keaton and Chaplin also had this. They set up their gag, then they'd get the gag and top it. You did this all the time. It's very carefully done and it's so beautifully worked out. It's sort of a lost art because it is peculiar to silent comedy, yet there's no reason why it couldn't work in sound pictures.

HL: No, it could work just the same.

AFI: But nobody does it. How did you come up with the gags?

HL: First, all the comics of that day—Buster, Charlie, all of them—were students of comedy. Now, Harry Langdon wasn't, and that was Harry's toughest part of it. Harry was a great comedian and could have been infinitely better, but he really wasn't a student of comedy like the other boys were. It was lucky that he got men like Frank Capra to direct; when he had those people he made the best pictures. But as far as the development of gags, we had a gag room—not to keep you still, but to think up comedy ideas. Why they called them gags I don't know, but that was the accepted parlance of the day. I

would keep anywhere from four to seven or eight gagmen— as many as I could get. They were very expensive in those days—we'd pay several of them $800 a week. And I would have complete control over the boys. I'd come in and they'd throw ideas at me. I knew what we wanted and we worked out sort of a theme or storyline which could be changed at any moment.

I'll tell you something funny. I don't know whether you've ever heard of a very successful play on Broadway called *The First Year*. Frank Craven wrote it and played the lead. He was a splendid comedy writer, had written many pictures and Broadway plays that were just excellent. I was talking to him one time and [he] said, "How many writers do you have work for you on these pictures, Harold?" I said, "Oh, five, six, seven, eight—as many as I think are good." He said, "Wouldn't it be cheaper to have just one?" I said, "You're damn right, but we haven't been able to do it." He said, "I think I could do it." I said, "Gee, Frank, if you can do it, brother, I'm for that. When you have some time, come on out and sit in our gag room and see what you can do in thinking up business. All the sequences have been laid and we'll choose the basted suit sequence (this isn't the one that he worked on, but I'll use this as an example). Work with them and see what you can do, because we've got to have these kinds of gags. That's what we've more or less built up our reputation on." So he came to L.A., and he was in that room for about three days. He finally came out and said, "I'm cured. I sat in that damn room for three days and couldn't think of one gag." And it was true.

AFI: Did you shoot very specifically in making pictures? Did you shoot sequentially?

HL: No, we've never done that. We shot as much as we could in sequence, then we'd occasionally jump around. I can explain it with two pictures. Now, when we made *Safety Last!* we made the climb first. We knew that the boy had to come to the city to make good, that he was going to pretend to make good for his girl back home, that the girl was going to come out thinking he had made good, and that he then would have to actually make good. One of the devices was climbing. He was going to get his pal, who was an iron-girder worker, to climb this building. Now, we made the climb first, and when we got through with the climb we were very pleased with it. We thought we had something. Now, from there we went back and started the picture, because we had the finish. But that, as I say, was a gag picture. We tried the same thing with *The Freshman*. We went out to the Rose Bowl and for two weeks we tried to film a football game for the last scene and got no place at all. We'd look at our dailies and they were just sad. We had to start at the beginning because it's a character comedy, and we had to build it from there on. We knew that the whole picture was really about a boy who wanted to go to college with the idea of being the most popular boy, and he has a completely erroneous idea of how to go about it. So he's in nothing but trouble all the time, and something pulls him out. Now, that's about the kind of theme we had.

AFI: In the scene of the tailor there were a good number of shots and I take it that whole thing was to some degree structured.

HL: Yes, we certainly had to structure that. You must do that. But we did it on the cuff rather than on paper. We knew that it had to build, we knew that the boy was going to go with the basted suit, so I put all the gag writers on what would happen to a fellow that goes to a party with it. And it was up to me to routine how those different gags would fit into the scene. Then, as we went along, we had some freedom.

AFI: So, did you improvise gags?

HL: No. Now, in being spontaneous, we'd work out a series of scenes for the day; we knew we had little islands of what we were going to do in a scene. But in between those set ideas, we'd ad-lib them. Now, the next scene we'd ad-lib a little more. By the time we had shot it four times, little islands would be left out and maybe we'd change the whole idea, we'd have all new business. It's just things that we couldn't think of in the gag room but came to us, and that's the reason you got adept at ad-libbing, creating as you went through and thinking of different things.

AFI: I have difficulty actually conceptualizing the preview process. You actually shot the whole thing and then presented it to the audience after finishing filming that sequence, then went back and let everybody redo it? Did you have to restage that whole scene?

HL: Yes, we kept the sets up. I think we were one of the very first, even back in the old one-reel days, to start previews. We used to go out here to Glendale. I can remember the old gentleman who was manager of the theater; his name was Howard. He would always put on tails to come out to explain to the audience what was going on, that this picture had never been shown before. They expected to do a lot more work on it; they, the audience, were the judges. You see, I tried to tell the boys: "Now, let's not take a century to make this picture because we know we're going to make a hell of a lot of it over. So let's make it as good as we can for the first time, then after the audience has seen it, we're coming back really to go to work and find out what's wrong with it." Now, they don't do that today.

AFI: (George Stevens, Jr.) For one thing, once you start paying an actor and you stop filming, you've got to keep on paying him.

HL: Yes, well, we didn't have any trouble with our people because I carried my crew fifty-two weeks a year, up until they had to join unions. Then you couldn't do it anymore because it was prohibited. If we laid off for three months, their salary went on just the same. We had a whole group of people. If you saw a series of our pictures, you'd see fellows like Charlie Stevenson and Noah Young in every picture. Audiences would see them and say, "Oh, that fellow was the bully." "He was the cop in that." So we had no trouble getting our actors.

AFI: (GS) Can we take one gag—the business with the guy outside the taxicab fighting over the suitcase [in *Speedy*]. Can you tell us how that's set up?

HL: Well, that went along pretty close to the way it was shot. We got the idea that we were going to come up to get a fare with two fellows that were quarreling over, probably, rent. The fellow was going to get knocked out and that killed my fare. Then he got up and knocked the other fellow down, which changed the whole picture. So I was very happy until the fellow got up and knocked him down. "The hell with it; that spoils that." So I started to take him out. Then we said, "We've got to have a kickoff, a topper." So we got an idea — let's get the door and distract the first fellow's attention so that the other fellow would have a good shot at him and knock him into the taxicab and I would have my fare. We could have quit right there, but they said, "Suppose he goes right on out the door and lands on the street on the other side, and you don't know it?" And that is how we did it. A topper is generally the best way to go — not always, but a great many times. As I say, when you study comedy, there are so many times when you've got to judge. Is it good to let the audience in on your gag and let them enjoy knowing what's going to happen, or should you surprise them? They don't know any more about it until they see it finalized. I've had many gags that we had to shoot both ways because we weren't sure. I would say that three-fourths of the time, surprise is best; but sometimes the others turn out to be much funnier when they're in on it and enjoying what's happening against the comic.

AFI: Could you think of an example of being in on the gag?

HL: In *Safety Last!* I'm in an office, trying to show off to my girl, [pretending I am a manager of a department store]. I've [accidentally] rung a bell, and the office boy comes in. [He knows] I'm not supposed to be there because I'm no better than he is. I show him this dollar bill [to keep him quiet] and he sees it and he's happy to get it. So I tell him to take the wastepaper basket, take it out and empty it, and I drop the dollar bill in it.

He gives me a wink, but as he starts out, I crumble a piece of paper and say, "Oh boy, come here. You'd better pick that up." As he picks that up, I reach in and get my dollar bill back. Now, those kinds of things you want the audience in on. Retrieving your money, that's always a good one.

AFI: I don't believe you ever took credit on your pictures as a director. And Keaton very rarely did. How did you function with the director? How were you in control?

HL: I think that in better than 60 percent of the pictures I could have taken full credit for direction because I took writers, idea men, people who had never directed pictures before — men like Ted Wilde, Tim Whelan, Sam Taylor, and Fred Newmeyer — and made them directors. I could mention scores of them, and they got credit for directing the pictures. My thinking was that I was getting all the credit I needed by being the main comic, and the audience was giving me the full credit. Why did I have to have the credit for doing the direction? I enjoyed being the comic. That's nothing against other people. Charlie Chaplin didn't choose to do that, and he did direct all his pictures. He has a perfect right to, and there's no reason he shouldn't take credit for directing, because he damn well did. Everything he takes credit for he deserves. I just didn't choose to do it, that's all.

AFI: When you were making a picture, there was more physical than verbal humor. You don't have that kind today.

HL: Yes, well, I wouldn't say physical as much as visual, because an awful lot of the gags were not really physical. That's a very good point, because we did have pretty good gags in our pictures right straight through, and because I didn't have on comedy clothes — I wasn't an incongruous type of character with big shoes always on the wrong feet and clothes that no one could visualize except as a comedy costume — which I *had* worn, with Lonesome Luke and, before that, Willie Work. Because of that, a lot of people got the idea that you were a kind of act where you could just do gags. But that's not true, because gags are done from inside. You must feel them, you must know how they are, you must time them, you must react to them. There's just one thing after another that a comic, to get a piece of business over, has got to know. And you could generally prove that if you had ten comics doing the same piece of business: one will invariably do it much funnier if it suits him, if it's his type of business, than someone who doesn't know that technique and doesn't have that feeling. You must have that feeling of comedy within you; and my character, you see, was a funny character in that. That's the reason I used him: he belied his appearance, especially in the early days, when somebody put horn-rimmed glasses on for a mollycoddle type — he was a kind of weakling in those days.

AFI: (GS) So it's the character rather than the gag thing?

HL: That's right. Now, one thing I had to do was to stay within the semblance of reasonability. Lots of people ruin the whole thing because they do an impossible gag and they ask you to believe them from then on. But practically all the gags that I did — with one or two exceptions — were all something that could happen. It wasn't very probable, but it could happen. Now, one time I did a gag that couldn't have happened. It was a pictures called *Get Out and Get Under* and I couldn't resist it. We were fixing a car and we had the hood up. I stuck my head into it and I went in a little further, and a little further, until finally I went all the way in. The last scene was showing my feet going down in there. Well, now, that couldn't happen with the motor in there, but we took a license on that one. So many comics don't do that. They get into a situation and they do something that spoils everything. Bob Hope used to try and mix oil and water all the time because he'd go along with a cartoon gag and then he'd want a very serious gag. You can't make them go both ways. Preston Sturges used to do that, and the audience would get confused. They don't know where you want to go. If you want to make a cartoon-type of picture, then make a cartoon. There's nothing wrong with that. It may be better than the other way. But stick to it. Don't try to blend the two and ask the audience to believe two things.

AFI: This has been wonderful. Thank you for speaking to us.

HL: It's a pleasure to have been your guest tonight. I feel highly honored being in the initial opening. I'm happy to say that I have the honor of being one of the original men of the Academy of Motion Picture Arts and Sciences, and I don't believe it was as big as this when we started, to tell the truth. I'm sure that everyone here, every guest you have, is rooting that it's going to go tremendous places. Thank you, gentlemen.

Notes

Introduction

1. Gilbert Seldes, *The Seven Lively Arts* (New York: Harper & Brothers, 1924), 15.
2. *The Kid* (1921), *The Pilgrim* (1923), *The Gold Rush* (1925), and *The Circus* (1928).

Main Text

1. Unsourced clipping in Harold Lloyd's personal scrapbook.
2. Harold Lloyd interview by Bob and Joan Franklin, Columbia University Oral History Research Office, 1959, transcript p. 7.
3. Dwight Whiting would follow Linthicum in the partnership. After a period of serving as partner and general manager, Whiting eventually resigned from Rolin in April 1918.
4. Harold Lloyd and Wesley W. Stout, *An American Comedy* (New York: Longmans, Green and Co., 1928), 84.
5. Ibid., 86.
6. Ibid., 92.
7. Hal Roach interview by Jeffrey Vance, 1991.
8. Harold Lloyd, "The Autobiography of Harold Lloyd," *Photoplay* 26, no. 1 (June 1924), 110.
9. Franklin, transcript p. 19.
10. Information provided to the authors by Kevin Brownlow. According to Brownlow, "Harold Lloyd always said that he got the idea for the glasses from a western film about a mild-mannered parson in spectacles who displays fighting fury when roused. He could not remember the title of the film, but recalled that it was not a feature, more likely a two-reeler. While I was in California in 1970, I interviewed veteran director George Marshall, and he brought along one of his old albums of stills. Inside, to my amazement, was a still of a bespectacled parson in a western setting. Marshall told me the title was *When Paris Green Saw Red*. I took a copy and showed it to Lloyd, and while he was not a hundred percent certain, he thought that was the one." *When Paris Green Saw Red* was released August 26, 1918 as a one-reel film produced by the Nestor Film Company and distributed by Universal Film Manufacturing Company with Neal Hart portraying the parson. Another film with a similar story released around the same time is *Cyclone Higgins, D.D.* (1918) released May 13, 1918 as a five-reel feature film produced and distributed by Metro Pictures and starring Francis X. Bushman.
11. Harold Lloyd, "The Funny Side of Life," *Films and Filming*, 10, no. 4 (January 1964), 19.
12. Byron Y. Newman, O.D., in "Harold Lloyd, The Man Who Popularized Eyeglasses in America," *Journal of the American Optometric Association* 66, no. 5 (1995), 310–11, writes: "For optometrists in the 1920s he was the man who popularized the use of glasses, especially horn-rimmed glasses, to a population who resisted the use of spectacles. Suddenly, there he was on the silent screen demonstrating for all to see that the wearing of eyeglasses added to one's personality."
13. William Cahn, *Harold Lloyd's World of Comedy* (New York: Duell, Sloan and Pearce, 1964), 144–45.
14. Lloyd and Stout, 105.
15. Ibid., 102.
16. Horatio Alger, Jr. (1832–1899) was an American writer of book for boys, among the most popular being the *Ragged Dick* series (1867), the *Luck and Pluck* series (1869), and the *Tattered Tom* series (1871). As a result of his stories—where virtue was always rewarded with success—his name has become identified with the American ideal of rising from hardship to success through hard work and self-reliance.
17. George C. Pratt, "Mind Over Matter: Harold Lloyd Reminisces," in *"Image" on the Art and Evolution of the Film.* Edited by Marshall Deutelbaum. (New York: Dover Publications, 1979), 210.
18. Harold Lloyd, "The Autobiography of Harold Lloyd." *Photoplay* 26, no. 2

(July 1924), 56

19. Ibid., 116.

20. Kevin Brownlow, "Harold Lloyd: A Renaissance Palace for One of the Silent Era's Great Comic Pioneers." *Architectural Digest* 47, no. 4 (April 1990), 162.

21. Mary B. Mullett, "A Movie Star Who Knows What Makes You Laugh," *American Magazine*, XCIV (July 1922), 36–39, 110–13.

22. James Marion Fidler, "Ta Ta Harold Take Care o' Yourself," *Motion Picture* (December 1926), 55, 89.

23. Mullett, 36–39, 110–13.

24. Kevin Brownlow, *The Parade's Gone By . . .* (New York: Alfred A. Knopf, 1968), 464.

25. Gilbert Seldes links Harold Lloyd and Charles Ray in *The Seven Lively Arts* (New York: Harper & Brothers, 1924), 16. However, Ray's characters were never as brash as Harold's characterizations. According to an article on page 9 of the *Why Worry?* press book, Lloyd thought highly of Ray's work. "Harold thinks his friend, Charles Ray, is a wonderful actor. When there is a Ray picture on the boards, he goes." However, in his book, *Three Classic Screen Comedies Starring Harold Lloyd* (Rutherford, N.J.: Fairleigh Dickson University Press, 1976) Donald W. McCaffrey, regarding his June 12, 1965 interview with Lloyd, writes that "Lloyd was very severe in his

judgment of Ray's work. He said he didn't 'admire' his films and felt that the actor could never obtain 'depth' in his comic character. 'To be blunt about it,' he declared, 'I had plenty of rivals, but Ray was not even a very good actor.'" (page 252). This is uncharacteristically uncharitable of Lloyd. It is interesting to point out that as Lloyd borrowed more elements from the Ray films, his popularity increased while Ray's popularity declined; audiences preferred the Charles Ray-type scenarios with the visual comedy that the Harold Lloyd films provided.

26. Charles Chaplin to Robert Wagner, scrapbook, May 23, 1922. Chaplin was not known to openly praise other comedians. Lloyd would later explain to Richard Correll that "Chaplin discussed with his publicist how much he liked *Grandma's Boy*, and the publicist wrote a letter to Harold telling him how much Chaplin liked the film. Harold then contacted Chaplin to thank him. Later, Harold found out that Chaplin was upset that his publicist should write him. Chaplin said to his publicist, 'Why did you do that? Why did you encourage my competition?'" Richard Correll interview by Jeffrey Vance, 1997.

27. "The best comedy, to my way of thinking, was Harold Lloyd's *Grandma's Boy*. Lloyd never misses fire — he's

always dependable." "Which Pictures Do You Like Best?" (unsigned article) in *Picture Play Magazine*, vol. 22 no. 4, 118.

28. Seldes, 15–16.

29. Arthur B. Friedman, "Interview with Harold Lloyd," *Film Quarterly* 15, no. 4 (Summer 1962), 8.

30. Tom Dardis, *Harold Lloyd: The Man on the Clock* (New York: The Viking Press, 1983), 128.

31. Orson Welles and Peter Bogdanovich. *This is Orson Welles*. Editor: Jonathan Rosenbaum (New York: Da Capo Press, 1998), 38.

32. Lloyd and Stout, 149.

33. Lloyd and Stout, 154.

34. *Variety*, April 2, 1924 in *Variety Film Reviews 1907–1980* (New York: Garland Publishing, Inc., 1983), vol. 2.

35. Harold Lloyd, "The Serious Business of Being Funny," *Film Comment* (Fall 1969), 57.

36. Harold was one of the many Hollywood dignitaries invited to watch the filming of the *Ben-Hur* chariot race on May 24, 1924, while he was filming *The Freshman*. Indeed, Lloyd stood beside Niblo on a hightower for approximately eight hours. See "Forty-Two Cameras Used on Scenes for *Ben-Hur*." *The New York Times*, November 1, 1925, section 8, 5.

37. The plot of *Girl Shy* is somewhat similar to the plot of the modern-age episode in Buster Keaton's *Three Ages*.

Harold seated on the rim of the
water well at Greenacres, 1927.

38. Lloyd, "The Serious Business of Being Funny," 49.

39. A. L. Woodbridge, "Yes Men Need Not Apply," unsourced clipping in Lloyd's *For Heaven's Sake* and *The Kid Brother* clipping book (book 1).

40. Lloyd and Stout, 158.

41. Pratt, 212.

42. Harold Lloyd, "The Funny Side of Life," 20.

43. "American Film Institute seminar with Harold Lloyd," transcript p. 28. According to Harold's autobiography, prominent screenwriter Frances Marion, who was a good friend of the Lloyd family, was also one of the advocates, insisting, "Harold, you've got to lose your pants," after watching the preliminary edit at the studio projection room. Lloyd and Stout, 174.

44. Harold Lloyd Corporation et al v. Witwer, No. 6398, U. S. Court of Appeals.

45. Brownlow, 471.

46. Sandburg, Carl. *Carl Sandburg at the Movies: A Poet in the Silent Era, 1920–1927,* ed. Dale Fetherling and Doug Fetherling. Scarecrow Press, 1985.

47. The plot of *The White Sheep* involves a mayor of a small town who has three sons, two burly men and the gentle Tobias (Glenn Tryon). The mayor is framed for murder; Tobias locates the alleged murder victim alive and well in hiding. He brings him back to town, and saves his father's life. According to film historian Richard W. Bann, the scenario of *The White Sheep* was developed jointly by Lloyd and Roach as a Harold Lloyd vehicle prior to Lloyd's leaving Roach in 1923. After Lloyd left Roach, Roach made *The White Sheep* with Glenn Tryon. Lloyd, with equal proprietary rights to the same scenario material, developed *The Kid Brother* three years later. Lloyd took directly from Roach in one casting choice: he hired Leo Willis to play virtually the same role he plays in *The White Sheep* in *The Kid Brother.*

48. The similarities of *The Kid Brother* to *Tol'able David* are the rural setting, the protagonist being treated like a boy in a family of men, a violent battle to defeat the murderous villain, the race-to-the-rescue climax in a hack, and the casting of Ralph Yearsly.

49. Lloyd, "The Serious Business of Being Funny," 49.

50. The monkey of *The Kid Brother* is frequently identified as Josephine, the monkey who appears with Buster Keaton in *The Cameraman* (1928), and as one of the three mischievous simians that attack Chaplin on the tightrope in *The Circus* (1928). Lloyd, however, refers to the monkey as Chicago in an article with his byline on page 4 of the *Welcome Danger* press book. A 1929 *Picture Play* article (Ruth M. Tildesley, "The Temperamental Dumb," *Picture Play* 29, no. 6 [February 1929], 112) also identifies the monkey as being named Chicago as well as many cited and uncited newspaper articles in the Harold Lloyd *The Kid Brother* clipping books.

51. Lloyd and Stout, 167–68.

52. Harold Lloyd, "The Funny Side of Life," 20.

53. Pratt, 208. Although Lloyd believed the climb in *Feet First* was the best he ever did from a technical standpoint, he believed the film was not as good as a whole as *Safety Last!*.

54. Lloyd, "The Serious Business of Being Funny," 49.

55. Constance Cummings interview by Jeffrey Vance, 2000.

56. Pratt, 208.

57. Harold Lloyd, "The Funny Side of Life," 20.

58. See "Harold Lloyd: The Man and His Times" by John Belton in Adam Reilly, *Harold Lloyd: The King of Daredevil Comedy* (New York: Macmillan Publishing Co., 1977), 191–98.

59. Pratt, 209.

60. Phyllis Welch interview by Jeffrey Vance, 2001.

61. Pratt, 210.

62. Franklin, transcript p. 70–71.

63. Lloyd and Stout, 199.

64. Lloyd and Stout, 198.

65. Richard Correll interview by Jeffrey Vance, 1997.

Bibliography

Books

Allen, Frederick Lewis. *Only Yesterday*. New York: Blue Ribbon Books, Inc., 1931.

Bergson, Henri. *"Laughter," Comedy*, edited by Wylie Sypher. Garden City, N Y: Doubleday and Company, 1956.

Brownlow, Kevin. *The Parade's Gone By . . .* New York: Alfred A. Knopf, 1968.

Cahn, William. *Harold Lloyd's World of Comedy*. New York: Duell, Sloan, and Pearce, 1964.

D'Agostino, Annette M. *Harold Lloyd: A Bio-Bibliography*. Westport, Conn.: Greenwood Press, 1994.

Daniels, Bebe and Lyon, Ben. *Life with the Lyons: The Autobiography of Bebe Daniels and Ben Lyon*. London: Oldhams Press Limited, 1953.

Dardis, Tom. *Harold Lloyd: The Man on the Clock*. New York: The Viking Press, 1983.

Goldwyn, Samuel. *Behind the Screen*. New York: George H. Doran Company, 1923.

Hayes, Suzanne Lloyd, ed. *3-D Hollywood*. New York: Simon and Schuster, 1992.

Hofstadter, Richard. *The Age of Reform: From Bryan to F. D. R*. New York: Alfred A. Knopf, 1955.

Kerr, Walter. *The Silent Clowns*. New York: Alfred A. Knopf, 1975.

Kozarski, Richard. *An Evening's Entertainment: The Age of the Silent Feature Picture, 1915–1928*. New York: Scribner, 1991.

Leuchtenburg, William E. *The Perils of Prosperity 1914–1932*. Chicago: University of Chicago Press, 1958.

Lloyd, Harold. "Comedy Development." In *The Truth About the Movies by the Stars*. Edited by Laurence A. Hughes. Hollywood: Hollywood Publishers, 1924.

Lloyd, Harold. "Introduction." In *Stereo Realist Manual* by Willard D. Morgan and Henry M. Lester. New York: Morgan & Lester, 1954.

Lloyd, Harold and Stout, Wesley W. *An American Comedy*. New York: Longmans, Green and Co., 1928.

Mast, Gerald. *The Comic Mind: Comedy and the Movies*. Indianapolis: The Bobbs-Merrill Company, 1973.

McCaffrey, Donald. *Four Great Comedians: Chaplin, Lloyd, Keaton, Langdon*. London: A. Zwemmer Ltd., New York: A. S. Barnes & Co., 1968.

———. *Three Classic Silent Screen Comedies Starring Harold Lloyd*. Rutherford, NJ: Fairleigh Dickinson University Press, 1975.

Montgomery, John. *Comedy Films*. London: George Allen and Unwin Ltd., 1954.

Pratt, George C. *Spellbound in Darkness*. Greenwich, Conn.: New York Graphic Society, 1973.

Reilly, Adam. *Harold Lloyd: The King of Daredevil Comedy*. New York: Macmillan Publishing Co., 1977.

Sandburg, Carl. *Carl Sandburg at the Movies: A Poet in the Silent Era, 1920–1927*, edited by Dale Fetherling and Doug Fetherling. Metuchen, N.J.: Scarecrow Press, 1985.

Schickel, Richard. *Harold Lloyd: The Shape of Laughter*. Boston: New York Graphic Society, 1974.

Schlesinger, Arthur M. Jr., *A Life in the Twentieth Century: Innocent Beginnings, 1917–1950*. Boston: Houghton Mifflin Company, 2000.

Seldes, Gilbert. *The Seven Lively Arts*. New York: Harper & Brothers, 1924.

Sherwood, Robert. *The Best Moving Pictures of 1922–1923*. Boston: Small, Maynard and Company, 1923.

Sullivan, Mark. *Our Times: The United States 1900–1925. The Twenties*. New York: Charles Scribner's Sons, 1935.

Periodicals

Agee, James. "Comedy's Greatest Era." *Life* 3 (September 1949): 70–88.

Brownlow, Kevin. "Harold Lloyd: A Renaissance Palace for One of the Silent Era's Great Comic Pioneers." *Architectural Digest* (April 1990): 160–65.

———. "Preserved in Amber." *Film Comment* 29, no. 2 (March–April 1993): 26–34.

Cohen, Hubert I. "The Serious Business of Being Funny." *Film Comment* (Fall 1969): 46–57.

Fredericks, James. "Lloyd: Laughsmith." *Motion Picture Magazine* 19, nos 3–4 (April–May 1920): 38–39.

Friedman, Arthur B. "Interview with Harold Lloyd." *Film Quarterly* 15, no. 4 (Summer 1962): 7–13.

Grafton, S. "Harold Lloyd." *Good Housekeeping* (May 1955): 54–57, 182.

Granger, Nelson E. "Harold Lloyd." *Films in Review* 13, no. 7 (August–September 1962): 407–22.

Hall, Gladys and Adele Whitely Fletcher. "We Interview 'The Boy'." *Motion Picture Magazine* XXIII, no. 6 (July 1922): 20–21, 92.

Howe, Milton. "Behind Harold's Spectacles." *Motion Picture Magazine* 33, no. 4 (May 1927): 24–25, 81.

Kaminsky, Stuart. "Harold Lloyd: A Reassessment of His Film Comedy." *Silent Picture* no. 16 (Autumn 1972): 21–29.

Lloyd, Elizabeth, as told to Phyllis Perlman. "The Boyhood of Harold Lloyd." *Motion Picture* (July 1923): 38–40, 88–89.

Lloyd, Harold. "My Ideal Girl." *Motion Picture Magazine* 15, no. 6 (July 1918): 32–33, 113.

———. as told to Marcel H. Wallenstein. "For the People, By the People." *Filmplay Journal* (April 1922): 12, 52.

———. "The Autobiography of Harold Lloyd." *Photoplay*, 25, 26, no. 6, 1, 2 (May, June, and July 1924).

———. What is Love? Twelve Men of the Screen Give Their Ideas." *Photoplay* 27, no. 3 (February 1925): 36.

———. "Harold Lloyd Tells the Most Dramatic Moments of His Life." *Motion Picture Magazine* 30, no. 5 (December 1925): 40–41, 110.

———. "The Hardships of Fun-Making." *Ladies Home Journal* (May 1926): 32, 50, 234. Reprinted in *Hollywood Directors: 1914–1940*. edited by Richard Koszarski. New York: Oxford University Press, 1976: 128–41.

———. "When They Gave Me Air." *Ladies Home Journal*. (February 1928): 19.

———. "The Funny Side of Life." *Films and Filming* 10, no. 4 (January 1964): 19–21.

Lloyd, Harold, as told to Louis Hochman. "My Adventures in Stereo." *Photography* 34, no. 4 (April 1954): 52–53, 122, 124–25.

Lloyd, Harold interviewed by Robert Steele. *Flashbacks*, 1 no. 3 (September 1972): 44–51.

McCaffery, Donald. "The Mutual Approval of Keaton and Lloyd." *Cinema Journal* 6 (1967): 8–15.

Reddy, Joseph. "Thrills and Chills in the Filming of Harold's *Feet First*." *Screen Mirror* vol. 1 no. 6 (October 1930): 13.

St. John, Adela Rogers. "How Lloyd Made *Safety Last*." *Photoplay* 24 no. 2 (July 1923): 33.

Slide, Anthony. "Harold Lloyd." *The Silent Picture*, nos. 11 and 12 (Summer/Autumn 1971): 5–8.

Thomajan, P. K. "The Lafograph." *American Cinematographer* 60, no. 1 (April 1928): 36–38.

Tildesley, Ruth M. "The Temperamental Dumb." *Picture Play* 29, no. 6 (February 1929): 89–90, 112.

"The World of Hiram Abif." *Time* 54, no. 4 (July 25, 1949): 13–17.

Interviews

Carter, Gaylord. Interviewed by Jeffrey Vance, 1991.

Cartwright, Peggy. Interviewed by Jeffrey Vance, 1997.

Correll, Richard. Interviewed by Jeffrey Vance, 1997.

Cummings, Constance. Interviewed by Jeffrey Vance, 2000.

Lloyd, Harold. "The American Film Institute Seminar with Harold Lloyd." September 23, 1969. Center for Advanced Film Studies, The American Film Institute.

———. Interviews by Kevin Brownlow, 1963, 1964, and 1970.

———. Interview by Bob and Joan Franklin. Columbia University Oral History Research Office, January 1959.

———. Interview by Arthur B. Friedman, 1955.

———. Interview by George C. Pratt for the International Museum of Photography at the George Eastman House, April 1958.

———. Interview by Harry Reasoner. *Calendar*. CBS television program, April 16, 1962.

———. Social Security in Action Interview, 1965.

Ramsden, Frances. Interviewed by Jeffrey Vance, 2000.

Roach, Hal. Interviewed by Jeffrey Vance, 1991.

Roberts, Gloria Lloyd. Interviewed by Jeffrey Vance, 2000.

Welch, Phyllis. Interviewed by Jeffrey Vance, 2001.

Miscellaneous

Bowser, Eileen. *Harold Lloyd's Short Comedies*. New York: Department of Film, The Museum of Modern Art, 1974.

Lloyd, Harold, as told to Joe Hyams. "The Golden Age of Visual Comedy: Its Decline and Pratfall." Unpublished article, 1964.

Robinson, David. *Harold Lloyd: The Third Genius*. London: Thames Television, 1989.

Fred Guiol Screen Script Collection, California State University, Fullerton, Pollak Library, University Archives and Special Collections.

The Harold Lloyd Corporation Collection, Margaret Herrick Library, Academy of Motion Picture Arts and Sciences.

Harold Lloyd Corpoation ledger and cost of production ledger books.

Harold Lloyd and His Comedies, bound volume of film scenarios 1919–1925.

Last Will and Testament of Harold C. Lloyd, March 2, 1971.

The Hal Roach Collection, University of Southern California Cinema–Television Library.

Delta Kappa Alpha celebration honoring Harold Lloyd and Mary Pickford at the University of Southern California, January 6, 1963.

Captain Kidd's Kids press book

Now or Never press book

Grandma's Boy press book

Dr. Jack press book

Why Worry? press book

Girl Shy press book

Hot Water press book

The Freshman press book

For Heaven's Sake press book

The Kid Brother press book

Speedy press book

Welcome Danger press book

Feet First press book

Movie Crazy press book

The Cat's-Paw press book

The Milky Way press book

Professor Beware press book

Harold Lloyd's World of Comedy press book

Filmography

Early Film Appearances

THE OLD MONK'S TALE (1913)
Released: February 15, 1913. Produced by Edison Picture Company. Length: 1 reel. Producer: Thomas A. Edison. Director: J. Searle Dawley. Cast: Laura Sawyer, Benjamin Wilson, Charles Sutton, Jessie McCallister, Harold Lloyd

CUPID IN A DENTAL PARLOR (1913)
Released: March 12, 1913. Distributed by Mutual Film Corporation. Produced by Keystone Film Company. Length: ½ reel. Producer: Mack Sennett. Director: Henry Lehrman. Cast: Fred Mace, Joseph Swickard, Harold Lloyd

HIS CHUM, THE BARON (1913)
Released: March 21, 1913. Distributed by Mutual Film Corporation. Produced by Keystone Film Company. Length: ½ reel. Producer: Mack Sennett. Cast: Ford Sterling, Harold Lloyd

ALGY ON THE FORCE (1913)
Released: March 28, 1913. Distributed by Mutual Film Corporation. Produced by Keystone Film Company. Length: ½ reel. Producer: Mack Sennett. Director: Henry Lehrman. Cast: Nick Cogley, Dot Farley, Ed Kennedy, Fred Mace, Harold Lloyd

'TWIXT LOVE AND FIRE (1913)
Released: April 19, 1913. Distributed by Mutual Film Corporation. Produced by Keystone Film Company. Length: ½ reel. Producer: Mack Sennett, Director: Henry Lehrman. Cast: Harold Lloyd

RORY O'THE BOGS (1913)
Released: December 20, 1913. Distributed by Universal Film Manufacturing Company. Produced by Universal Film Manufacturing Company. Length: 3 reels. Director: J. Farrell MacDonald. Cast: J. Warren Kerrigan, Jessalyn Van Trump, Harold Lloyd, Hal Roach

SAMSON (1914)
Released: April 30, 1914. Distributed by Universal Film Manufacturing Company. Produced by Universal Film Manufacturing Company. Length: 6 reels. Director: J. Farrell MacDonald. Scenario: James Dayton. Art Director: Frank Ormston. Cast: J. Warren Kerrigan, George Periolat, Lule Warrenton, Kathleen Kerrigan, Edith Bostwick, Hal Roach, Frank Borzage, Harold Lloyd

THE PATCHWORK GIRL OF OZ (1914)
Released: September 28, 1914. Produced by Paramount Pictures Corporation. Length: 5 reels. Producer: L. Frank Baum. Assistant Producer: Harold Ostrom. Director: J. Farrell MacDonald. Scenario: L. Frank Baum. Cameraman: James A. Crosby. Original Music: Louis F. Gottschalk. Cast: Pierre Couderc, Violet MacMillan, Fred Woodward, Marie Wayne, Frank Moore, Dick Rosson, Hal Roach, Harold Lloyd

BEYOND HIS FONDEST HOPES (1915)
Released: January 30, 1915. Distributed by Eclectic. Produced by Rolin Film Company. Length: 1 reel. Producer: Hal Roach. Director: Hal Roach. Cast: Harold Lloyd

CLOSE-CROPPED CLIPPINGS (1915)
Released: January 30, 1915. Distributed by Eclectic. Produced by Rolin Film Company. Length: 1 reel. Producer: Hal Roach. Director: Hal Roach. Cast: Harold Lloyd

PETE THE PEDAL POLISHER (1915)
Released: January 30, 1915. Distributed by Eclectic. Produced by Rolin Film Company. Length: 1 reel. Producer: Hal Roach. Director: Hal Roach. Cast: Harold Lloyd

WILLIE RUNS THE PARK (1915)
Released: February 1915. Distributed by Warner's Features. Produced by: Rolin Film Company. Producer: Hal Roach. Director: Hal Roach. Cast: Harold Lloyd, Roy Stewart, Jane Novak.

HOGAN'S ROMANCE UPSET (1915)
Released: February 13, 1915. Distributed by Mutual Film Corporation. Produced by Keystone Film Company. Length: 1 reel. Producer: Mack Sennett. Cast: Roscoe "Fatty" Arbuckle, Charlie Murray, Harold Lloyd

JUST NUTS (1915)
Released: April 19, 1915. Distributed by Pathé Exchange. Produced by Rolin Film Company. Length: 1 reel. Producer: Hal Roach. Director: Hal Roach. Cast: Harold Lloyd, Roy Stewart, Jane Novak

LOVE, LOOT AND CRASH (1915)
Released: April 24, 1915. Distributed by Mutual Film Corporation. Produced by Keystone Film Company. Length: 1 reel. Producer: Mack Sennett. Director: Nick Cogley. Cast: Charles (Charley) Chase, Dora Rodgers, Josef Swickard, Fritz Schade, Harold Lloyd

THEIR SOCIAL SPLASH (1915)
Released: April 26, 1915. Distributed by Mutual Film Corporation. Produced by Keystone Film Company. Length: split reel. Producer: Mack Sennett. Director: Arvid E. Gillstrom. Cast: Dixie Chene, Slim Summerville, Polly Moran, Charlie Murray, Harold Lloyd

Harold Lloyd caught in a hair-raising moment from *High and Dizzy* (1920), his second "thrill" picture.

MISS FATTY'S SEASIDE LOVERS (1915)
Released: May 15, 1915. Distributed by Mutual Film Corporation. Produced by Keystone Film Company. Length: 1 reel. Producer: Mack Sennett. Director: Roscoe "Fatty" Arbuckle. Cast: Roscoe "Fatty" Arbuckle, Billy Gilbert, Edgar Kennedy, Harold Lloyd

FROM ITALY'S SHORES (1915)
Released: May 19, 1915. Distributed by Universal Film Manufacturing Company. Produced by Rolin Film Company. Length: 2 reels. Producer: Carl Laemmle. Director: Otis Turner. Scenario: James Dayton. Cast: Roy Stewart, Harold Lloyd, Jane Novak

COURTHOUSE CROOKS (1915)
Released: July 5, 1915. Produced by Keystone Film Company. Length: 2 reels. Producer: Mack Sennett. Director: Charles Parrott. Cast: Ford Sterling, Minta Durfee, Harold Lloyd

The Lonesome Luke Films

SPIT-BALL SADIE (1915)
Released: July 31, 1915. Distributed by Pathé Exchange. A Phunfilms comedy produced by Rolin Film Company. Length: 1 reel. Producer: Hal Roach. Director: Hal Roach. Scenario: Tad Dorgan. Cast: Harold Lloyd

TERRIBLY STUCK UP (1915)
Released: August 28, 1915. Distributed by Pathé Exchange. A Phunfilms comedy produced by Rolin Film Company. Length: 1 reel. Producer: Hal Roach. Director: Hal Roach. General Manager: Dwight Whiting. Cast: Harold Lloyd

A MIXUP FOR MAZIE (1915)
Released: September 6, 1915. Distributed by Pathé Exchange. A Phunfilms comedy produced by Rolin Film Company. Length: 1 reel. Producer: Hal Roach. Director: Hal Roach. General Manager: Dwight Whiting. Cast: Harold Lloyd

SOME BABY (1915)
Released: September 20, 1915. Distributed by Pathé Exchange. A Phunfilms comedy produced by Rolin Film Company. Length: 1 reel. Producer: Hal Roach. Director: Hal Roach. General Manager: Dwight Whiting. Cast: Harold Lloyd

FRESH FROM THE FARM (1915)
Released: October 4, 1915. Distributed by Pathé Exchange: A Phunfilms comedy produced by Rolin Film Company. Length: 1 reel. Producer: Hal Roach. Director: Hal Roach. General Manager: Dwight Whiting. Cast: Harold Lloyd

GIVING THEM FITS (1915)
Released: November 1, 1915. Distributed by Pathé Exchange. A Phunfilms comedy produced by Rolin Film Company. Length: 1 reel. Producer: Hal Roach. Director: Hal Roach. General Manager: Dwight Whiting. Cast: Harold Lloyd, Harry Pollard, Gene Marsh, Bebe Daniels

BUGHOUSE BELLHOPS (1915)
Released: November 8, 1915. Distributed by Pathé Exchange. A Phunfilms comedy produced by Rolin Film Company. Length: 1 reel. Producer: Hal Roach. Director: Hal Roach. General Manager: Dwight Whiting. Cast: Harold Lloyd, Harry Pollard, Gene Marsh, Bebe Daniels

TINKERING WITH TROUBLE (1915)
Released: November 17, 1915. Distributed by Pathé Exchange. A Phunfilms comedy produced by Rolin Film Company. Length: 1 reel. Producer: Hal Roach. Director: Hal Roach. General Manager: Dwight Whiting. Cast: Harold Lloyd, Harry Pollard, Gene Marsh, Bebe Daniels

GREAT WHILE IT LASTED (1915)
Released: November 24, 1915. Distributed by Pathé Exchange. A Phunfilms comedy produced by Rolin Film Company. Length: 1 reel. Producer: Hal Roach. Director: Hal Roach. General Manager: Dwight Whiting. Cast: Harold Lloyd, Harry Pollard, Gene Marsh, Bebe Daniels

RAGTIME SNAP SHOTS (1915)
Released: December 1, 1915. Distributed by Pathé Exchange. A Phunfilms comedy produced by Rolin Film Company. Length: 1 reel. Producer: Hal Roach. Director: Hal Roach. General Manager: Dwight Whiting. Cast: Harold Lloyd, Harry Pollard, Earl Mohan, Gene Marsh, Bebe Daniels

THE NEW ADVENTURES OF TERENCE O'ROURKE (1915)
Released: December 4, 1915. Distributed by Universal Film Manufacturing Company. Produced by Universal Film Manufacturing Company. Length: 2 reels each. Serial Episodes: "The Palace of Dust," "When a Queen Loved O'Rourke," and The Road to Paradise." Director: Otis Turner. Scenario: Walter Woods, F. McGrew Willis from a story by Louis Joseph Vance. Cast: J. Warren Kerrigan, Ray Gallagher, George Periolat, Lois Wilson, Harold Lloyd (extra).

A FOOZLE AT THE TEE PARTY (1915)
Released: December 8, 1915. Distributed by Pathé Exchange. A Phunfilms comedy produced by Rolin Film Company. Length: 1 reel. Producer: Hal Roach. Director: Hal Roach. General Manager: Dwight Whiting. Cast: Harold Lloyd, Harry Pollard, Earl Mohan, Gene Marsh, Bebe Daniels

RUSES, RHYMES, AND ROUGHNECKS (1915)
Released: December 15, 1915. Distributed by Pathé Exchange. A Phunfilms comedy produced by Rolin Film Company. Length: 1 reel. Director: Hal Roach. General Manager: Dwight Whiting. Cast: Harold Lloyd, Harry Pollard, Gene Marsh, Bebe Daniels

PECULIAR PATIENTS' PRANKS (1915)
Released: December 22, 1915. Distributed by Pathé Exchange. A Phunfilms comedy produced by Rolin Film Company. Length: 1 reel. Producer: Hal Roach. Director: Hal Roach. General Manager: Dwight Whiting. Cast: Harold Lloyd, Harry Pollard, Gene Marsh, Bebe Daniels

LONESOME LUKE, SOCIAL GANGSTER (1915)
Released: December 29, 1915. Distributed by Pathé Exchange. A Phunfilms comedy produced by Rolin Film Company. Length: 1 reel. Producer: Hal Roach. Director: Hal Roach. General Manager: Dwight Whiting. Cast: Harold Lloyd, Harry Pollard, Gene Marsh, Bebe Daniels

LONESOME LUKE LEANS TO THE LITERARY (1916)
Released: January 5, 1916. Distributed by Pathé Exchange. A Phunfilms comedy produced by Rolin Film Company. Length: 1 reel. Producer: Hal Roach. Director: Hal Roach. General Manager: Dwight Whiting. Cast: Harold Lloyd, Harry Pollard, Gene Marsh, Bebe Daniels

LUKE LUGS LUGGAGE (1916)
Released: January 10, 1916. Distributed by Pathé Exchange. A Phunfilms comedy produced by Rolin Film Company. Length: 1 reel. Producer: Hal Roach. Director: Hal Roach. General Manager: Dwight Whiting. Cast: Harold Lloyd, Harry Pollard, Gene Marsh, Bebe Daniels

LONESOME LUKE LOLLS IN LUXURY (1916)
Released: January 19, 1916. Distributed by Pathé Exchange. A Phunfilms comedy produced by Rolin Film Company. Length: 1 reel. Producer: Hal Roach. Director: Hal Roach. General Manager: Dwight Whiting. Cast: Harold Lloyd, Harry Pollard, Gene Marsh, Bebe Daniels

LUKE, THE CANDY CUT-UP (1916)
Released: January 31, 1916. Distributed by Pathé Exchange. A Phunfilms comedy produced by Rolin Film Company. Length: 1 reel. Producer: Hal Roach. Director: Hal Roach. General Manager: Dwight Whiting. Cast: Harold Lloyd, Harry Pollard, Gene Marsh, Bebe Daniels

LUKE FOILS THE VILLAIN (1916)
Released: February 16, 1916. Distributed by Pathé Exchange. A Phunfilms comedy produced by Rolin Film Company. Length: 1 reel. Producer: Hal Roach. Director: Hal Roach. General Manager: Dwight Whiting. Cast: Harold Lloyd, Harry Pollard, Gene Marsh, Bebe Daniels

LUKE AND THE RURAL ROUGHNECKS (1916)
Released: March 1, 1916. Distributed by Pathé Exchange. A Phunfilms comedy produced by Rolin Film Company. Length: 1 reel. Producer: Hal Roach. Director: Hal Roach. General Manager: Dwight Whiting. Cast: Harold Lloyd, Harry Pollard, Earl Mohan, Bebe Daniels

LUKE PIPES THE PIPPINS (1916)
Released: March 15, 1916. Distributed by Pathé Exchange. A Phunfilms comedy produced by Rolin Film Company. Length: 1 reel. Producer: Hal Roach. Director: Hal Roach. General Manager: Dwight Whiting. Cast: Harold Lloyd, Harry Pollard, Bebe Daniels

LONESOME LUKE, CIRCUS KING (1916)
Released: March 29, 1916. Distributed by Pathé Exchange. A Phunfilms comedy produced by Rolin Film Company. Length: 1 reel. Producer: Hal Roach. Director: Hal Roach. General Manager: Dwight Whiting. Cast: Harold Lloyd, Harry Pollard, Bebe Daniels

LUKE'S DOUBLE (1916)
Released: April 12, 1916. Distributed by Pathé Exchange. A Phunfilms comedy produced by Rolin Film Company. Length: 1 reel. Producer: Hal Roach. Director: Hal Roach. General Manager: Dwight Whiting. Cast: Harold Lloyd, Harry Pollard, Bebe Daniels

THEM WAS THE HAPPY DAYS (1916)
Released: April 26, 1916. Distributed by Pathé Exchange. A Phunfilms comedy produced by Rolin Film Company. Length: 1 reel. Producer: Hal Roach. Director: Hal Roach. General Manager: Dwight Whiting. Cast: Harold Lloyd, Harry Pollard, Bebe Daniels

LUKE AND THE BOMB THROWERS (1916)
Released: May 8, 1916. Distributed by Pathé Exchange. Produced by Rolin Film Company. Length: 1 reel. Producer: Hal Roach. Director: Hal Roach. General Manager: Dwight Whiting. Cast: Harold Lloyd, Harry Pollard, Bebe Daniels

LUKE'S LATE LUNCHERS (1916)
Released: May 22, 1916. Distributed by Pathé Exchange. Produced by Rolin Film Company. Length: 1 reel. Producer: Hal Roach. Director: Hal Roach. General Manager: Dwight Whiting. Cast: Harold Lloyd, Harry Pollard, Bebe Daniels

LUKE LAUGHS LAST (1916)
Released: June 5, 1916. Distributed by Pathé Exchange. Produced by Rolin Film Company. Length: 1 reel. Producer: Hal Roach. Director: Hal Roach. General Manager: Dwight Whiting. Cast: Harold Lloyd, Harry Pollard, Bebe Daniels

LUKE'S FATAL FLIVVER (1916)
Released: June 19, 1916. Distributed by Pathé Exchange. Produced by Rolin Film Company. Length: 1 reel. Producer: Hal Roach. Director: Hal Roach. General Manager: Dwight Whiting. Cast: Harold Lloyd, Harry Pollard, Bebe Daniels

LUKE'S SOCIETY MIXUP (1916)
Released: June 26, 1916. Distributed by Pathé Exchange. Produced by Rolin Film Company. Length: 1 reel. Producer: Hal Roach. Director: Hal Roach. General Manager: Dwight Whiting. Cast: Harold Lloyd, Harry Pollard, Bebe Daniels

LUKE'S WASHFUL WAITING (1916)
Released: July 3, 1916, Distributed by Pathé Exchange. Produced by Rolin Film Company. Length: 1 reel. Producer: Hal Roach. Director: Hal Roach. General Manager: Dwight Whiting. Cast: Harold Lloyd, Harry Pollard, Bebe Daniels

LUKE RIDES ROUGH-SHOD (1916)
Released: July 10, 1916. Distributed by Pathé Exchange. Produced by Rolin Film Company. Length: 1 reel. Producer: Hal Roach. Director: Hal Roach. General Manager: Dwight Whiting. Cast: Harold Lloyd, Harry Pollard, Bebe Daniels

LUKE, CRYSTAL GAZER (1916)
Released: July 24, 1916. Distributed by Pathé Exchange. Produced by Rolin Film Company. Length: 1 reel. Producer: Hal Roach. Director: Hal Roach. General Manager: Dwight Whiting. Cast: Harold Lloyd, Harry Pollard, Bebe Daniels

LUKE'S LOST LAMB (1916)
Released: August 7, 1916. Distributed by Pathé Exchange. Produced by Rolin Film Company. Length: 1 reel. Producer: Hal Roach. Director: Hal Roach. General Manager: Dwight Whiting. Cast: Harold Lloyd, Harry Pollard, Bebe Daniels

LUKE DOES THE MIDWAY (1916)
Released: August 21, 1916. Distributed by Pathé Exchange. Produced by Rolin Film Company. Length: 1 reel. Producer: Hal Roach. Director: Hal Roach. General Manager: Dwight Whiting. Cast: Harold Lloyd, Harry Pollard, Bebe Daniels

LUKE JOINS THE NAVY (1916)
Released: September 3, 1916. Distributed by Pathé Exchange. Produced by Rolin Film Company. Length: 1 reel. Producer: Hal Roach. Director: Hal Roach. General Manager: Dwight Whiting. Cast: Harold Lloyd, Harry Pollard, Bebe Daniels

LUKE AND THE MERMAIDS (1916)
Released: September 17, 1916. Distributed by Pathé Exchange. Produced by Rolin Film Company. Length: 1 reel. Producer: Hal Roach. Director: Hal Roach. General Manager: Dwight Whiting. Cameraman: Jim Crosby. Cast: Harold Lloyd, Harry Pollard, Bebe Daniels

LUKE'S SPEEDY CLUB LIFE (1916)
Released: October 1, 1916. Distributed by Pathé Exchange. Produced by Rolin Film Company. Length: 1 reel. Producer: Hal Roach. Director: Hal Roach. General Manager: Dwight Whiting. Cast: Harold Lloyd, Harry Pollard, Earl Mohan, Bebe Daniels

LUKE AND THE BANG-TAILS (1916)
Released: October 15, 1916. Distributed by Pathé Exchange. Produced by Rolin Film Company. Length: 1 reel. Producer: Hal Roach. Director: Hal Roach. General Manager: Dwight Whiting. Cast: Harold Lloyd, Harry Pollard, Bebe Daniels

LUKE, THE CHAUFFEUR (1916)
Released: October 29, 1916. Distributed by Pathé Exchange. Produced by Rolin Film Company. Length: 1 reel. Producer: Hal Roach. Director: Hal Roach. General Manager: Dwight Whiting. Cast: Harold Lloyd, Harry Pollard, Bebe Daniels

LUKE'S PREPAREDNESS PREPARATIONS (1916)
Released: November 5, 1916. Distributed by Pathé Exchange. Produced by Rolin Film Company. Length: 1 reel. Producer: Hal Roach. Director: Hal Roach. General Manager: Dwight Whiting. Cast: Harold Lloyd, Harry Pollard, Bebe Daniels

LUKE, THE GLADIATOR (1916)
Released: November 12, 1916. Distributed by Pathé Exchange. Produced by Rolin Film Company. Length: 1 reel. Producer: Hal Roach. Director: Hal Roach. General Manager: Dwight Whiting. Cast: Harold Lloyd, Harry Pollard, Bebe Daniels

LUKE, PATIENT PROVIDER (1916)
Released: November 19, 1916. Distributed by Pathé Exchange. Produced by Rolin Film Company. Length: 1 reel. Producer: Hal Roach. Director: Hal Roach. General Manager: Dwight Whiting. Cast: Harold Lloyd, Harry Pollard, Bebe Daniels

LUKE'S NEWSIE KNOCKOUT (1916)
Released: November 26, 1916. Distributed by Pathé Exchange. Produced by Rolin Film Company. Length: 1 reel. Producer: Hal Roach. Director: Hal Roach. General Manager: Dwight Whiting. Cast: Harold Lloyd, Harry Pollard, Bebe Daniels

LUKE'S MOVIE MUDDLE (1916)
Released: December 3, 1916. Distributed by Pathé Exchange. Produced by Rolin Film Company. Length: 1 reel. Producer: Hal Roach. Director: Hal Roach. General Manager: Dwight Whiting. Cast: Harold Lloyd, Harry Pollard, Bebe Daniels

At this point the direction of the Harold Lloyd comedies alternated principally between Gilbert Pratt, Alf Goulding, and Hal Roach.

LUKE, RANK IMPERSONATOR (1916)
Released: December 10, 1916. Distributed by Pathé Exchange. Produced by Rolin Film Company. Length: 1 reel. Producer: Hal Roach. General Manager: Dwight Whiting. Cast: Harold Lloyd, Harry Pollard, Bebe Daniels

LUKE'S FIREWORKS FIZZLE (1916)
Released: December 17, 1916. Distributed by Pathé Exchange. Produced by Rolin Film Company. Length: 1 reel. Producer: Hal Roach. General Manager: Dwight Whiting. Cast: Harold Lloyd, Harry Pollard, Bebe Daniels

LUKE LOCATES THE LOOT (1916)
Released: December 24, 1916. Distributed by Pathé Exchange. Produced by Rolin Film Company. Length: 1 reel. Producer: Hal Roach. General Manager: Dwight Whiting. Cast: Harold Lloyd, Harry Pollard, Bebe Daniels

LUKE'S SHATTERED SLEEP (1916)
Released: December 31, 1916. Distributed by Pathé Exchange. Produced by Rolin Film Company. Length: 1 reel. Producer: Hal Roach. General Manager: Dwight Whiting. Cast: Harold Lloyd, Harry Pollard, Bebe Daniels

LUKE'S LOST LIBERTY (1917)
Released: January 7, 1917. Distributed by Pathé Exchange. Produced by Rolin Film Company. Length: 1 reel. Producer: Hal Roach. General Manager: Dwight Whiting. Cast: Harold Lloyd, Harry Pollard, Bebe Daniels

LUKE'S BUSY DAY (1917)
Released: January 21, 1917. Distributed by Pathé Exchange. Produced by Rolin Film Company. Length: 1 reel. Producer: Hal Roach. General Manager: Dwight Whiting. Cast: Harold Lloyd, Harry Pollard, Bebe Daniels

LUKE'S TROLLEY TROUBLES (1917)
Released: February 4, 1917. Distributed by Pathé Exchange. Produced by Rolin Film Company. Length: 1 reel. Producer: Hal Roach. General Manager: Dwight Whiting. Cast: Harold Lloyd, Harry Pollard, Bebe Daniels

LONESOME LUKE, LAWYER (1917)
Released: February 18, 1917. Distributed by Pathé Exchange. Produced by Rolin Film Company. Length: 1 reel. Producer: Hal Roach. General Manager: Dwight Whiting. Cast: Harold Lloyd, Harry Pollard, Bebe Daniels

LUKE WINS YE LADYE FAIRE (1917)
Released: February 25, 1917. Distributed by Pathé Exchange. Produced by Rolin Film Company. Length: 2 reels. Producer: Hal Roach. General Manager: Dwight Whiting. Cast: Harold Lloyd, Harry Pollard, Bebe Daniels

LONESOME LUKE'S LIVELY LIFE (1917)
Released: March 18, 1917. Distributed by Pathé Exchange. Produced by Rolin Film Company. Length: 2 reels. Producer: Hal Roach. General Manager: Dwight Whiting. Cast: Harold Lloyd, Harry Pollard, Bebe Daniels

LONESOME LUKE ON TIN CAN ALLEY (1917)
Released: April 15, 1917. Distributed by Pathé Exchange. Produced by Rolin Film Company. Length: 2 reels. Producer: Hal Roach. General Manager: Dwight Whiting. Cast: Harold Lloyd, Harry Pollard, Bebe Daniels

LONESOME LUKE'S HONEYMOON (1917)
Released: May 20, 1917. Distributed by Pathé Exchange. Produced by Rolin Film Company. Length: 2 reels. Producer: Hal Roach. General Manager: Dwight Whiting. Cast: Harold Lloyd, Harry Pollard, Bebe Daniels

LONESOME LUKE, PLUMBER (1917)
Released: June 17, 1917. Distributed by Pathé Exchange. Produced by Rolin Film Company. Length: 2 reels. Producer: Hal Roach. General Manager: Dwight Whiting. Cast: Harold Lloyd, Harry Pollard, Bebe Daniels

STOP! LUKE! LISTEN! (1917)
Released: July 15, 1917. Distributed by Pathé Exchange. Produced by Rolin Film Company. Length: 2 reels. Producer: Hal Roach. General Manager: Dwight Whiting. Cast: Harold Lloyd, Harry Pollard, Bebe Daniels

LONESOME LUKE, MESSENGER (1917)
Released: August 5, 1917. Distributed by Pathé Exchange. Produced by Rolin Film Company. Length: 2 reels. Producer: Hal Roach. General Manager: Dwight Whiting. Cast: Harold Lloyd, Harry Pollard, Bebe Daniels

LONESOME LUKE, MECHANIC (1917)
Released: August 19, 1917. Distributed by Pathé Exchange. Produced by Rolin Film Company. Length: 2 reels. Producer: Hal Roach. General Manager: Dwight Whiting. Cast: Harold Lloyd, Harry Pollard, Bebe Daniels

LUKE'S WILD WOMEN (1917)
Released: September 2, 1917. Distributed by Pathé Exchange. Produced by Rolin Film Company. Length: 2 reels. Producer: Hal Roach. General Manager: Dwight Whiting. Cast: Harold Lloyd, Harry Pollard, Bebe Daniels

The One-Reel Glass Character Films

The one-reel Glass Character comedies would alternate with the final two-reel Lonesome Luke comedies, the last Lonesome Luke film being WE NEVER SLEEP.

OVER THE FENCE (1917)
Released: September 9, 1917. Distributed by Pathé Exchange. Produced by Rolin Film Company. Length: 1 reel. Producer: Hal Roach. Directors: Harold Lloyd and J. Farrell MacDonald. General Manager: Dwight Whiting. Titles: H. M. Walker. Cast: Harold Lloyd, Harry Pollard, Bebe Daniels, J. Darsie Lloyd

LONESOME LUKE LOSES PATIENTS (1917)
Released: September 16, 1917. Distributed by Pathé Exchange. Produced by Rolin Film Company. Length: 2 reels. Producer: Hal Roach. General Manager: Dwight Whiting. Titles: H. M. Walker. Cast: Harold Lloyd, Harry Pollard, Bebe Daniels

PINCHED (1917)
Released: September 23, 1917. Distributed by Pathé Exchange. Produced by Rolin Film Company. Length: 1 reel. Producer: Hal Roach. Directors: Harold Lloyd and Gilbert Pratt. General Manager: Dwight Whiting. Photography: Walter Lundin. Titles: H. M. Walker. Cast: Harold Lloyd, Harry Pollard, Bebe Daniels

BY THE SAD SEA WAVES (1917)
Released: September 30, 1917. Distributed by Pathé Exchange. Produced by Rolin Film Company. Length: 1 reel. Producer: Hal Roach. Director: Alf Goulding. General Manager: Dwight Whiting. Titles: H. M. Walker. Cast: Harold Lloyd, Harry Pollard, Bebe Daniels

BIRDS OF A FEATHER (1917)
Released: October 7, 1917. Distributed by Pathé Exchange. Produced by Rolin Film Company. Length: 2 reels. Producer: Hal Roach. General Manager: Dwight Whiting. Titles: H. M. Walker. Cast: Harold Lloyd, Harry Pollard, Bebe Daniels

BLISS (1917)
Released: October 14, 1917. Distributed by Pathé Exchange. Produced by Rolin Film Company. Length: 1 reel. Producer: Hal Roach. Director: Alf Goulding. General Manager: Dwight Whiting. Titles: H. M. Walker. Cast: Harold Lloyd, Harry Pollard, Bebe Daniels

FROM LONDON TO LARAMIE (1917)
Released: October 21, 1917. Distributed by Pathé Exchange. Produced by Rolin Film Company. Length: 2 reels. Producer: Hal Roach. General Manager: Dwight Whiting. Titles: H. M. Walker. Cast: Harold Lloyd, Harry Pollard, Bebe Daniels

RAINBOW ISLAND (1917)
Released: October 28, 1917. Distributed by Pathé Exchange. Produced by Rolin Film Company. Length: 1 reel. Producer: Hal Roach. Director: Gilbert Pratt. General Manager: Dwight Whiting. Titles: H. M. Walker. Cast: Harold Lloyd, Harry Pollard, Bebe Daniels

LOVE, LAUGHS AND LATHER (1917)
Released: November 4, 1917. Distributed by Pathé Exchange. Produced by Rolin Film Company. Length: 2 reels. Producer: Hal Roach. General Manager: Dwight Whiting. Titles: H. M. Walker. Cast: Harold Lloyd, Harry Pollard, Bebe Daniels

THE FLIRT (1917)
Released: November 11, 1917. Distributed by Pathé Exchange. Produced by Rolin Film Company. Length: 1 reel. Producer: Hal Roach. Director: Gilbert Pratt. General Manager: Dwight Whiting. Titles: H. M. Walker. Cast: Harold Lloyd, Harry Pollard, Bebe Daniels

CLUBS ARE TRUMP (1917)
Released: November 18, 1917. Distributed by Pathé Exchange. Produced by Rolin Film Company. Length: 2 reels. Producer: Hal Roach. General Manager: Dwight Whiting. Titles: H. M. Walker. Cast: Harold Lloyd, Harry Pollard, Bebe Daniels

ALL ABOARD (1917)
Released: November 25, 1917. Distributed by Pathé Exchange. Produced by Rolin Film Company. Length: 1 reel. Producer: Hal Roach. Director: Alf Goulding. General Manager: Dwight Whiting. Titles: H. M. Walker. Cast: Harold Lloyd, Harry Pollard, Bebe Daniels

WE NEVER SLEEP (1917)
Released: December 2, 1917. Distributed by Pathé Exchange. Produced by Rolin Film Company. Length: 2 reels. Producer: Hal Roach. General Manager: Dwight Whiting. Titles: H. M. Walker. Cast: Harold Lloyd, Harry Pollard, Bebe Daniels

MOVE ON (1917)
Released: December 9, 1917. Distributed by Pathé Exchange. Produced by Rolin Film Company. Length: 1 reel. Producer: Hal Roach. Director: Gilbert Pratt. General Manager: Dwight Whiting. Titles: H. M. Walker. Cast: Harold Lloyd, Harry Pollard, Bebe Daniels

BASHFUL (1917)
Released: December 23, 1917. Distributed by Pathé Exchange. Produced by Rolin Film Company. Length: 1 reel. Producer: Hal Roach. Director: Alf Goulding. General Manager: Dwight Whiting. Titles: H. M. Walker. Cast: Harold Lloyd, Harry Pollard, Bebe Daniels

STEP LIVELY (1917)
Released: December 30, 1917. Distributed by Pathé Exchange. Produced by Rolin Film Company. Length: 1 reel. Producer: Hal Roach. Director: Alf Goulding. General Manager: Dwight Whiting. Titles: H. M. Walker. Cast: Harold Lloyd, Harry Pollard, Bebe Daniels

THE TIP (1918)
Released: January 6, 1918. Distributed by Pathé Exchange. Produced by Rolin Film Company. Length: 1 reel. Producer: Hal Roach. Director: Gilbert Pratt. General Manager: Dwight Whiting. Photography: Walter Lundin. Titles: H. M. Walker. Cast: Harold Lloyd, Harry Pollard, Bebe Daniels

THE BIG IDEA (1918)
Released: January 20, 1918. Distributed by Pathé Exchange. Produced by Rolin Film Company. Length: 1 reel. Producer: Hal Roach. Directors: Gilbert Pratt and Hal Mohr. General Manager: Dwight Whiting. Photography: Walter Lundin. Titles: H. M. Walker. Cast: Harold Lloyd, Harry Pollard, Bebe Daniels

THE LAMB (1918)
Released: February 3, 1918. Distributed by Pathé Exchange. Produced by Rolin Film Company. Length: 1 reel. Producer: Hal Roach. Directed by Harold Lloyd, Gilbert Pratt, and Hal Mohr. General Manager: Dwight Whiting. Photography: Walter Lundin. Titles: H. M. Walker. Cast: Harold Lloyd, Harry Pollard, Bebe Daniels

HIT HIM AGAIN (1918)
Released: February 17, 1918. Distributed by Pathé Exchange. Produced by Rolin Film Company. Length: 1 reel. Producer: Hal Roach. Director: Gilbert Pratt. General Manager: Dwight Whiting. Photography: Walter Lundin. Titles: H. M. Walker. Cast: Harold Lloyd, Harry Pollard, Bebe Daniels

BEAT IT (1918)
Released: February 24, 1918. Distributed by Pathé Exchange. Produced by Rolin Film Company. Length: 1 reel. Producer: Hal Roach. Director: Gilbert Pratt. General Manager: Dwight Whiting. Photography: Walter Lundin. Titles: H. M. Walker. Cast: Harold Lloyd, Harry Pollard, Bebe Daniels

A GASOLINE WEDDING (1918)
Released: March 3, 1918. Distributed by Pathé Exchange. Produced by Rolin Film Company. Length: 1 reel. Producer: Hal Roach. Director: Alf Goulding. General Manager: Dwight Whiting. Photography: Walter Lundin. Titles: H. M. Walker. Cast: Harold Lloyd, Harry Pollard, Bebe Daniels

LOOK PLEASANT PLEASE (1918)
Released: March 10, 1918. Distributed by Pathé Exchange. Produced by Rolin Film Company. Length: 1 reel. Producer: Hal Roach. Director: Alf Goulding. General Manager: Dwight Whiting. Photography: Walter Lundin. Titles: H. M. Walker. Cast: Harold Lloyd, Harry Pollard, Bebe Daniels

HERE COME THE GIRLS (1918)
Released: March 17, 1918. Distributed by Pathé Exchange. Produced by Rolin Film Company. Length: 1 reel. Producer: Hal Roach. Director: Attributed to Jefferson. General Manager: Dwight Whiting. Photography: Walter Lundin. Titles: H. M. Walker. Cast: Harold Lloyd, Harry Pollard, Bebe Daniels

LET'S GO (1918)
Released: March 24, 1918. Distributed by Pathé Exchange. Produced by Rolin Film Company. Length: 1 reel. Producer: Hal Roach. Director: Alf Goulding. General Manager: Dwight Whiting. Photography: Walter Lundin. Titles: H. M. Walker. Cast: Harold Lloyd, Harry Pollard, Bebe Daniels

ON THE JUMP (1918)
Released: March 31, 1918. Distributed by Pathé Exchange. Produced by Rolin Film Company. Length: 1 reel. Producer: Hal Roach. Director: Alf Goulding. General Manager: Dwight Whiting. Photography: Walter Lundin. Titles: H. M. Walker. Cast: Harold Lloyd, Harry Pollard, Bebe Daniels

FOLLOW THE CROWD (1918)
Released: April 7, 1918. Distributed by Pathé Exchange. Produced by Rolin Film Company. Length: 1 reel. Producer: Hal Roach. Director: Alf Goulding. General Manager: Dwight Whiting. Photography: Walter Lundin. Titles: H. M. Walker. Cast: Harold Lloyd, Harry Pollard, Bebe Daniels

PIPE THE WHISKERS (1918)
Released: April 14, 1918. Distributed by Pathé Exchange. Produced by Rolin Film Company. Length: 1 reel. Producer: Hal Roach. Director: Alf Goulding. General Manager: Dwight Whiting. Photography: Walter Lundin. Titles: H. M. Walker. Cast: Harold Lloyd, Harry Pollard, Bebe Daniels

IT'S A WILD LIFE (1918)
Released: April 21, 1918. Distributed by Pathé Exchange. Produced by Rolin Film Company. Length: 1 reel. Producer: Hal Roach. Director: Gilbert Pratt. General Manager: Dwight Whiting. Photography: Walter Lundin. Titles: H. M. Walker. Cast: Harold Lloyd, Harry Pollard, Bebe Daniels

HEY THERE (1918)
Released: April 28, 1918. Distributed by Pathé Exchange. Produced by Rolin Film Company. Length: 1 reel. Producer: Hal Roach. Director: Gilbert Pratt. Photography: Walter Lundin. Titles: H. M. Walker. Cast: Harold Lloyd, Harry Pollard, Bebe Daniels

KICKED OUT (1918)
Released: May 5, 1918. Distributed by Pathé Exchange. Produced by Rolin Film Company. Length: 1 reel. Producer: Hal Roach. Director: Alf Goulding. Photography: Walter Lundin. Titles: H. M. Walker. Cast: Harold Lloyd, Harry Pollard, Bebe Daniels

THE NON-STOP KID (1918)
Released: May 12, 1918. Distributed by Pathé Exchange. Produced by Rolin Film Company. Length: 1 reel. Producer: Hal Roach. Director: Gilbert Pratt. Photography: Walter Lundin. Titles: H. M. Walker. Cast: Harold Lloyd, Harry Pollard, Bebe Daniels

TWO-GUN GUSSIE (1918)
Released: May 19, 1918. Distributed by Pathé Exchange. Produced by Rolin Film Company. Length: 1 reel. Producer: Hal Roach. Director: Alf Goulding. Photography: Walter Lundin. Titles: H. M. Walker. Cast: Harold Lloyd, Harry Pollard, Bebe Daniels

FIREMAN, SAVE MY CHILD (1918)
Released: May 26, 1918. Distributed by Pathé Exchange. Produced by Rolin Film Company. Length: 1 reel. Producer: Hal Roach. Director: Alf Goulding. Photography: Walter Lundin. Titles: H. M. Walker. Cast: Harold Lloyd, Harry Pollard, Bebe Daniels

THE CITY SLICKER (1918)
Released: June 2, 1918. Distributed by Pathé Exchange. Produced by Rolin Film Company. Length: 1 reel. Producer: Hal Roach. Director: Gilbert Pratt. Photography: Walter Lundin. Titles: H. M. Walker. Cast: Harold Lloyd, Harry Pollard, Bebe Daniels

SIC 'EM TOWSER (1918)
Released: June 8, 1918. Distributed by Pathé Exchange. Produced by Rolin Film Company. Length: 1 reel. Producer: Hal Roach. Director: Gilbert Pratt. Photography: Walter Lundin. Titles: H. M. Walker. Cast: Harold Lloyd, Harry Pollard, Bebe Daniels

SOMEWHERE IN TURKEY (1918)
Released: June 16, 1918. Distributed by Pathé Exchange. Produced by Rolin Film Company. Length: 1 reel. Producer: Hal Roach. Director: Alf Goulding. Photography: Walter Lundin. Titles: H. M. Walker. Cast: Harold Lloyd, Harry Pollard, Bebe Daniels

ARE CROOKS DISHONEST? (1918)
Released: June 23, 1918. Distributed by Pathé Exchange. Produced by Rolin Film Company. Length: 1 reel. Producer: Hal Roach. Director: Gilbert Pratt. Photography: Walter Lundin. Titles: H. M. Walker. Cast: Harold Lloyd, Harry Pollard, Bebe Daniels

AN OZARK ROMANCE (1918)
Released: July 7, 1918. Distributed by Pathé Exchange. Produced by Rolin Film Company. Length: 1 reel. Producer: Hal Roach. Director: Alf Goulding. Photography: Walter Lundin. Titles: H. M. Walker. Cast: Harold Lloyd, Harry Pollard, Bebe Daniels

KICKING THE GERM OUT OF GERMANY (1918)
Released: July 21, 1918. Distributed by Pathé Exchange. Produced by Rolin Film Company. Length: 1 reel. Producer: Hal Roach. Director: Alf Goulding. Photography: Walter Lundin. Titles: H. M. Walker. Cast: Harold Lloyd, Harry Pollard, Bebe Daniels

THAT'S HIM (1918)
Released: August 4, 1918. Distributed by Pathé Exchange. Produced by Rolin Film Company. Length: 1 reel. Producer: Hal Roach. Director: Gilbert Pratt. Photography: Walter Lundin. Titles: H. M. Walker. Cast: Harold Lloyd, Harry Pollard, Bebe Daniels

BRIDE AND GLOOM (1918)
Released: August 18, 1918. Distributed by Pathé Exchange. Produced by Rolin Film Company. Length: 1 reel. Producer: Hal Roach. Director: Alf Goulding. Photography: Walter Lundin. Titles: H. M. Walker. Cast: Harold Lloyd, Harry Pollard, Bebe Daniels

TWO SCRAMBLED (1918)
Released: September 1, 1918. Distributed by Pathé Exchange. Produced by Rolin Film Company. Length: 1 reel. Producer: Hal Roach. Director: Gilbert Pratt. Photography: Walter Lundin. Titles: H. M. Walker. Cast: Harold Lloyd, Harry Pollard, Bebe Daniels

BEES IN HIS BONNET (1918)
Released: September 15, 1918. Distributed by Pathé Exchange. Produced by Rolin Film Company. Length: 1 reel. Producer: Hal Roach. Director: Gilbert Pratt. Photography: Walter Lundin. Titles: H. M. Walker. Cast: Harold Lloyd, Harry Pollard, Bebe Daniels

SWING YOUR PARTNERS (1918)
Released: September 29, 1918. Distributed by Pathé Exchange. Produced by Rolin Film Company. Length: 1 reel. Producer: Hal Roach. Director: Alf Goulding. Photography: Walter Lundin. Titles: H. M. Walker. Cast: Harold Lloyd, Harry Pollard, Bebe Daniels

WHY PICK ON ME? (1918)
Released: October 18, 1918. Distributed by Pathé Exchange. Produced by Rolin Film Company. Length: 1 reel. Producer: Hal Roach. Director: Gilbert Pratt. Photography: Walter Lundin. Titles: H. M. Walker. Cast: Harold Lloyd, Harry Pollard, Bebe Daniels

NOTHING BUT TROUBLE (1918)
Released: October 27, 1918. Distributed by Pathé Exchange. Produced by Rolin Film Company. Length: 1 reel. Producer: Hal Roach Director: Alf Goulding. Photography: Walter Lundin. Titles: H. M. Walker. Cast: Harold Lloyd, Harry Pollard, Bebe Daniels

HEAR 'EM RAVE (1918)
Released: November 10, 1918. Distributed by Pathé Exchange. Produced by Rolin Film Company. Length: 1 reel. Producer: Hal Roach. Director: Gilbert Pratt. Photography: Walter Lundin. Titles: H. M. Walker. Cast: Harold Lloyd, Harry Pollard, Bebe Daniels

TAKE A CHANCE (1918)
Released: November 24, 1918. Distributed by Pathé Exchange. Produced by Rolin Film Company. Length: 1 reel. Producer: Hal Roach. Director: Alf Goulding. Photography: Walter Lundin. Titles: H. M. Walker. Cast: Harold Lloyd, Harry Pollard, Bebe Daniels

SHE LOVES ME NOT (1918)
Released: December 29, 1918. Distributed by Pathé Exchange. Produced by Rolin Film Company. Length: 1 reel. Producer: Hal Roach. Director: Alf Goulding. Photography: Walter Lundin. Titles: H. M. Walker. Cast: Harold Lloyd, Harry Pollard, Bebe Daniels

WANTED—$5,000 (1919)
Released: January 12, 1919. Distributed by Pathé Exchange. Produced by Rolin Film Company. Length: 1 reel. Producer: Hal Roach. Director: Gilbert Pratt. Photography: Walter Lundin. Titles: H. M. Walker. Cast: Harold Lloyd, Harry Pollard, Bebe Daniels

GOING! GOING! GONE! (1919)
Released: January 26, 1919. Distributed by Pathé Exchange. Produced by Rolin Film Company. Length: 1 reel. Producer: Hal Roach. Director: Gilbert Pratt. Photography: Walter Lundin. Titles: H. M. Walker. Cast: Harold Lloyd, Harry Pollard, Bebe Daniels

ASK FATHER (1919)
Released: February 9, 1919. Distributed by Pathé Exchange. Produced by Rolin Film Company. Length: 1 reel. Producer: Hal Roach. Director: Hal Roach. Photography: Walter Lundin. Titles: H. M. Walker. Cast: Harold Lloyd, Harry Pollard, Bebe Daniels

ON THE FIRE (1919)
Released: February 23, 1919. Distributed by Pathé Exchange. Produced by Rolin Film Company. Length: 1 reel. Producer: Hal Roach. Director: Alf Goulding. Photography: Walter Lundin. Titles: H. M. Walker. Cast: Harold Lloyd, Harry Pollard, Bebe Daniels

I'M ON MY WAY (1919)
Released: March 9, 1919. Distributed by Pathé Exchange. Produced by Rolin Film Company. Length: 1 reel. Producer: Hal Roach. Director: Alf Goulding. Photography: Walter Lundin. Titles: H. M. Walker. Cast: Harold Lloyd, Harry Pollard, Bebe Daniels

LOOK OUT BELOW! (1919)
Released: March 16, 1919. Distributed by Pathé Exchange. Produced by Rolin Film Company. Length: 1 reel. Producer: Hal Roach. Director: Hal Roach. Photography: Walter Lundin. Titles: H. M. Walker. Cast: Harold Lloyd, Harry Pollard, Bebe Daniels

THE DUTIFUL DUB (1919)
Released: March 23, 1919. Distributed by Pathé Exchange. Produced by Rolin Film Company. Length: 1 reel. Producer: Hal Roach. Director: Alf Goulding. Photography: Walter Lundin. Titles: H. M. Walker. Cast: Harold Lloyd, Harry Pollard, Bebe Daniels

NEXT AISLE OVER (1919)
Released: March 30, 1919. Distributed by Pathé Exchange. Produced by Rolin Film Company. Length: 1 reel. Producer: Hal Roach. Director: Alf Goulding. Photography: Walter Lundin. Titles: H. M. Walker. Cast: Harold Lloyd, Harry Pollard, Bebe Daniels

A SAMMY IN SIBERIA (1919)
Released: April 6, 1919. Distributed by Pathé Exchange. Produced by Rolin Film Company. Length: 1 reel. Producer: Hal Roach. Director: Hal Roach. Photography: Walter Lundin. Titles: H. M. Walker. Cast: Harold Lloyd, Harry Pollard, Bebe Daniels

JUST DROPPED IN (1919)
Released: April 13, 1919. Distributed by Pathé Exchange. Produced by Rolin Film Company. Length: 1 reel. Producer: Hal Roach. Director: Hal Roach. Photography: Walter Lundin. Titles: H. M. Walker. Cast: Harold Lloyd, Harry Pollard, Bebe Daniels

CRACK YOUR HEELS (1919)
Released: April 20, 1919. Distributed by Pathé Exchange. Produced by Rolin Film Company. Length: 1 reel. Producer: Hal Roach. Director: Alf Goulding. Photography: Walter Lundin. Titles: H. M. Walker. Cast: Harold Lloyd, Harry Pollard, Bebe Daniels

RING UP THE CURTAIN (1919)
Released: April 27, 1919. Distributed by Pathé Exchange. Produced by Rolin Film Company. Length: 1 reel. Producer: Hal Roach. Director: Alf Goulding. Photography: Walter Lundin. Titles: H. M. Walker. Cast: Harold Lloyd, Harry Pollard, Bebe Daniels

YOUNG MR. JAZZ (1919)
Released: May 4, 1919. Distributed by Pathé Exchange. Produced by Rolin Film Company. Length: 1 reel. Producer: Hal Roach. Director: Hal Roach. Photography: Walter Lundin. Titles: H. M. Walker. Cast: Harold Lloyd, Harry Pollard, Bebe Daniels

SI, SENOR (1919)
Released: May 11, 1919. Distributed by Pathé Exchange. Produced by Rolin Film Company. Length: 1 reel. Producer: Hal Roach. Director: Alf Goulding. Photography: Walter Lundin. Titles: H. M. Walker. Cast: Harold Lloyd, Harry Pollard, Bebe Daniels

BEFORE BREAKFAST (1919)
Released: May 18, 1919. Distributed by Pathé Exchange. Produced by Rolin Film Company. Length: 1 reel. Producer: Hal Roach. Director: Hal Roach. Photography: Walter Lundin. Titles: H. M. Walker. Cast: Harold Lloyd, Harry Pollard, Bebe Daniels

THE MARATHON (1919)
Released: May 25, 1919. Distributed by Pathé Exchange. Produced by Rolin Film Company. Length: 1 reel. Producer: Hal Roach. Director: Alf Goulding. Photography: Walter Lundin. Titles: H. M. Walker. Cast: Harold Lloyd, Harry Pollard, Bebe Daniels

BACK TO THE WOODS (1919)
Released: June 1, 1919. Distributed by Pathé Exchange. Produced by Rolin Film Company. Length: 1 reel. Producer: Hal Roach. Director: Hal Roach. Photography: Walter Lundin. Titles: H. M. Walker. Cast: Harold Lloyd, Harry Pollard, Bebe Daniels

PISTOLS FOR BREAKFAST (1919)
Released: June 8, 1919. Distributed by Pathé Exchange. Produced by Rolin Film Company. Length: 1 reel. Producer: Hal Roach. Director: Alf Goulding. Photography: Walter Lundin. Titles: H. M. Walker. Cast: Harold Lloyd, Harry Pollard, Bebe Daniels

SWAT THE CROOK (1919)
Released: June 15, 1919. Distributed by Pathé Exchange. Produced by Rolin Film Company. Length: 1 reel. Producer: Hal Roach. Director: Hal Roach. Photography: Walter Lundin. Titles: H. M. Walker. Cast: Harold Lloyd, Harry Pollard, Bebe Daniels

OFF THE TROLLEY (1919)
Released: June 22, 1919. Distributed by Pathé Exchange. Produced by Rolin Film Company. Length: 1 reel. Producer: Hal Roach. Director: Alf Goulding. Photography: Walter Lundin. Titles: H. M. Walker. Cast: Harold Lloyd, Harry Pollard, Bebe Daniels

SPRING FEVER (1919)
Released: June 29, 1919. Distributed by Pathé Exchange. Produced by Rolin Film Company. Length: 1 reel. Producer: Hal Roach. Directors: Hal Roach and Frank Terry. Photography: Walter Lundin. Titles: H. M. Walker. Cast: Harold Lloyd, Harry Pollard, Bebe Daniels

BILLY BLAZES, ESQ. (1919)
Released: July 6, 1919. Distributed by Pathé Exchange. Produced by Rolin Film Company. Length: 1 reel. Producer: Hal Roach. Director: Hal Roach. Photography: Walter Lundin. Titles: H. M. Walker. Cast: Harold Lloyd, Harry Pollard, Bebe Daniels

JUST NEIGHBORS (1919)
Released: July 13, 1919. Distributed by Pathé Exchange. Produced by Rolin Film Company. Length: 1 reel. Producer: Hal Roach. Directors: Harold Lloyd and Frank Terry. Photography: Walter Lundin. Titles: H. M. Walker. Cast: Harold Lloyd, Harry Pollard, Bebe Daniels

AT THE OLD STAGE DOOR (1919)
Released: July 20, 1919. Distributed by Pathé Exchange. Produced by Rolin Film Company. Length: 1 reel. Producer: Hal Roach. Director: Hal Roach. Photography: Walter Lundin. Titles: H. M. Walker. Cast: Harold Lloyd, Harry Pollard, Bebe Daniels

NEVER TOUCHED ME (1919)
Released: July 27, 1919. Distributed by Pathé Exchange. Produced by Rolin Film Company. Length: 1 reel. Producer: Hal Roach. Director: Alf Goulding. Photography: Walter Lundin. Titles: H. M. Walker. Cast: Harold Lloyd, Harry Pollard, Bebe Daniels

A JAZZED HONEYMOON (1919)
Released: August 3, 1919. Distributed by Pathé Exchange. Produced by Rolin Film Company. Length: 1 reel. Producer: Hal Roach. Director: Hal Roach. Photography: Walter Lundin. Titles: H. M. Walker. Cast: Harold Lloyd, Harry Pollard, Bebe Daniels

COUNT YOUR CHANGE (1919)
Released: August 10, 1919. Distributed by Pathé Exchange. Produced by Rolin Film Company. Length: 1 reel. Producer: Hal Roach. Director: Alf Goulding. Photography: Walter Lundin. Titles: H. M. Walker. Cast: Harold Lloyd, Harry Pollard, Bebe Daniels

CHOP SUEY & CO. (1919)
Released: August 17, 1919. Distributed by Pathé Exchange. Produced by Rolin Film Company. Length: 1 reel. Producer: Hal Roach. Director: Hal Roach. Photography: Walter Lundin. Titles: H. M. Walker. Cast: Harold Lloyd, Harry Pollard, Bebe Daniels

HEAP BIG CHIEF (1919)
Released: August 24, 1919. Distributed by Pathé Exchange. Produced by Rolin Film Company. Length: 1 reel. Producer: Hal Roach. Director: Alf Goulding. Photography: Walter Lundin. Titles: H. M. Walker. Cast: Harold Lloyd, Harry Pollard, Bebe Daniels

DON'T SHOVE (1919)
Released: August 31, 1919. Distributed by Pathé Exchange. Produced by Rolin Film Company. Length: 1 reel. Producer: Hal Roach. Director: Alf Goulding. Photography: Walter Lundin. Titles: H. M. Walker. Cast: Harold Lloyd, Harry Pollard, Bebe Daniels

BE MY WIFE (1919)
Released: September 7, 1919. Distributed by Pathé Exchange. Produced by Rolin Film Company. Length: 1 reel. Producer: Hal Roach. Director: Hal Roach. Photography: Walter Lundin. Titles: H. M. Walker. Cast: Harold Lloyd, Harry Pollard, Bebe Daniels

THE RAJAH (1919)
Released: September 14, 1919. Distributed by Pathé Exchange. Produced by Rolin Film Company. Length: 1 reel. Producer: Hal Roach. Director: Hal Roach. Photography: Walter Lundin. Titles: H. M. Walker. Cast: Harold Lloyd, Harry Pollard, Bebe Daniels

HE LEADS, OTHERS FOLLOW (1919)
Released: September 21, 1919. Distributed by Pathé Exchange. Produced by Rolin Film Company. Length: 1 reel. Producer: Hal Roach. Directors: Hal Roach and Vincent Bryan. Photography: Walter Lundin. Titles: H. M. Walker. Cast: Harold Lloyd, Harry Pollard, Bebe Daniels

SOFT MONEY (1919)
Released: September 28, 1919. Distributed by Pathé Exchange. Produced by Rolin Film Company. Length: 1 reel. Producer: Hal Roach. Directors: Hal Roach and Vincent Bryan. Photography: Walter Lundin. Titles: H. M. Walker. Cast: Harold Lloyd, Harry Pollard, Bebe Daniels

COUNT THE VOTES (1919)
Released: October 5, 1919. Distributed by Pathé Exchange. Produced by Rolin Film Company. Length: 1 reel. Producer: Hal Roach. Director: Hal Roach. Photography: Walter Lundin. Titles: H. M. Walker. Cast: Harold Lloyd, Harry Pollard, Bebe Daniels

PAY YOUR DUES (1919)
Released: October 12, 1919. Distributed by Pathé Exchange. Produced by Rolin Film Company. Length: 1 reel. Producer: Hal Roach. Directors: Hal Roach and Vincent Bryan. Photography: Walter Lundin. Titles: H. M. Walker. Cast: Harold Lloyd, Harry Pollard, Bebe Daniels

HIS ONLY FATHER (1919)
Released: October 19, 1919. Distributed by Pathé Exchange. Produced by Rolin Film Company. Length: 1 reel. Producer: Hal Roach. Directors: Hal Roach and Frank Terry. Photography: Walter Lundin. Titles: H. M. Walker. Cast: Harold Lloyd, Harry Pollard, Bebe Daniels

The Two- and Three-Reel Glass Character Films

BUMPING INTO BROADWAY (1919)
Released: November 2, 1919. Distributed by Pathé Exchange. Produced by Rolin Film Company. Length: 2 reels. Producer: Hal Roach. Director: Hal Roach. Photography: Walter Lundin. Titles: H. M. Walker. Cast: Harold Lloyd, Bebe Daniels, Harry Pollard, Helen Gilmore, Fred Newmeyer, Gus Leonard

CAPTAIN KIDD'S KIDS (1919)
Released: November 30, 1919. Distributed by Pathé Exchange. Produced by Rolin Film Company. Length: 2 reels. Producer: Hal Roach. Director: Hal Roach. Photography: Walter Lundin. Titles: H. M. Walker. Cast: Harold Lloyd, Bebe Daniels, Harry Pollard, Fred Newmeyer, Helen Gilmore

FROM HAND TO MOUTH (1919)
Released: December 28, 1919. Distributed by Pathé Exchange. Produced by Rolin Film Company. Length: 2 reels. Producer: Hal Roach. Director: Alf Goulding. Photography: Walter Lundin. Titles: H. M. Walker. Cast: Harold Lloyd, Mildred Davis, Harry Pollard, Peggy Cartwright

HIS ROYAL SLYNESS (1920)
Released: February 8, 1920. Distributed by Pathé Exchange. Produced by Rolin Film Company. Length: 2 reels. Producer: Hal Roach. Director: Hal Roach. Photography: Walter Lundin. Titles: H. M. Walker. Cast: Harold Lloyd, Mildred Davis, Harry Pollard, Gus Leonard, Bob O'Connor, Gaylord Lloyd

HAUNTED SPOOKS (1920)
Released: March 31, 1920. Distributed by Pathé Exchange. Produced by Rolin Film Company. Length: 2 reels. Producer: Hal Roach. Directors: Hal Roach and Alf Goulding. Photography: Walter Lundin. Titles: H. M. Walker. Cast: Harold Lloyd, Mildred Davis, Wallace Howe, Ernest Morrison

AN EASTERN WESTERNER (1920)
Released: May 2, 1920. Distributed by Pathé Exchange. Produced by Rolin Film Company. Length: 2 reels. Producer: Hal Roach. Director: Hal Roach. Photography: Walter Lundin. Story: Frank Terry. Titles: H. M. Walker. Cast: Harold Lloyd, Mildred Davis, Noah Young

HIGH AND DIZZY (1920)
Released: July 11, 1920. Distributed by Pathé Exchange. Produced by Rolin Film Company. Length: 2 reels. Producer: Hal Roach. Director: Hal Roach. Photography: Walter Lundin. Story: Frank Terry. Titles: H. M. Walker. Cast: Harold Lloyd, Mildred Davis, Roy Brooks, Wallace Howe, Charles Stevenson

GET OUT AND GET UNDER (1920)
Released: September 12, 1920. Distributed by Pathé Exchange. Produced by Hal E. Roach Studios. Length: 2 reels. Producer: Hal Roach. Director: Hal Roach. Photography: Walter Lundin. Titles: H. M. Walker. Cast: Harold Lloyd, Mildred Davis, Fred McPherson, Ernest Morrison

NUMBER, PLEASE? (1920)
Released: December 26, 1920. Distributed by Pathé Exchange. Produced by Hal E. Roach Studios. Length: 2 reels. Producer: Hal Roach. Directors: Hal Roach and Fred Newmeyer. Photography: Walter Lundin. Titles: H. M. Walker. Cast: Harold Lloyd, Mildred Davis, Roy Brooks, Charles Stevenson, Ernest Morrison

NOW OR NEVER (1921)
Released: May 5, 1921. Distributed by Pathé Exchange. Presented by: Associated Exhibitors, Inc. Produced by Hal E. Roach Studios. Length: 3 reels. Producer: Hal Roach. Directors: Hal Roach and Fred Newmeyer. Scenario: Sam Taylor. Photography: Walter Lundin. Editor: Thomas J. Crizer. Titles: H. M. Walker. Cast: Harold Lloyd, Mildred Davis, Anna May Bilson

AMONG THOSE PRESENT (1921)
Released: July 3, 1921. Distributed by Pathé Exchange. Presented by: Associated Exhibitors, Inc. Produced by Hal E. Roach Studios. Length: 3 reels. Producer: Hal Roach. Director: Fred Newmeyer. Story: Hal Roach and Sam Taylor. Photography: Walter Lundin. Film Editor: Thomas J. Crizer. Titles: H. M. Walker. Cast: Harold Lloyd, Mildred Davis, Aggie Herring, James Kelly, Vera White, William Gillespie

I DO (1921)
Released: September 11, 1921. Distributed by Pathé Exchange. Presented by: Associated Exhibitors, Inc. Produced by Hal E. Roach Studios. Length: 2 reels. Producer: Hal Roach. Director: Fred Newmeyer. Story: Hal Roach and Sam Taylor. Photography: Walter Lundin. Film Editor: Thomas J. Crizer. Titles: H. M. Walker. Cast: Harold Lloyd, Mildred Davis, Noah Young, Jackie Morgan, Jackie Edwards

NEVER WEAKEN (1921)
Released: October 22, 1921. Distributed by Pathé Exchange. Presented by: Associated Exhibitors, Inc. Produced by Hal E. Roach Studios. Length: 3 reels. Producer: Hal Roach. Director: Fred Newmeyer. Story: Hal Roach and Sam Taylor. Photography: Walter Lundin. Film Editor: Thomas J. Crizer. Titles: H. M. Walker. Cast: Harold Lloyd, Mildred Davis, Roy Brooks, Mark Jones, Charles Stevenson

The Silent Features

A SAILOR-MADE MAN (1921)
Released: December 25, 1921. Distributed by Pathé Exchange. Presented by: Associated Exhibitors, Inc. Produced by Hal E. Roach Studios. Length: 4 reels. Producer: Hal Roach. Director: Fred Newmeyer. Story: Hal Roach, Sam Taylor, and Jean Havez. Photography: Walter Lundin. Film Editor: Thomas J. Crizer. Titles: H. M. Walker. Cast: Harold Lloyd, Mildred Davis, Noah Young, Dick Sutherland

GRANDMA'S BOY (1922)
Released: September 3, 1922. Distributed by Pathé Exchange. Presented by: Associated Exhibitors, Inc. Produced by Hal E. Roach Studios. Length: 5 reels. Producer: Hal Roach. Director: Fred Newmeyer. Story: Hal Roach, Sam Taylor, and Jean Havez. Photography: Walter Lundin. Film Editor: Thomas J. Crizer. Titles: H. M. Walker. Cast: Harold Lloyd, Mildred Davis, Anna Townsend, Charles Stevenson, Dick Sutherland, Noah Young

DR. JACK (1922)

Released: December 19, 1922. Distributed by Pathé Exchange. Presented by: Associated Exhibitors, Inc. Produced by Hal E. Roach Studios. Length: 5 reels. Producer: Hal Roach. Director: Fred Newmeyer. Assistant Director: Robert A. Golden. Story: Hal Roach, Sam Taylor, and Jean Havez. Photography: Walter Lundin. Film Editor: Thomas J. Crizer. Titles: H. M. Walker. Cast: Harold Lloyd, Mildred Davis, John T. Prince, Eric Mayne, C. Norman Hammond

SAFETY LAST! (1923)

Released: April 1, 1923. Distributed by Pathé Exchange. Produced by Hal E. Roach Studios. Length: 7 reels. Producer: Hal Roach. Directors: Fred Newmeyer and Sam Taylor. Assistant Director: Robert A. Golden. Story: Hal Roach, Sam Taylor, and Tim Whelan. Photography: Walter Lundin. Art Direction: Fred Guiol. Technical Assistants: C. E. Christensen and John L. Murphy. Editor: Thomas J. Crizer. Titles: H. M. Walker. Cast: Harold Lloyd, Mildred Davis, Bill Strother, Noah Young, Westcott B. Clarke

WHY WORRY? (1923)

Released: September 16, 1923. Distributed by Pathé Exchange. Produced by Hal E. Roach Studios. Length: 6 reels. Producer: Hal Roach. Directors: Fred Newmeyer and Sam Taylor. Assistant Director: Robert A. Golden. Story: Sam Taylor, Ted Wilde, Tim Whelan. Photography: Walter Lundin. Editor: Thomas J. Crizer. Titles: H. M. Walker. Cast: Harold Lloyd, Jobyna Ralston, Johan Aasen, Wallace Howe, James Mason, Leo White, Gaylord Lloyd, Mark Jones

GIRL SHY (1924)

Released: April 20, 1924. Distributed by Pathé Exchange. Produced by Harold Lloyd Corporation. Length: 8 reels. Producer: Harold Lloyd. Directors: Fred Newmeyer and Sam Taylor. Assistant Director: Robert A. Golden. Story: Sam Taylor, Ted Wilde, Tim Whelan. Photography: Walter Lundin. Photography Assistant: Henry N. Kohler. Editor: Allen McNeil. Production Manager: John L. Murphy. Technical Director: William MacDonald. Art Director: Liell K. Vedder. Cast: Harold Lloyd, Jobyna Ralston, Richard Daniels, Carlton Griffin

HOT WATER (1924)

Released: November 2, 1924. Distributed by Pathé Exchange. Produced by Harold Lloyd Corporation. Length: 5 reels. Producer: Harold Lloyd. Directors: Sam Taylor and Fred Newmeyer. Assistant Director: Robert A. Golden. Story and Titles: Sam Taylor, John Grey, Tim Whelan, Thomas J. Gray. Photography: Walter Lundin. Photography Assistant: Henry N. Kohler. Editor: Allen McNeil. Technical Director: William MacDonald. Art Director: Liell K. Vedder. Cast: Harold Lloyd, Jobyna Ralston, Josephine Crowell, Charles Stevenson, Mickey McBan

THE FRESHMAN (1925)

Released: September 20, 1925. Distributed by Pathé Exchange. Produced by Harold Lloyd Corporation. Length: 7 reels. Producer: Harold Lloyd. Directors: Sam Taylor and Fred Newmeyer. Assistant Director: Robert A. Golden. Story: Sam Taylor, Ted Wilde, John Grey, Tim Whelan. Photography: Walter Lundin. Photography Assistant: Henry N. Kohler. Editor: Allen McNeil. Titles: Thomas J. Grey. Production Manager: John L. Murphy. Technical Director: William MacDonald. Art Director: Liell K. Vedder. Cast: Harold Lloyd, Jobyna Ralston, Brooks Benedict, James Anderson, Hazel Keener, Joseph Harrington, Pat Harmon

FOR HEAVEN'S SAKE (1926)

Released: April 5, 1926. Distributed by Paramount Pictures. Produced by Harold Lloyd Corporation. Length: 6 reels. Producer: Harold Lloyd. Director: Sam Taylor. Assistant Director: Robert A. Golden. Story: Ted Wilde, John Grey, and Clyde Bruckman. Titles: Ralph Spence. Photography: Walter Lundin. Photography Assistant: Henry N. Kohler. Art Director: Liell K. Vedder. Technical Director: William MacDonald. Editor: Allen McNeil. Production Manager: John L. Murphy. Cast: Harold Lloyd, Jobyna Ralston, Noah Young, James Mason, Paul Weigel

THE KID BROTHER (1927)

Released: January 22, 1927. Distributed by Paramount Pictures. Produced by Harold Lloyd Corporation. Length: 8 reels. Producer: Harold Lloyd. Directors: Ted Wilde and J. A. Howe. Assistant Director: Gaylord F. Lloyd. Story: John Grey, Ted Wilde and Thomas J. Crizer. Scenario: John Grey, Lex Neal, and Howard Green. Photography: Walter Lundin. Photography Assistant: Henry N. Kohler. Production Manager: John L. Murphy. Editor: Allen McNeil. Art Director: Leill K. Vedder. Technical Director: William MacDonald. Cast: Harold Lloyd, Jobyna Ralston, Walter James, Leo Willis, Olin Francis, Constantine Romanoff, Eddie Boland, Frank Lanning, Ralph Yearsley

SPEEDY (1928)

Released: April 7, 1928. Distributed by Paramount Pictures. Produced by Harold Lloyd Corporation. Length: 8 reels. Producer: Harold Lloyd. Director: Ted Wilde. Assistant Director: Gaylord F. Lloyd. Story and Scenario: John Grey, Lex Neal, Howard Rogers, and Jay Howe. Photography: Walter Lundin. Special Photography: Henry N. Kohler. Titles: Albert De Mond. Art Director: Leill K. Vedder. Technical Director: William MacDonald. Editor: Carl Himm. Production Manager: John L. Murphy. Cast: Harold Lloyd, Ann Christy, Bert Woodruff, George Herman "Babe" Ruth, Byron Douglas, Brooks Benedict

The Sound Feature Films

WELCOME DANGER (1929)

Released: October 12, 1929. Distributed by Paramount Pictures. Produced by Harold Lloyd Corporation. Length: 12 reels. Producer: Harold Lloyd. Directors: Clyde Bruckman (sound version) Ted Wilde, Mal St. Clair, and Clyde Bruckman (silent version). Assistant Director: Gaylord F. Lloyd. Story: Felix Adler, Lex Neal, and Clyde Bruckman. Dialogue: Paul Gerard Smith. Photography: Walter Lundin and Henry N. Kohler. Musical Arrangement: Bakaleinikoff. Sound Technicians: Cecil Bardwell and Lodge Cunningham. Editors: Bernard Burton and Carl Himm. Art Direction: Leill K. Vedder. Technical Director: William MacDonald. Production Manager: John L. Murphy. Production Assistant: Tom Gubbins. Cast: Harold Lloyd, Barbara Kent, Noah Young, Charles Middleton, William Walling

FEET FIRST (1930)

Released: November 8, 1930. Distributed by Paramount-Publix Corporation. Produced by Harold Lloyd Corporation., Producer: Harold Lloyd. Director: Clyde Bruckman. Assistant Directors: Gaylord Lloyd and Mal DeLay. Story: John Grey, Al Cohn, and Clyde Bruckman. Scenario: Felix Adler and Lex Neal. Photography: Walter Lundin and Henry N. Kohler. Film Editor: Bernard Burton. Technical Director: William MacDonald. Art Director: Leill K. Vedder. Sound Technicians: William Fox, Cecil Bardwell. Production Manager: John L. Murphy. Cast: Harold Lloyd, Barbara Kent, Robert McWade, Lillianne Leighton, Henry Hall, Noah Young, Alec Francis, Arthur Housman, Sleep 'n Eat (Willie Best)

MOVIE CRAZY (1932)

Released: September 23, 1932. Distributed by Paramount Pictures. Produced by Harold Lloyd Corporation. Producer: Harold Lloyd. Director: Clyde Bruckman. Assistant Director: Gaylord Lloyd. Story: Agnes Christine Johnston, John Grey, and Felix Adler. Continuity: Clyde Bruckman, Frank Terry, and Lex Neal. Screenplay and Dialogue: Vincent Lawrence. Photography: Walter Lundin. Editor: Bernard Burton. Art Directors: Harry Oliver and William MacDonald. Production Manager: John L. Murphy. Cast: Harold Lloyd, Constance Cummings, Kenneth Thomson, Louise Closser Hale, Spencer Charters, Robert McWade, Eddie Featherstone, Sydney Jarvis, Harold Goodwin, Mary Doran, DeWitt Jennings, Lucy Beaumont, Arthur Housman

THE CAT'S-PAW (1934)

Released: August 7, 1934. Distributed by Fox Film Corporation. Produced by Harold Lloyd Corporation. Producer: Harold Lloyd. Director: Sam Taylor. Story: Clarence Budington Kelland. Screenplay: Sam Taylor. Photography: Walter Lundin. Musical Direction: Alfred Newman. Music and Lyrics: Harry Akst and Roy Turk. Art Director: Harry Oliver. Choreography: Larry Ceballos. Editor: Bernard Burton. Production Manager: John L. Murphy. Cast: Harold Lloyd, Una Merkel, George Barbier, Nat Pendleton, Grace Bradley, Alan Dinehart, Grant Mitchell, Fred Warren, J. Farrell MacDonald, James Donald, Edwin Maxwell, Frank Sheridan, Fuzzy Knight, Vincent Barnett

THE MILKY WAY (1936)

Released: February 7, 1936. Distributed by Paramount Pictures. Presented by Adolph Zukor. Producer: E. Lloyd Sheldon. Director: Leo McCarey. Screenplay: Grover Jones, Frank Butler, and Richard Connell. From a play by Lynn Root and Harry Clork. Photography: Alfred Gilks. Art Directors: Hans Dreier and Bernerd Herzbrun. Editor: LeRoy Stone. Sound Recording: Earl Hayman and Louis Messenkop. Interior Decorations: A. E. Freudeman. Cast: Harold Lloyd, Adolphe Menjou, Verree Teasdale, Helen Mack, William Gargan, George Barbier, Dorothy Wilson, Lionel Stander, Marjorie Gateson

PROFESSOR BEWARE (1938)

Released: July 29, 1938. Distributed by Paramount Pictures. Presented by Adolph Zukor. Producer: Harold Lloyd. Director: Elliott Nugent. Screenplay: Delmer Daves. Adaptation by Jack Cunningham and Clyde Bruckman. Based on a story by Crampton Harris, Francis M. and Marian B. Cockrell. Photography: Archie Stout. Film Editor: Duncan Mansfield. Art Director: Al D'Agostino. Sound: Earl Sitar. Cast: Harold Lloyd, Phyllis Welch, Raymond Walburn, Lionel Stander, William Frawley, Thurston Hall, Cora Witherspoon, Sterling Holloway

THE SIN OF HAROLD DIDDLEBOCK (1947)

Released: April 4, 1947. Distributed by United Artists Corporation. Re-edited and Re-released by RKO-Radio as MAD WEDNESDAY on October 28, 1950. Produced by California Pictures Corporation. Producer: Preston Sturges. Director: Preston Sturges. Screenplay: Preston Sturges. Music: Werner R. Heymann. Photography: Robert Pittack. Technical Director: Curtis Courant. Special Effects: John Fulton. Art Director: Robert Usher. Set Decorations: Victor A. Gangelin. Film Editor: Thomas Neff. Sound: Fred Lau. Makeup: Ted Larsen. Hair Stylist: Elaine Ramsey. Production Manager: Cliff Bourghton. Cast: Harold Lloyd, Frances Ramsden, Jimmy Conlin, Raymond Walburn, Rudy Vallee, Edgar Kennedy, Arline Judge, Franklin Pangborn, Lionel Stander, Margaret Hamilton, Jack Norton, Robert Dudley, Arthur Hoyt, Julius Tannen, Al Bridge, Robert Grieg, Georgia Caine, Torben Meyer, Vic Potel, Jackie the lion

Cameo Appearance

DOGS OF WAR (1923)

Released: July 1, 1923. Distributed by Pathé Exchange. Produced by Hal Roach Studios. Length: 2 reels. Producer: Hal Roach. Director: Robert F. McGowan. Story: Hal Roach. Titles: H. M. Walker. Cast: Our Gang, Harold Lloyd, Jobyna Ralston

Harold Lloyd Productions

Harold Lloyd was the producer of a series of eight silent two-reel comedies starring Edward Everett Horton, produced by Lloyd's Hollywood Productions, Inc. and distributed by Paramount Pictures. The titles are: NO PUBLICITY (1927), FIND THE KING (1927), DAD'S CHOICE (1928), BEHIND THE COUNTER (1928), HORSE SHY (1928) SCRAMBLED WEDDINGS (1928), VACATION WAVES (1928), and CALL AGAIN (1928)

TOO MANY CROOKS (1927)

Released: April 2, 1927. Distributed by: Paramount Pictures. Presented by: Adolph Zukor, Jesse Lasky. Produced by: Famous Players-Lasky. Length: 6 reels. Producer: Harold Lloyd. Director: Fred Newmeyer. Screenplay: Rex Taylor. Photography: Harry Jackson. Cast: Mildred Davis, Lloyd Hughes, George Bancroft, El Brendel

A GIRL, A GUY, AND A GOB (1941)

Released: March 14, 1941. Distributed by; RKO-Radio Pictures. Producer: Harold Lloyd. Director: Richard Wallace. Screenplay: Frank Ryan and Bert Granet. Story by Grover Jones. Musical Score: Roy Webb. Director of Photography: Russell Metty. Special Effects: Vernon L. Walker. Art Director: Van Nest Polglase. Associate: Albert D'Agostino. Wardrobe: Edward Stevenson. Set Decorations: Darrell Silvera. Recorded by: Hugh McDowell, Jr. Edited by: George Crone. Assistant Director: James H. Anderson. Cast: George Murphy, Lucille Ball, Edmond O'Brien, Henry Travers, Franklin Pangborn

MY FAVORITE SPY (1942)

Released: June 12, 1942. Distributed by RKO-Radio Pictures. Producer: Harold Lloyd. Director: Tay Garnett. Screenplay: Sig Nerzig and William Bowers. Original Story: M. Coastes Webster. Director of Photography: Robert de Grasse. Special Effects: Vernon L. Walker. Art Directors: Albert S. D'Agostino and Carroll Clark. Gowns: Edward Stevenson. Set Decorations: Darrell Silvera. Recorded by: Earl A. Wolcott. Edited by: Desmond Marquette. Assistant Director: James A. Anderson. Musical Score: Roy Webb. Musical Director: C. Bakaleinikoff. Lyrics: Johnny Burke. Music: James Van Heusen. Musical Arrangements: George Duning. Cast: Kay Kyser, Ellen Drew, Jane Wyman, Robert Armstrong, Helen Westley, William Demarest, Una O'Connor, and Kay Kyser's Band (Harry Babbitt, Ish Kabibble, Sully Mason, Truby Irwin, Dorothy Dunn)

Compilation Films

DOWN MEMORY LANE (1949)

A compilation of excerpts from the Lloyd films made for the July 15, 1949, Shriners Chicago convention. The compilation concludes with new footage of Mildred, Gloria, Peggy, and Harold, Jr. outside Greenacres.

HAROLD LLOYD'S LAUGH PARADE (1951)

Producer and Narrator: Harold Lloyd. Editorial Supervision: Harvey C. Johnston. A compilation of excerpts from the Lloyd films made for the Shriners.

HAROLD LLOYD'S WORLD OF COMEDY (1962)
First shown: May 12, 1962. Released: June 4, 1962. Distributed by Continental Distributing Inc. Produced by Harold Lloyd. Producer: Harold Lloyd. Associate Producer: Jack Murphy. Narration written by: Art Ross. Music: Walter Scharf. Orchestration: Lew Shuken, Jack Hayes. Production Editor: Duncan Mansfield. Music Editor: Sid Sidney. Sound Effects: Del Harris. Music Recordings: Vinton Vernon. Story Consultant: Harold Lloyd, Jr. A compilation of excerpts from many of the Lloyd films, including SAFETY LAST!, WHY WORRY?, GIRL SHY, HOT WATER, THE FRESHMAN, FEET FIRST, MOVIE CRAZY, and PROFESSOR BEWARE.

HAROLD LLOYD'S FUNNY SIDE OF LIFE (1963)
First shown: August 1, 1963. Released: November 9, 1966. Distributed by Janus Films. Produced by Harold Lloyd. Producer: Harold Lloyd. Associate Producer: Jack Murphy. Narration written by: Arthur Ross. Music: Walter Scharf. Lyrics of Song "There Was a Boy, There Was a Girl" by: Ned Washington. Production Editor: Duncan Mansfield. Music Editor: Sid Sidney. Sound Effects: Del Harris. Music Recordings: Vinton Vernon. Story Consultant: Harold Lloyd, Jr. A compilation of excerpts from GIRL SHY, FOR HEAVEN'S SAKE, THE KID BROTHER, SPEEDY, MOVIE CRAZY, and Lloyd's 1959 revision of THE FRESHMAN, with an introduction in which he appears on screen.

Radio

THE HAROLD LLOYD COMEDY THEATRE
Harold Lloyd's involvement with radio began in 1940 when he was one of the founders of radio station KMPC in Los Angeles. However, it was Preston Sturges who encouraged Lloyd to undertake the master of ceremonies duties for an NBC radio network program, eventually titled THE HAROLD LLOYD COMEDY THEATRE, which lasted one season (from October 29, 1944 until June 10, 1945). The program, modeled after the popular Lux Radio Theater, featured hour-long adaptations of current films. Unless otherwise indicated, the program originated from Hollywood.

THE PALM BEACH STORY
Air date: October 29, 1944. Cast: Claudette Colbert, Robert Young

BALL OF FIRE
Air date: November 5, 1944. Cast: Walter Pidgeon, Lucille Ball

TRUE TO LIFE
Air date: November 12, 1944. Cast: Dick Powell, Victor Moore, Rosemary DeCamp

VIVACIOUS LADY
Air date: November 19, 1944. Cast: Lee Bowman, Linda Darnell

CLARENCE
Air date: November 26, 1944. Cast: Joseph Cotton

TAKE A LETTER, DARLING
Air date: December 3, 1944. Cast: John Hodiak, Susan Hayward

LOUDER, PLEASE
Air date: December 10, 1944. Cast: Adolphe Menjou, Julie Bishop

LUCKY PARTNERS
Air date: December 17, 1944. Cast: Herbert Marshall, Jane Wyman, Sheldon v nard

BACHELOR MOTHER
Air date: December 24, 1944. Cast: Louis Hayward, Brenda Marshall

ROOM SERVICE
Air date: December 31, 1944. Cast: Jack Oakie, Stuart Erwin, Donald McBride, Cara Williams

THE LADY EVE
Air date: January 7, 1945. Cast: Ralph Bellamy, Betty Field, Guy Kibbe. Program originated from New York

NOTHING BUT THE TRUTH
Air date: January 14, 1945. Cast: Alan Young, Anne Baxter. Program originated from New York

THE SHOW-OFF
Air date: January 21, 1945. Cast: Fred Allen, Alice Frost, Joseph Curtin, Claudia Morgan. Program originated from New York

APPOINTMENT FOR LOVE
Air date: January 28, 1945. Cast: Paul Henreid, Virginia Bruce

MY FAVORITE WIFE
Air date: February 4, 1945. Cast: Joel McCrea, Constance Moore, Gail Patrick

A GIRL, A GUY, AND A GOB
Air date: February 11, 1945. Cast: George Murphy, Lucille Ball

THE MILKY WAY
Air date: February 18, 1945. Cast: Robert Walker, Jimmy Gleason, Eve Arden

YOU CAN'T RATION LOVE
Air date: March 4, 1945. Cast: Paulette Goddard, Burgess Meredith

THE MAGNIFICENT DOPE
Air date: March 11, 1945. Cast: William Gargan, Janet Blair, Tom Drake

A LADY TAKES A CHANCE
Air date: March 18, 1945. Cast: Randolph Scott, Gene Tierney

BREWSTER'S MILLIONS
Air date: March 25, 1945. Cast: Dennis O'Keefe, Helen Walker, Mischa Auer

THE MAJOR AND THE MINOR
Air date: April 1, 1945. Cast: Joan Fontaine, Sonny Tufts

A SLIGHT CASE OF MURDER
Air date; April 8, 1945. Cast: Edward G. Robinson, Allen Jenkins

THE NERVOUS WRECK
Air date: April 22, 1945. Cast: Jack Haley, Martha O'Driscoll

SCATTERBRAIN
Air date: April 29, 1945. Cast: Judy Canova

HIRED WIFE
Air date: May 6, 1945. Cast: Joan Bennett, Robert Paige

SHE LOVES ME NOT
Air date: May 13, 1945. Cast: Maria Montez, Tom Drake, Freddie Bartholomew

BOY MEETS GIRL
Air date: May 20, 1945. Cast: Ann Sothern, Chester Morris, Lee Tracy

JUNE MOON
Air date: May 27, 1945. Cast: Jack Carson, Frank McHugh

HAVING WONDERFUL TIME
Air date: June 3, 1945. Cast: Pat O'Brien, June Duprez, Tom Conway

TOM, DICK AND HARRY
Air date: June 10, 1945. Cast: June Allyson

Acknowledgments

This book could not have been possible without the help of Robert Cushman, Photograph Curator of the Margaret Herrick Library of the Academy of Motion Picture Arts and Sciences, who served as photographic coordinator on this book. I am also appreciative of his reading of the manuscript and improving it with his suggestions.

I am very grateful to Manoah Bowman who printed all the superb photographs for this book and served as photographic editor.

I am also grateful to Kevin Brownlow for generously providing the introduction as well as making available his unpublished manuscript on Harold Lloyd; to Jack Lemmon for kindly providing the book's foreword; to Gloria Lloyd Roberts for her encouragement, enthusiasm, and memories; to Jon S. Bouker for his friendship and numerous contributions to this project; to David Shepard for his support and guidance with the manuscript; to Robert S. Birchard for his excellent suggestions to the manuscript; and to Casey Shaw for his friendship and for giving up many Saturdays to help archive the photographic holdings of The Harold Lloyd Trust (and, as a result, finding some of the best images used in this book).

I thank my editors Elisa Urbanelli for her patience and expert editing and Karyn Gerhard for her superb editing and excellent suggestions which greatly improved the text. I am also grateful to Richard W. Bann, Marc Wanamaker of Bison Archives, Ron Burkle, the late Gaylord Carter, Richard Correll, Dorothy Davis, Jake DeHaan, Douglas Doty, Randy Haberkamp, Linda Hoppe, Phil Moad of the Kobal Collection, Dave Nowell, David Robinson, Richard Simonton, Jr., Anthony Slide, Robert Gitt and Jere Guldin of the UCLA Film and Television Archive, Ned Comstock of the Cinema-Television Library of the University of Southern California, Meredith Walters, Constance Williams, Hazel Zimmerman, and my family, especially my mother, Sandra Vance, and my grandparents, Robert E. and Edith A. Patterson, for their love and support.

Jeffrey Vance

Photo Credits

James Abbe: 78 bottom; Peter Basch: 203; Bennett: 18; Campbell Studios: 33; John Engstead: 205; Leo Fuchs: 9; Philippe Halsman: 211; Louis Hochman: 201; Gene Kornman: 1, 7, 46–7 all, 50 all, 51 all, 52, 54 top, bottom, 56, 57, 60, 61 top, 62, 63 all, 65, 66–7, 68 all, 69, 70, 72–3 all, 75, 76, 77, 78 top, 79 all, 80, 81, 84–5, 86, 87, 88, 89 all, 91, 92, 93, 94–5, 96, 97, 98–9, 101, 102 all, 103, 104–5, 106 all, 107, 109, 110 all, 111, 112–3, 114 all, 115 all, 116–17 all, 119, 120, 121, 122, 123 all, 124, 125, 127, 128, 129 all, 130 all, 131 all, 132, 133, 134–5, 137, 138–9 all, 140, 141 all, 142–3 all, 145, 146 all, 147 all, 149 all, 150, 151 all, 153, 154–5 all, 156, 157 all, 158, 159 all, 161, 162–3 all, 164 all, 165, 167, 168–9 all, 170, 171, 173, 174, 175, 176 all, 177, 178–9, 221; J. C. Milligan: 2, 4, 14, 28 all, 29, 30 all, 31, 32 all, 34–5 all, 36, 37, 38–9 all, 40 all, 41, 42, 43, 45, 71; Talmage Morrison: 189, 191; Strauss Peyton: 54 right; Photoplayers Studio: 21; Schellenberg Studio: 19

Index

Project Manager: Elisa Urbanelli
Editor: Karyn Gerhard
Designer: Robert McKee

Library of Congress Cataloging-in-Publication Data
Vance, Jeffrey, 1970–
    Harold Lloyd : master comedian / Jeffrey Vance and Suzanne Lloyd;
    introduction by Kevin Brownlow; Manoah Bowman, photographic editor.
          p. cm.
    Includes bibliographical references and index.
    ISBN 0–8109–1674–6
    1. Lloyd, Harold, 1893–1971 2. Motion picture actors and actresses — United States--Biography.
    3. Comedians — United States — Biography. I. Lloyd, Suzanne. II. Title.
    PN2287.L5 V36 2001
    791.43'028'092 — dc21

                                    2001006014

Printed and bound in Japan
10 9 8 7 6 5 4 3 2 1

Harry N. Abrams, Inc.
100 Fifth Avenue
New York, N.Y. 10011
www.abramsbooks.com

Abrams is a subsidiary of